The Spirit of the
Alberta Indian Treaties

edited by
Richard Price

Institute for Research on Public Policy/Institut de recherches politiques

Distributed by
Butterworth & Co. (Canada) Ltd.
Toronto

ISBN 0 920380 23 9

Legal Deposit Third Quarter
Bibliothèque nationale du Québec

Institute for Research on Public Policy/Institut de recherches politiques
3535, chemin Queen Mary, Bureau 514
Montréal, Québec H3V 1H8

Typesetting by Tri-Graphic Printing (Ottawa) Ltd.

Foreword

Recent controversy regarding the rights of native peoples and their position in Canadian society has made it clear that native peoples are suffering from many real and pressing socio-economic needs. The Indian people would argue that they arise, at least in part, from the failure of the Canadian government to fulfil the spirit of its obligations under the land-surrender treaties negotiated with Indian leaders late in the last century.

It is the belief of the authors of this report that current difficulties and misunderstandings in the interpretation of these treaties are largely a result of the fundamentally different perceptions of Indians and government representatives as to the meaning of these treaties. While Indian leaders base their interpretation on a historical understanding that emphasizes the ''spirit'' or original ''intent'' of the agreement, most government positions have been based on a legal interpretation of the ''letter'' of the agreement.

IRPP is publishing this report in the hope that the development of a common understanding of the spirit of the treaties will provide a sound basis for negotiations between government and native groups, and thus make it possible to arrive at satisfactory legislation, policies, and programs to answer the socio-economic needs of Indian peoples.

Although this particular study deals with the Indians of Alberta, there are clear implications for all native groups, and hence for the issue of native rights—a public policy issue of national importance. Through this essay, we are pleased to contribute to the national debate and to help improve public understanding on this issue.

Although I am certain its conclusions will spark controversy, I recommend this study to you as a thoughtful and well-researched treatment of an important and timely public policy issue. As such, it should be of interest to government policy makers and indeed to all concerned Canadians.

Michael J.L. Kirby
President
April 1979

Avant-propos

Les autochtones éprouvent de nombreux besoins socio-économiques réels et pressants: c'est ce qu'a clairement démontré la récente controverse concernant leurs droits et leur situation au sein de la société canadienne. Le peuple indien affirmerait que le gouvernement canadien en est responsable, tout au moins partiellement, pour n'avoir pas respecté les obligations qui lui incombent en vertu des traités de cession des terres négociés avec les chefs indiens à la fin du siècle dernier.

Les auteurs de ce rapport croient que les obstacles et les mésententes actuelles dans l'interprétation de ces traités proviennent largement des différences fondamentales opposant la perception des Indiens à celle des représentants gouvernementaux relativement au sens de ces traités. Alors que les chefs indiens fondent leur interprétation sur une dimension historique mettant en relief "l'esprit" ou "l'intention" originale de l'accord, la plupart des positions du gouvernement se justifient dans l'interprétation juridique de la "lettre" de l'accord.

L'IRP publie ce rapport dans l'espoir que l'élaboration d'une intelligence commune de l'esprit des traités fournira une base solide aux négociations entre le gouvernement et les groupes autochtones, concrétisant ainsi la formulation d'une législation, de politiques et de programmes qui puissent répondre adéquatement aux besoins socio-économiques des Indiens.

Bien que cette étude traite spécifiquement des Indiens de l'Alberta, certaines conséquences s'appliquent clairement à tous les groupes autochtones et, donc, à la question des droits des autochtones—question de politiques d'importance nationale. Nous sommes heureux de contribuer, grâce à cet essai, au débat national et d'aider le public à approfondir ses connaissances sur le sujet.

Tout en étant persuadé que les conclusions de cet ouvrage feront éclater la controverse, j'en recommande la lecture, puisqu'il constitue une étude réfléchie et bien documentée d'une importante question d'actualité du domaine des politiques. Voilà d'ailleurs pourquoi il devrait intéresser les responsables de l'élaboration des politiques au sein du gouvernement et, bien sûr, tous les Canadiens.

Michael J.L. Kirby
Président
Avril 1979

Preface

I am pleased to express my personal appreciation and satisfaction that this book on the Alberta Indian treaties will finally be published. We have waited a long time for the views of our elders to be given a proper hearing and a wider circulation. Indeed, the Indian understanding of the treaties has been long neglected. This book takes a real step forward in rectifying that situation.

Many of us remember the presentation of the "Red Paper," *Citizens Plus*, by the Alberta Indian chiefs and the Indian Association of Alberta in 1970. While much has changed since that presentation, many of the themes of the Red Paper regarding treaty rights still remain relevant today. Two main themes were as follows:

a. The need to have the federal government recognize the treaties
b. The need to modernize the treaties

In this regard, the Indian Association of Alberta is taking the necessary measures to accomplish this difficult task. To be more specific, the Red Paper recommended that:

> The Government of Canada must declare that it accepts the treaties as binding and must pledge that it will incorporate the treaties in updated terms in an amendment to the Canadian Constitution.

However, the constitutional proposals put forward by the prime minister of Canada in 1978 do not mention our treaties, although one section does mention aboriginal rights. We will continue to press the government to recognize our treaties and to have them included in the new constitution.

The emphasis on modernizing the treaties in the Red Paper included the following statements:

> The intent and spirit of the treaties must be our guide, not the precise letter of a foreign language. Treaties that run forever must have room for changes in the conditions of life. The undertaking of the government to provide teachers was a commitment to provide Indian children the educational opportunity equal to their white neighbors. The machinery and livestock symbolized economic development. . . . Indians have the right to receive, without payment, all healthcare services without exception and paid by the Government of Canada.

It is true that the Government of Canada in 1973 referred to its obligation to honour the spirit and terms of the treaties. However, there is yet today no common understanding of the spirit of our treaties; much discussion must still take place on this issue.

Thus, the Indian people of Alberta are still struggling to insure that *Citizens Plus* is followed up adequately and fairly, and implemented by the Government of Canada. In my view, *The Spirit of the Alberta Indian Treaties* can contribute positively to our efforts. I would like to thank all those who contributed to this book, and to recommend it to all Canadians—whether Indian or non-Indian—for their careful study and reflection.

Joe Dion
President
Indian Association of Alberta
September 1978

Préface

Je suis heureux de pouvoir exprimer personnellement la satisfaction et le contentement que j'éprouve à la publication de ce livre sur les traités des Indiens de l'Alberta. Il nous a fallu attendre longtemps pour que les opinions de nos aînés soient plus convenablement présentées et plus largement diffusées. En effet, l'interprétation indienne des traités a longtemps été négligée. Ce livre pose un important jalon en rectifiant la situation.

Plusieurs d'entre nous se souviennent de la présentation du "Livre rouge", *Citizens Plus*, par les chefs indiens de l'Alberta et l'Association indienne de l'Alberta en 1970. Bien des choses ont changé depuis; néanmoins, plusieurs des thèmes du Livre rouge concernant les droits des traités demeurent pertinents aujourd'hui. Parmi ces thèmes figurent principalement:

a. La nécessité de faire reconnaître les traités par le gouvernement fédéral

b. La nécessité de rajeunir les traités

Dans cette optique, l'Association indienne de l'Alberta prend les mesures qui s'imposent pour accomplir cette tâche ardue. Le Livre rouge recommandait plus précisément:

> Le Gouvernement du Canada doit reconnaître explicitement ses obligations en vertu des traités et doit s'engager à incorporer une version mise à jour des traités à la Constitution canadienne, sous forme d'amendement.

Toutefois, les propositions constitutionnelles mises de l'avant par le premier ministre du Canada en 1978 ne font pas mention de nos traités, bien que les droits des aborigènes y soient à l'occasion signalés. Nous continuerons d'exercer des pressions auprès du gouvernement pour que soient reconnus nos traités et pour qu'ils soient inclus dans la nouvelle constitution.

Le Livre rouge insistait sur le rajeunissement des traités en ces termes:

> C'est l'intention et l'esprit des traités qui doivent nous guider et non pas la lettre précise d'une langue étrangère. Des traités qui se veulent irrévocables doivent s'ajuster au changement des conditions de vie. En promettant de fournir des professeurs, le gouvernement s'engageait à donner aux jeunes Indiens les mêmes

chances au plan de l'éducation qu'à leurs voisins blancs. L'outillage et le cheptel symbolisaient le développement économique. . . . Les Indiens ont le droit de se prévaloir gratuitement de tous les services d'hygiène sans exception, aux frais du Gouvernement du Canada.

Il est vrai que le Gouvernement du Canada, en 1973, a fait allusion à l'obligation qui lui incombe de respecter l'esprit et les termes des traités. Toutefois, l'interprétation de l'esprit de nos traités demeure encore aujourd'hui un point de divergence; cette question doit à nouveau faire l'objet de nombreuses discussions.

Donc, le peuple indien de l'Alberta lutte sans relâche pour que le Livre rouge soit équitablement et fidèlement observé et mis en application par le Gouvernement du Canada. Selon moi, *The Spirit of the Alberta Indian Treaties* peut réellement soutenir nos efforts. J'aimerais remercier tous ceux qui ont collaboré à ce livre et recommander à tous les Canadiens, Indiens ou non-Indiens, de l'étudier avec soin et d'y réfléchir.

Joe Dion
Président
Association indienne de l'Alberta
Septembre 1978

Table of Contents

Introduction

The recent centennial commemoration of Indian Treaties Six and Seven has focused attention on the meaning of these documents. At the Treaty Seven centennial in 1977, the seven chiefs expressed their displeasure that the treaty promises have not been kept and therefore that many of their people live in poverty. Prince Charles, speaking on behalf of the Government of Canada, acknowledged these hardships and stressed that the government wished to work out solutions jointly with the Indian people.

This book is directed to the question—what is the meaning of the Alberta Indian treaties? The Indian Association of Alberta is making available years of research work in the form of this unique collection of articles and interviews with Indian elders. It is our belief that Indian people and governments have conflicting perceptions of these Indian treaties; not only are these perspectives at the root of many contemporary Indian-government problems and misunderstandings, but their basis resides in the Indian treaty negotiations of the last century. In fact, government and Indian leaders tend to operate within two different systems of knowledge and perceptions of reality regarding basic ''treaty rights'' issues.

This manuscript is devoted to an accurate portrayal of the differing government and Indian interpretations of the Indian Treaties Six, Seven, and Eight in Alberta—with special attention given to the Indian understanding. However, the main theme regarding the vital importance of these conflicting treaty interpretations has implications beyond Alberta, because these same elements appear to be present in all the Indian treaties after 1870 (i.e., Treaties One, Two, and Five in Manitoba; Treaties Four, Six, Eight, and Ten in Saskatchewan; Treaties Eight and Eleven in the Northwest Territories; Treaty Eight in British Columbia; and Treaties Three and Nine in Ontario).

It is our hope that these essays and interviews with elders, with their rich variety of content and focus on a common concern, will produce a greater mutual understanding on the part of both leaders of government and the Indian people. We believe that greater mutual understanding does allow the potential for governments to respond with a more sympathetic, enlightened public policy regarding the Indian treaties, and for Indian leaders to be more flexible in their dealings with governments.

Different historical experiences and interpretations, coupled with different, current perceptions of reality, have led Indians and government to their current impasse over treaty rights discussions and negotiations. However, a conscious attempt on both sides to understand the perspective of the other and a willingness to compromise may be the bases for a workable future relationship and solutions.

Before briefly highlighting some problems of federal public policy on Indian treaties, I would be remiss in not pointing out that we believe that this book should hold a real interest for a wide readership, both Indian and non-Indian. For example, many young Indians who are particularly concerned with questions of identity in relation to the political and social history of their people may well find new insights in this manuscript, especially regarding:

1. The significant Indian input into important terms of treaties
2. The special, spiritual meanings attached to the treaty ceremonies and the treaty itself by the Indian elders and the Indian chiefs who signed the treaties

For many non-Indian Canadians, who wish both to gain a better knowledge of a key historical interaction between the Indian people and white Euro-Canadian society, and to influence their governments on current policy in this regard, this book presents the following important results:

a. The real differences between Indians and governments as to the meaning of the basic land surrender clause of the treaties
b. The symbolic meaning of the treaties for Indians, implying to them a trust relationship with the Crown
c. The broader, more all-inclusive Indian view of the various economic and social terms of the treaties
d. The sense of betrayal expressed by many Indians that the treaties were not fulfilled

These points also have real significance for governments and their future policy making in this area.

The term "governments" is used advisedly because provincial governments, particularly the Prairie provincial governments, have treaty rights obligations in the areas of reserve land entitlements and hunting, fishing, and trapping. These areas are, at least in part, a provincial responsibility under the terms of the Natural Resources Transfer Legislation of 1930.

However, conflicting treaty interpretations and their implications for Indian-provincial government relations can only be noted here; I wish to highlight briefly Indian-federal government policy differences regarding Indian treaties. The main federal statement of policy in this regard was made 8 August 1973, by the Honourable Jean Chrétien in a Statement on Claims of Indian and Inuit People:

As the government pledged some years ago, legal obligations must be recognized. This remains the basis of government policy. The Federal Government's commitment to honour the treaties was most recently restated by Her Majesty . . . ''You may be assured that the Government of Canada recognizes the importance of full compliance with the spirit and terms of your treaties.''

In many ways this statement contains certain contradictory elements that are at the centre of current misunderstandings and impasses. By contradictory elements, I mean the references to ''legal obligations'' on the one hand, and the ''spirit'' of the treaties on the other. The Modern Canadian Dictionary defines spirit as ''true intent or meaning as opposed to outward formal observance: the spirit of the law.''

The federal government has a strong tendency to follow the legal obligations option and to look for advice from the law officers of the Crown. This advice tends to restrict treaty interpretations to the strict written terms of the treaties and to a century of case law from the European-influenced Canadian court system. No one in the federal government has been bold enough to try publicly to define or interpret what was meant by the reference to spirit of the treaties contained in the policy statement.

On the Indian side, however, there is no such hesitation to try to define the spirit of the treaties. Indian leaders believe that certain Indian elders have knowledge of the true intent or spirit of the treaties. The Indian leaders are often the contemporary spokesmen for the elders' interpretations of the treaties. The elders do not rely on case law or written documents, but on oral history. Knowledge of the treaty negotiation events has been passed down from generation to generation, starting with the chiefs and headmen who actually signed the treaty. Thus, we have two quite different systems of knowledge and perceptions of reality, and it is therefore no accident that recent deliberations between Indian leaders and the federal Cabinet ministers in the National Indian Brotherhood/Cabinet Joint Committee have broken down over the meaning of ''education as a treaty right.''

For many government policy makers, the strict written terms of the treaties are clear; for example, Treaty Seven reads:

Further, Her Majesty agrees to pay the salary of such teachers to instruct the children of said Indians as to Her Government of Canada may seem advisable, when said Indians are settled on their reserves and shall desire teachers.

For the Indian leaders, education is a right guaranteed in the treaties and through Indian aboriginal rights. Most Indian leaders believe that their education rights, negotiated at treaty time, guaranteed them free education at all levels and in perpetuity, that is, in return for some land and natural resources, the Indian people believed that they were to receive prepaid education from the government as a right.

When governments make financial cutbacks, as they have done recently, and when those cutbacks come in areas related to treaty promises, then they symbolize and reaffirm in the minds of Indians the governmental betrayal or contravention of treaty rights.

The one avenue that seems open to federal policy makers and Indian leaders has already been suggested by the former Indian Claims commissioner of Canada, Dr. Lloyd Barber, in a speech to the Canadian Managing Editors' Conference, in Regina, on 27 May 1976:

> In my mind, the key to resolution of the treaty problems is to look to the spirit of the treaties. If the issues are approached in this way, I think that we will find that while there is substantial disagreement about what the Government was legally bound to provide, there is very good potential for agreement in terms of what the government might, in fact, provide in the way of developmental assistance today.

In his work as Indian Claims commissioner, Dr. Barber made a solid effort to really understand both Indian and government perceptions of the treaties, and his suggestion does present a concrete possibility for examining the contemporary implications of the spirit of the treaties. If the goal of a common or even a closer understanding of this spirit is kept in the forefront of the minds of the government and Indian negotiators, then hopefully the present basis of common co-operation—the real and obvious socio-economic needs of Indian people—can be enhanced and translated into long-term, mutually acceptable policies, legislation, and programs. As Dr. Barber would attest, these are the types of issues that must be negotiated face-to-face by Indian leaders and government ministers because these are not problems that can be litigated by lawyers for the respective sides, if there is to be a real resolution of the Indian sense of grievance regarding broken treaties.

For our part, as researchers, we have tried to examine the spirit of the treaties by studying carefully the actual treaty negotiations to get a clearer picture of the meanings and associations that were given to the treaty terms at that time. This is the goal of part one of this book. The spirit of the treaties also involves an examination of the various interpretations given by the respective parties. In part two, we concentrate on the Indian interpretations of the treaties, in order to do justice to the Indian historical experience in its own right—not as an appendage of Euro-Canadian history.

The essays and interviews of elders in this book represent close to four years of work by a team of staff and consultants of the Treaty and Aboriginal Rights Research (T.A.R.R.) group of the Indian Association of Alberta. In light of the fact that I was research director for most of that time, I was asked to edit this manuscript and to write this introduction.

At this stage, I would like to acknowledge the various sources of support for our research team. First, we received a great deal of encouragement for our work from successive Indian Association of Alberta boards and executives. Second, we are grateful for the financial research grants from the Department of Indian Affairs and Northern Development. Third, a special note of thanks is due to the Indian Claims Commission of Canada for allowing John Taylor to work with us on this project and to use John's essay for this publication. Finally, a word of thanks to the National Museum of Man for the use of John Taylor's essay on Canada's Northwest policy.

In closing, I should also make clear that the research results contained in this manuscript represent the views of individuals involved in the T.A.R.R. research group and various Indian elders, but do not necessarily represent the position or views of the Indian Association of Alberta Board of Directors and Executive.

Richard Price
Indian Association of Alberta
September 1978

Introduction

La récente commémoration du centenaire des Traités des Indiens six et sept s'est attardée sur le sens de ces documents. Lors du centenaire du Traité sept, en 1977, les chefs indiens ont exprimé leur mécontentement du fait que les conventions du traité n'ayant pas été respectées, leur peuple est maintenu dans la pauvreté. Le Prince Charles, au nom du gouvernement du Canada, reconnaissant cet état de fait, a certifié que le gouvernement souhaite mettre au point des solutions en collaboration avec le peuple indien.

Ce livre porte sur la question suivante: Quelle est la signification des traités des Indiens de l'Alberta? L'Association indienne de l'Alberta met à la disposition du public le fruit de plusieurs années de recherche sous la forme d'une série originale d'articles et d'entrevues avec les Indiens de l'ancienne génération. Nous croyons que le peuple indien et les gouvernements conçoivent les traités indiens de façon tout à fait différente. Ces conceptions ne sont pas seulement à l'origine des nombreux problèmes et des mésententes qui divisent Indiens et gouvernements, mais leur source réside surtout dans les accords conclus par traité au siècle dernier. En réalité, le gouvernement et les dirigeants indiens tendent à agir dans deux systèmes différents de connaissance et de perception de la réalité en ce qui a trait aux questions fondamentales des ''droits des traités''.

L'objet de cet ouvrage est de tracer un portrait exact des divergences d'interprétation des Traités des Indiens six, sept et huit en Alberta, par le gouvernement d'une part et les Indiens d'autre part—en portant une attention particulière à l'interprétation des Indiens. Cependant, le thème principal concernant l'importance vitale de ces interprétations antagonistes a des implications s'étendant au-delà de l'Alberta, car il semble que les mêmes éléments se retrouvent dans tous les traités des Indiens postérieurs à 1870 (cf. les Traités un, deux et cinq au Manitoba; les Traités quatre, six, huit et dix en Saskatchewan; les Traités huit et onze dans les Territoires du Nord-Ouest; le Traité huit en Colombie-Britannique; les Traités trois et neuf en Ontario).

Nous espérons voir naître, grâce à ces articles et ces entrevues avec les Indiens de l'ancienne génération, la richesse de leur contenu et leur préoccupation commune, une plus grande compréhension mutuelle entre les dirigeants du gouvernement et le peuple indien. Nous avons la conviction qu'une meilleure compréhension réciproque permettra aux gouvernements de répondre avec plus de bienveillance et de discernement, dans le choix de politiques concernant les traités indiens, et assouplira les arguments des dirigeants indiens dans leurs discussions avec les gouvernements.

Les différentes expériences et interprétations du passé, associées aux différentes perceptions présentes de la réalité, ont conduit les Indiens et le gouvernement à l'impasse à laquelle se heurtent aujourd'hui les discussions et les négociations des droits des traités. Cependant, un effort réel des deux parties pour comprendre l'optique de l'autre et la volonté d'en arriver à un compromis pourraient servir de base aux discussions éventuelles et aux solutions.

Avant d'exposer brièvement certains problèmes de politiques fédérales sur les affaires indiennes, il ne faudrait pas omettre de souligner que ce livre nous apparaît d'un grand intérêt pour un vaste public de lecteurs, indiens et non indiens. A titre d'exemple, beaucoup de jeunes Indiens, particulièrement préoccupés par les questions d'identité relatives à l'histoire politique et sociale de leur peuple, pourraient bien trouver de nouveaux horizons dans cet ouvrage, particulièrement en ce qui concerne:
1. l'importante contribution indienne aux principales clauses des accords;
2. le sens spirituel particulier que les Indiens de l'ancienne génération et les chefs signataires des traités attachent aux cérémonies du traité de paix et au traité en tant que tel.

Pour beaucoup de Canadiens non indiens qui souhaitent approfondir leur connaissance de l'interaction historique primordiale du peuple indien et de la société blanche euro-canadienne et influencer leur gouvernement dans les politiques actuelles, ce livre présente les principaux éléments qui suivent:
a. les différences réelles d'interprétation, entre Indiens et gouvernements, de la clause fondamentale de cession des terres, aux termes des traités;
b. la signification symbolique des traités aux yeux des Indiens, impliquant pour eux des liens de confiance avec la Couronne;
c. une vue globale plus large, chez les Indiens, des diverses conditions économiques et sociales des traités;
d. le sentiment de trahison qu'éprouvent plusieurs Indiens vis-à-vis le non-respect des traités.
Tous ces points ont également leur signification pour les gouvernements et l'élaboration de leurs politiques futures dans ce domaine.

Le terme ''gouvernements'' est utilisé à dessein, car les gouvernements provinciaux, particulièrement ceux des Prairies, ont des obligations contractuelles dans les domaines des droits sur la propriété des réserves ainsi que des droits concernant la chasse, la pêche et la chasse au piège. Ces responsabilités sont du ressort, au moins en partie, de la province, suivant les termes de la législation du transfert des ressources naturelles de 1930.

Cependant, les interprétations contradictoires des traités et leurs implications sur les relations entre les Indiens et les gouvernements provinciaux sont simplement signalées ici. Je souhaite exposer brièvement les différences entre le gouvernement fédéral et les Indiens en ce qui concerne la politique des traités indiens. Les grandes lignes de la position du gouvernement fédéral à cet égard étaient données par l'honorable Jean Chrétien, le 8 août 1973, lors d'une déclaration sur les revendications des peuples indien et inuit:

> Le gouvernement s'y étant engagé il y a quelques années, les obligations légales doivent être reconnues. Ceci reste la base de la politique du gouvernement. L'engagement du gouvernement fédéral de respecter les traités a été réitéré tout récemment par Sa Majesté . . . Vous pouvez être assurés que le gouvernement du Canada reconnaît l'importance du respect intégral de l'esprit et des clauses de vos traités.*

A bien des égards, cette déclaration contient certains éléments contradictoires qui sont au coeur des mésententes et des impasses actuelles. Par éléments contradictoires, j'entends les références aux ''obligations légales'' d'une part et à ''l'esprit'' des traités d'autre part. Le dictionnaire canadien moderne définit l'esprit comme l'intention réelle ou la signification, par opposition à l'observation formelle apparente: l'esprit de la loi.

Le gouvernement fédéral a une forte tendance à opter pour ''l'obligation légale'' et à demander les conseils des juristes de la Couronne. Ces conseils tendent à limiter les interprétations des traités au sens strict des termes écrits et à se reporter à un siècle de jurisprudence fondée sur un système juridique canadien d'influence européenne. Personne au gouvernement fédéral n'a été assez téméraire pour tenter de définir ou d'interpréter publiquement ce qu'est ''l'esprit'' des traités auquel fait référence la déclaration en question.

Du côté indien, cependant, pareille hésitation n'existe pas. Les dirigeants indiens croient que certains de leurs aînés possèdent la connaissance de la véritable intention ou de ''l'esprit'' des traités. Les dirigeants indiens sont souvent les porte-parole contemporains des anciennes générations, transmettant leur interprétation des traités. Les aînés ne s'appuient ni sur la jurisprudence ni sur les documents écrits, mais sur l'histoire orale. La connaissance des événements relatifs aux négociations de traités a été transmise d'une génération à la suivante, à partir des dirigeants et chefs de tribus qui ont personnellement ratifié les traités. Ainsi avons-nous deux systèmes de connaissance et de perception de la réalité totalement différents, et ce n'est donc pas le fait du hasard que les délibérations entre les dirigeants indiens et les ministres du Cabinet fédéral au comité bipartite Cabinet-Fraternité des Indiens du Canada aient achoppé sur la signification du ''droit à l'éducation au sens des traités''.

----

* Traduction

Pour plusieurs responsables de l'élaboration des politiques au sein du gouvernement, l'écrit des traités, au sens strict, est clair; le Traité sept stipule, par exemple:

En outre, Sa Majesté consent à payer le salaire de tels enseignants pour l'instruction des enfants desdits Indiens dans la mesure où le gouvernement du Canada le jugera préférable, quand lesdits Indiens seront installés dans leur réserves et voudront des enseignants.*

Pour les dirigeants indiens, l'éducation est un droit garanti dans les traités et par les droits des aborigènes indiens. La plupart des dirigeants indiens croient que les droits à l'éducation, négociés au moment du traité, leur garantissent l'éducation sans frais à tous les niveaux et à perpétuité. En d'autres mots, le peuple indien croit qu'en échange des terres et des ressources naturelles, le gouvernement doit obligatoirement assumer les coûts de l'éducation.

Lorsque les gouvernements diminuent les crédits budgétaires, comme ils l'ont fait récemment, et que ces réductions touchent des domaines propres aux accords des traités, leur trahison ou leur violation des droits des traités se trouvent alors réaffirmées dans l'esprit des Indiens.

La seule voie qui semble ouverte aux responsables fédéraux de l'élaboration des politiques et aux dirigeants indiens a déjà été suggérée par l'ex-commissaire aux revendications des Indiens, M. Lloyd Barber, lors d'une allocution à la *Canadian Managing Editors' Conference*, à Regina, le 27 mai 1976:

Dans mon esprit, la clé de la solution aux problèmes des traités est de se pencher sur l'esprit des traités. Si les questions sont abordées sous cet angle, nous découvrirons, je crois, que malgré le désaccord à propos de ce que le gouvernement est légalement tenu de fournir, nous ne sommes pas loin d'une entente, sur ce point, dans le domaine de l'assistance au développement aujourd'hui.*

Dans son travail de commissaire aux revendications des Indiens, Barber a fait un réel effort pour comprendre à fond comment le gouvernement et les Indiens perçoivent les traités, et sa suggestion offre des perspectives concrètes d'analyse des implications présentes de l'esprit des traités. Si le gouvernement et les négociateurs indiens gardent en tête l'objectif d'une compréhension mutuelle ou même d'un rapprochement de cet esprit, les bases actuelles de collaboration—les besoins socio-économiques réels et manifestes du peuple indien—pourront être mises en valeur et traduites par des accords politiques réciproquement acceptables, des législations et des programmes à long terme. Comme le dirait M. Barber, c'est le genre de questions qui doivent être négociées face à face entre les dirigeants indiens et les ministres du gouvernement; il ne faut pas chercher l'apaisement de ce

---

* Traduction

sentiment d'injustice que nourrissent les Indiens, en raison de la violation des traités, dans l'affrontement d'avocats plaidant pour les deux parties.

Pour notre part, à titre de chercheurs, nous avons essayé d'analyser l'esprit des traités en étudiant soigneusement les négociations qui ont abouti aux traités existants afin de préciser la signification et les associations qu'on a voulu donner aux termes des traités, à cette époque. C'est l'objet du premier chapitre de cet ouvrage. L'esprit des traités demande également un examen des diverses interprétations qu'en font les parties respectives. Nous avons réservé le second chapitre aux interprétations indiennes des traités, afin de rendre justice à l'expérience historique des Indiens dans son droit propre—et non à titre de simple appendice de l'histoire euro-canadienne.

Les essais et les entrevues auprès des Indiens de l'ancienne génération représentent presque quatre ans de travail accompli par une équipe de personnel et d'experts du groupe de recherche sur les droits des autochtones et les droits des traités *(Treaty and Aboriginal Rights Research)* de l'Association indienne de l'Alberta. Puisque j'ai été Directeur de la recherche pour la majeure partie du travail, on m'a confié le rôle d'éditeur du document et le soin d'en rédiger l'introduction.

J'aimerais donc mentionner de quelles sources notre équipe de recherche a tiré ses appuis. Tout d'abord, nous avons reçu l'encouragement chaleureux de différents Conseils et Comités exécutifs de l'Association indienne de l'Alberta. Nous sommes reconnaissants au ministère des Affaires indiennes et du Nord pour ses subventions de recherche. En troisième lieu, nous devons des remerciements tout particuliers à la Commission d'étude des revendications des Indiens du Canada pour avoir permis à John Taylor de travailler avec nous à ce projet et pour avoir autorisé la publication de son essai. Enfin, un mot de remerciement au Musée national de l'homme pour nous avoir permis d'utiliser l'ouvrage de John Taylor traitant de la politique du Nord-Ouest canadien.

Pour terminer, je tiens à préciser que les conclusions de recherche que contient cet ouvrage traduisent l'opinion des membres du groupe de recherche T.A.R.R. et celle de quelques Indiens de l'ancienne génération, mais n'illustrent pas forcément la position ou le point de vue du Conseil et de l'exécutif de l'Association indienne de l'Alberta.

Richard Price
Association indienne de l'Alberta
Septembre 1978

Treaty and Aboriginal Rights Research (T.A.R.R.)
OF THE INDIAN ASSOCIATION OF ALBERTA

ᐁᑯᒪ ᒪᓭᓇᐃᑲᐣ ᑯᔭᐢᒥᑲᑌᐠ ᑕᑐ ᑫᑳᐩ ᑲᐯ ᒧᐢᑫᓇᒥᐠ ᐁᒪᒥᐢᑯᒥᑲᑌᑳᐤ

ᐁᑯᒪ ᐅᑕᐠ ᐯᒋ ᑲᑫ ᐃᐧᑰᑫᒧᑕᐧᐤ ᐊᐳᑕᐤ ᐅᒋ ᐁᐳᒍᐊᐧᐠ ᓂᐃᓭᐤᐊᐧᐠ ᐊᑎᐟ ᒣᓇ ᑲᐢᑫᑌᐤᐊᐧᓭᐢᑌᓇᐠ ᐅᐦᒋ ᓂᑯᑐᐧᓭᐠ ᑫᑕᓭᓇᐃᑳᑌᐤᑲᐧᐤ ᐅᑌᐸᐊᐢᑲᒍᐊᐧᐊᐧ ᐁᑲᐧ ᐁᑯ ᓂᐠ ᐅᑭ ᑌᐸᑯᐠ ᑫᐯᑕᓭᓇᐃᑲᑌᑲᐧᐤ ᐅᑌᐸᐊᐢᑲᒍᐊᐧᐊᐧ ᒪᒋᑲ ᐁᑯᐦ ᐁᑯᐢᐯ ᑲᑫ ᐃᐧᑯᑫᒧᑕᐧᐤ ᒣᐢᑕᐃ ᑫᑲᐧᐩ ᑫ ᐊᔭᒧᑕᒪᐧᐠ ᐁᑯᓀᐠ ᐅᑭ ᑫᓭᐊᔭᐠ ᒣᒣᐟ ᑫᑲᐧᐩᐯ ᒪᓄᒧᐃᑯᐊᐧᐠ ᑕᐯᐢᑯᐨ ᐁᑯᓀ ᐅᐃ ᑲᑫᓭᐤ ᑌᐸᐊᒧᐊᐧᑲᐠ ᐊᑯᑕᒪᑫᐤᓇ ᐅᑫᒪᓈ ᐅᐦᒋ ᒣᑲᐧᐨ ᑳ ᑲᑳᐯᑯᓇᒪᑯᔭᑲᐧᐤ ᐁᑯᓀ ᒣᐢᑕᐃ ᒣᑕᑕᒪᐧᐠ ᑭᐢᓭᐊᔭᐠ ᒪᒋᑲ ᐁᑯᒪ ᐊᓇᐨ ᒣᑲᐧᐨ ᐁᔭᒍᐊᐧᐠ ᒣᐢᑕᐃ ᑫᑌᒪᑫᓭᐤᐊᐧᐠ " ᐁᑲᐧᐊᐧ ᑫᑯ ᐅᑫᒪᐢᑭᐧᐤ ᐅᑯᐢ ᓭ ᑳᐢᑎᐢ ᐁᑯᐢᐯ ᐁᔭᒍᐊᐧ ᑲᑫ ᐯᑭᐢᑲᐧᑕᐟ ᐁᑯᒪ ᑫᑎᐧᐟ ᐅᑫᒪᓈᐠ ᐅᐦᒋᐅ ᑫᒪᐤᐊᐧᐠ ᐊᑳᐤᐊᐧᑕᒪᐧᐠ ᑕᑫ ᓂᑯᑲᒧᐊᐧᑕᐧᐤ ᐁᔭᒍᐊᐧ ᐁᑯᒪ ᐁᔮᑯᐠ ᑲᑲᐧᑕᑭ ᑕᔭᐟ " ᒪᒋᑲ ᐁᑯᒪ ᐅᐦᒋ ᑯᔭᐢᑕᒍᐅᐠ ᐅᒪ ᒪᓭᓇᐃᑲᐠ ᐁᐃᐧᒋᑲᑌᐠ ᑕᐠᓭ ᑫᒋ ᓇ ᐁᐃᑕᑫᑯᐟ ᑌᐸᐊᒧᐊᐧᑲᐠ ᐁᑯᒪ ᐯᒐᔭᐠ ᐅᑫᒪᐤ ᑌᐸᐊᐢᑲᐠ ᐊᐢᐳᐢᑕ" ᐁᑯᓀᐠ ᐃᑭ ᐊᑐᐢᑫᔭᑲᐧᐣᓇᐠ ᑌᐸᐊᒧᐊᐧᑲᐠ ᐊᐢᐯᔭᒧᐊᐧᒋᑲᓂᐠ ᐅᑕ ᐊᐢᐳᐢᑕ ᐅᐦᒋ ᐁᐊᐧ ᑯᓀᐠ ᑲᑫᐯ ᓇᑐᐢᑲᒪᑫᑕᐧᐤ ᑌᐸᐊᒧᐊᐧᑲᐠ ᐊᑯᑕᒪᑫᐤᓇ ᒪᒋ ᒣᐢᑕᐃ ᐯᒪᓄᐊᐧᒋᑕᐤᐊᐧ ᐠ ᑭᐢᑫᔭᑕᒪᐤᐃᐦ ᒣᓇ ᑫᔭᐃᐠ ᒣᒣᐟ ᑫᓭᐊᔭ ᑫᐯ ᐊᒋᒍᐁᐤᐊᐧᐠ ᒪᒋᑲ ᒪᓭᓇᐃ ᑲᓀᐠ ᒣᓇ ᑫᐯ ᒪᓭᓇᐊᒪᐧᐠ ᑕᑐ ᑫᑲᐧᐩ ᑲᐯ ᒧᐢᑫᓇᒪᑫᑕᐧᐤ

ᐁᑯᒪ ᑫᐢᑕᕽᐆᐧᑫᑕᒦᐠ ᐊᔭ ᐊᔭᑕᐤ ᐅᐦᒋ ᓂᐃᓭᐤ ᐅᓂᑲᓂᐢᑖᑫᐊᐧᐠ ᒣᓇ ᐅᑫᒪᓈ ᐅᐦᒋ ᐅᑫᒪᐤᐊᐧᐠ ᒣᐢᑕᐃ ᑫᐯ ᒍᑌᓇᒪᐧᐠ ᐅᐃ ᐊᑯᑕᒪᑫᐤᓇ ᒪᑲ ᐸᐯᑐᐢ ᐃᓭᑫ ᓭᒍᑌᓇᑲᐧᐤ ᐅᑫᒪᓈᐠ ᐅᒋ ᒍᑌᐯᑯᓇᒪᐧᐠ ᐊᑯᑕᒪᑫᐤᓇ ᓇᔭᐢᑕᐤ ᒪᒋᑲ ᐁᔭᓂᐤ ᐅᓂᑲᓂᐢᑕᒪᑫᐤᐊᐧᐠ ᒣᓭᑲᒣ ᐊᔭᒪᒍᐠ ᑳᐯ ᓂᐸᐃᐧᐃᑕᐧᐤ " ᐊᐧᑕ ᓂᐸᐃᐧᐢᑕᒪᑫ ᐊᐧᐠ ᑌᐸᐊᒧᐊᐧᑲᐠ ᐊᑯᑕᒪᑫᐤᓇ ᐁᑲᑭᐧ ᐯᒪᒋᑕᑕᐧᐤ ᒣᑕᑕᐟ ᑐᒣᑕᓈᐤ ᐊᐧᐢᑭᐩ ᐁᑲᐧ ᐅᒋ ᒣᐸᔦᐤ ᐊᐧᐢᐱᐠ ᐅᒋ ᐊᑯᑕᒪᑫᐤᓇ ᑲᐯ ᐯ ᑌᑲᐧᑕᒪᑕᐧᐤ ᐁᔭᒍᐊᐧᐠ ᐁᑯᓭ ᑫᔭᐯᐨ ᐅᒪ ᓇᒧ ᔭ ᑲᐧᔭᐢᐠᑯᐸᔭᓇᐧ " ᐁᑯᒪ ᒪᓭᓇᐃᑲᐠ ᑯᔭᐢᑕᒪᑫᐠ ᐅᐦᑕᐤ ᑕᐊᐧᐸᑌᐃᐃᐧᐠ ᑕᐢᓭ ᑫᒋᓇ ᐁ ᐃᑕᑲᑲᐠ ᒣᑲᐧᐨ ᐅᒪ ᐊᔭᑕᐤ ᐅᐦᒋ ᐅᓂᑲᓂᐢᑕᒪᑫᐤᐊᐧᐠ ᑕᐢᓭ ᒣᓇ ᑫᐢᓭ ᐁᑎᐧᐢᑕᒧᐊᐧᑕᑲᐧᐤ ᐁᑯᓀ ᑲᑫᓭᐤ ᑌᐸᐊᐢᑲᐣᓇ ᐁᑯᒪ ᑫᐢᐯᑲᐠ ᐅᑫᒪᐤ ᑌᐸᐊᒣᑲᐠ ᐊᐢᐳᐢᑕ ᐁᑯᒪ ᐊᑕ ᐁᓭᑫᑕᐠ ᑲ ᑲᑭᐧ ᓂᐢᑐᑕᒧᐃᐃᐧᐠ ᑕᐢᓭ ᑫᑕᒍᐊᐧᑌᑲᐧᐤ ᑌᐸ ᐊᒧᐊᐧᑲᐠ ᐊᑯᑕᒪᑫᐤᓇ

ᒪᑲ ᐅᑕᐤ ᐯᑯ ᐊᑎᑕᐧᓭᐠ ᐁᑕᓇᔭᑕᐤ ᐅ ᐃᐧᐸᔦᐤ ᐅᓭᒼ ᐁᑳ ᑲᐧᓭᐢᐠ ᐁᐃᑎᐧᐢᑕᒧᐊᐧᒋᑲᑌ ᑲᐧᐤ ᐊᑯᑕᒪᑫᐤᓇ ᒣᐢᑕᐃ ᐊᐧᐣᓭᒧᑕᑯᒪᑲᐣᓇ ᐁᑯᓭ ᒣᑲᐧᐨ ᓇᒪ ᐊᑲᒣ ᓇᒧᔭ ᓇᔭᐢᑕᐤ ᐅᑕ ᐅᐦᒋ ᑌᐸᐊᐢᑲᐣᒍᐃᐧᔭᒍᐊᐧᐠ ᐊᐢᐳᐢᑕ ᐅᒋ ᒪᑲ ᒣᓭᐃᐧ ᑯᐢᑲᐧᐨ ᐁᐃᐢᐯᒐᐠ ᐁᑯᒪ ᑫᑕᐢᑫᓇᐤ ᑲᑲᓇᑕᐠ ᐁᐃᑕᐢᑕᐧᐤ ᑌᐸᐊᒧᐊᐧᑲᐣᓇᐠ

ᐁᑯᒪ ᑫᓭᑲᓄᐊᐧᑕᒦᐠ ᑫᐢᐱᐠ ᑕᑫ ᓂᑯᑲᒪᑫᒪᑲᑲᐧᐤ ᐁᑯᓀ ᐅᐃ ᒪᓭᓇᐃᑲᐣᓇ ᑲᑫᒪᐧᐊ ᐧᓭᑯᓇᒪᐠ ᑕᐢᓭ ᑫᒋᓇ ᐁᓭ ᐅᐢᑫᓭᑲᐧᐊᒥᐠ ᒣᓇ ᒣᒣᐟ ᑫᓭᐊᔭᐠ ᓂᑫᐊᐸᒋᐊᐧᐠ ᓇᓈᐠ ᐁ ᐊᒋᒧᐊᔭᑲᐧᐤ ᑕᐢᓭ ᑲᑫ ᐯ ᐃᓭᑭᐢᑫᔭᑕᑲᐧᐤ ᐃᐧᓭᐤᐊᐧᐤ ᒪᒋᑲ ᐁᑯᓀ ᑲᐃᐧᐊᐸᒋᒋᑲᑌᑲᐧᐤ ᐅᑕ ᒣᓇ ᑕᐢᓭ ᑫᓭᑲᓄᐊᐧᑕᑲᐧᐤ ᐁᑯᒪ ᐊᑯᑕᒪᑫᐤᓇ ᐅᐦᒋ ᒪᒋᑲᐸᑯᓭᔭᑕᑲᐠ ᐊᔭᑕᐤ ᐅᐦᒋ ᐅᓂᑲᓂᐢᑕᒪᑫᐤᐊᐧᐠ ᑕᑐᓀᐢᑐᑕᑐᑕᐧᐤ ᐅᑫᒪᓈ ᐅᐦᒋ ᒣᓇ ᐁᔭᓂᐤ ᐅᓂᑲᓂᐤᐊᐧᐠ " ᐁᑯᒪ ᒣᓇ ᑳ ᑕᐳᐊᐧᑫᔭᑕᒦᐠ ᐅᑫᒪᓈᐠ ᐅᐦᒋᐅ ᑫᒪᐤᐊᐧᐠ ᑕᐢᓂᒋᐢᑐᑕᑲᐧᐤ ᑕᐊᐧᐸᐸᑲᐧᐤ ᒣᓇ ᑕᑭᐧᐢᑯᐃᐧᐱᐠᑫᑕᐧᐤ ᑕᑎᓂᑯᑲᒪᑫ ᑕᐧᐤ ᑌᐸᐊᒧᐊᐧᑲᐣᓇ ᐅᐦᒋ ᐁᑲᐧ ᒣᓇ ᑫᑐᓂᑲᐣᓂᑕᓇᐤᐊᐧᐠ ᑕ ᑕᐢᑕᐳᐃᐧᐱᐠᑫᑕᐧᐤ ᑕᒪᐢᑲᐤᐊᐧᐠ ᐯᑭᐢᑭᐃᐧᐠ ᑐᐯᓇᑲᐧᐤ ᐁᑯᒪ ᑕᑐ ᑫᑲᐧᐩ ᐅᑫᒪᓈᐠ ᑲᐃᐧᒪᓭᑕᑕᐧᐤ ᐁᑲᐧ ᒣᓇ ᑕᒪᓇᒋᑕᑕᐧᐤ ᐅᑕᑯᑕᒪᑫᐤᒍᐊᐧᐊᐧ ᐅᑫᒪᓈᐠ ᐅᐦᒋ ᐅᑫᒪᐤᐊᐧᐊᐧᐠ

ᐁᑲᐧ ᐸᐯᑐᐢ ᑳᑕᐠ ᑫᑲᐧᐩ ᑲᑫ ᐯ ᐃᐢᐸᔭᐠ ᒣᓇ ᐊᔭᑕᐤ ᐸᐯᑐᐢ ᑫ ᐃᓭᐃᐧᐱᐠ

ᒣᓂᑯ− ᐊᒋᑕᒪᑫᐅᓇ ᐅᑌᐢᑲᑌᑲᐧᐤ ᒪᑲ ᐁᑲᐧ ᑯᑲᐧᐠ ᐊᓄ− ᐅᑫᒪᓇᐠ ᐅᐦᒋ
ᐅᑫᒪᐤᐊᐧᐠ ᐯᑯᓇᒪᐠ ᐊᒋᑕᒪᑫᐃᐧᐠ ᐸᐯᐢᑯ− ᐁᑯᒪᓇᑯᔭ ᑲᔭ− ᒣᓭᐃᐧ ᑌᐸᐊ
ᐢᑲᒋᓇ ᒋᓂᔭᐤᐊᐧ ᑲᐢᑕᑕᐯᑕᒧᐊᐧᑕᐤ ᑌᐸᐊᒧᐊᐧᑲᒋᓇ ᒪᒋᑲ ᒋᐢᑲᐧ−ᐃ
ᐯᓇᒪᐧᐠ ᐁᑯᓭ ᐊᑌᓭᐁᑯᓇᒪᐧᐠ ᑕᐠᑫᑲᐧᐩ ᑲᑫ ᐊᒋᑕᒪᑫᑕᐧᐤ ᐃᐧᔭ ᑫᒋᐅᑫ
ᒪᐢᑭᐧᐤ ᐁᑫ ᐊᓭᐅᓇᒧᐊᐧᐠ ᑌᐸᐊᒧᐊᐧᑲᒋᓇ ᑕᑕᑕᓇᑕᐤ " ᐯᓭᑲᐧᔭᐠ ᑫᔭᐯ−
ᒣᓭᔭᑌᑯᑌᐤ ᐁᑯᑕ ᑌᐸᐊᒧᐊᐧᑲᓇᐠ ᑯᒋᔭᑕᐧᐤᒣᑲᐧ− ᐊᑕ ᐯᔭᐠ ᐅᓂᑲᓂ
ᐤᐊᐧ ᑫ ᐃᐧᑕᒪᑲᐧᐠ ᑲᒋᔭᑕᑲᐧᐤᒣᓇ ᑕᐊᐊᐧᔭᓇᐢᑕᑲᐧᐤ ᐅᔭᒋᐃ
ᐤᓇ ᐅᑫᒪᓇᐠ ᐅᐦᒋ ᐁᑲᐧᐊᐧ ᒣᐢᑌᑫᒪᐤ ᐁᔭᓂᐤ ᐊᐢᑭᔭ ᑲᑌᐯᔭᑕᒧᑲᒋᐠ
ᐁᑯᐦ ᑲᓂᑲᓇᐯᐢᑕᐠ ᐸᐧ3ᐳ3 ᑫᐃᓭᔭᑲᒋ ᐁᑯᒪ ᑲᑫ ᐃᑎᐧᐠ ᐁᑯᐢᐯ
ᒣᑲᐧ− ᐁᒪᒪᐤᐊᐧᐳᓂᑫᑕᐧᐤ ᐁᑯᒪ ᑯᑕᐠ ᐅᑫᒪᐤ ᑌᐸᐊᐢᑲᐠ ᑳᑭᐢᑲᔭᐊᐧᐠ
ᐅᐯᐁᔭᐤᐃᐧᐯᓂᑕ ᐁᑯᑫᒥᐟ ᓂᐢᑕᓇᐤ ᑌᐸᑯᑎᐸᓭᐠ ᐊᐢᑭᐩ ᐊᑫᑎᐟ 1976
ᓂᔭ ᐃᐧᔭ ᑌᐯᔭᐤ ᐁᓭᒫᑕᑐᓂᔭᑕᒪᐠ ᑕᐢᐳ ᑫᒋᓇ ᑕᑫ ᐃᐳ ᒣᓭᔭᐸᔭᐠ ᑌᓭᒪᓭᑕ
ᐠ ᐁᑯᓂ ᐅᐃᐊᒋᑕᒪᑫᐅᓇ ᒣᐢᑕᐃ ᑳᓇᑕᑌᐃᐧᐱᐢᑲᑫᒪᑲᑲᐧᐤ ᒣᑲᐧ− ᐁᑯᒪ
ᑲᐧᔭᐢᐠ ᑕᑫᓇᐅᐊᐧᐸᒋᑲᑌᑲᐧᐤ ᑕᐳᐳ ᑫᒋᓇ ᑲᑫ ᐃᑎᐧᐠᑕᑕᐧᐤ ᐅᑫᒪᓇᐠ ᐅᒋᐅᑫ
ᒪᐤᐊᐧᐠ ᐊᐳ ᑕᑫ ᓇᑕᐅᐃᐧᒋᑲᑌᐅᐊᐧ ᓇᐠᑕᐅ ᐃᐳ ᒪᒋᑲ ᑫᐢᐱᐠ ᐁᑯᐢᐁᐢ
ᒪᓭᑕᐠᒧᐊᐧ ᐁᑯᓂ ᑫᑕᓭᓇᐃᑲᑌᑲᐧᐤ ᒪᐢᑯ− ᑲᒋᐢᑯᔭᑌᓇᐳᑐᓇᐤ ᑕᐳᐳ ᑌᓭᐃᐧᐱᐠ
ᑫᔭᐠ ᒪᑌᐃᔭ ᑫᑲᐧᐩ ᑫᒋ ᑲᑫ ᐊᒋᑕᒪᑫᑕᐧᐤ ᐁᑯᓂᐠ ᐅᑫ ᐅᑫᒪᓇᐠ ᐅᐦᒋ ᐅᑫᒪᐤ
ᐊᐧᐠ ᐁᑯᒪ ᑌᓭᐃᐧᐸᐊᒪᑕᐧᐤ ᒪᐢᑯ− ᑕᐸᑲᑕᒥᐢᑲᑲᐧᐠ ᒪᒋᑲ ᐯᐳᐢ ᑫᑲᐧᐩ
ᓇᐅᐊᐧ− ᐁᒣᐊᐧᓭᐠ ᑕᒋᑕᒪᑫᐅᐊᐧᐠ ᒣᓇ ᑕᑲᓄᔭᑕᒪᐧᐠ ᑕᓂᒋᑲᒪᑫᑕᐧᐤ ᐊᓄ−
ᐁᑲᐧ ᑲᑫ ᓂᑲᓂᐢᑕᐠ ᐁᔭᓂᐤ ᐊᐢᑭᐩ ᑲᓇᐯᔭᑕᒧᑲᒋᐠ ᐸ3ᐳ3 ᒣᑐᓂ
ᒋᐢᑲᐧ− ᐁ ᐃᐢᐁᑕᑯᒋᐠ ᑫᓂᒋᑲᒪᐅᐃᐧᐤ ᐁᔭᒧᐊᐧ ᒣᓇ ᐁᓭᑲᐢᑫᑕᐟ ᑫᑲᑭᐧᓂ
ᐢᑐᑕᑕ ᐁᑯᓂ ᐅᐃ ᐊᒋᑕᒪᑫᐅᓇ ᑕᐳᓭ ᑫᒋᐠ ᐁᑕᑭᑌᑲᐧᐤ ᒣᓇ ᑫᑲᑭᐧᓂ
ᐢᑐᑕᐃᐧᐤ ᓇᓇᐳ ᐁᔭᒧᐊᐧ ᒣᓇ ᐅᑫᒪᓇᐠ ᐅᐦᒋ ᐅᑫᒪᐤᐊᐧ ᐁᑯᒪ ᑕᐳ ᑫᑲᐧᐩ
ᑲᒪᒥᐢᑯᑕᐠ ᒣᑐᓂ ᑲᐧᔭᐢᐠ ᐁᑕᐅᐊᐧᐊᐧᐠ ᒪᒋᑲ ᐁᑯᒪ ᐯᔭᐠᑲᐧᔭᐠ ᐯᑭᐢ
ᑭᐧᐃᐧᐠ ᑫᑎᐢᑕᒧᐊᐧᑕᒥᐠ ᐁᑯᐦ ᑕᓂᑲᒧᐃᐧᐯᓇᒪᑕᐧᐤ ᐅᑫᒪᐤᐊᐧᐠ ᒣᓇ ᐅᓂ
ᑲᓂᐢᑕᒪᑫᐅᐊᐧᐠ ᐊᐳ ᑫᑕᑕᐤᐃᐧ ᑕᓭᑯᑌᔭᒧᐊᐧᐠ ᑕᒪᒪᐤᐊᐧᐳᐢᑫᑕᐧᐤ
ᐁᑯᒪ ᒪᒪᐤᐊᐧᒋ ᑫᒋᓇ ᑲ ᑲᑭᐧᑕᒪᑕᐧᐤ ᒣᑲᐧ− ᐁᔭᓇᐊᐧᐠ ᑫᑲᓇᓇᑲᐧᐠᒣᓇ
ᐅᔭᒋᐃᐧᐤ ᓇ ᑫᐢᐱᐠ ᑫᑕᑕ ᐊᐢᑕᒪᑫᐅᐊᐧᐠ ᐅᑫᒪᐤᐊᐧᐠ ᓭᒫᐠ ᑌᑎᐢᑕᒧᐊᐧ
ᑕᑲᐧᐤ ᑭᐢᐱᐠ ᑕᑫ ᐊᐸᒋᐃᑯᐟ ᐅᑎ ᒣᓇ ᑌᐸᐊᒧᐊᐧᑲᐠ ᐁᑭᐧᔭᐠ ᐁᑯᑕ ᑕᑌ
ᐯᔭᒧᐊᐧᐠ ᑕᐸᒋᑕᑕᐧᐤ ᒪᑲ ᒣᓇ ᑕᑌᐯᔭᒧᑕᐤ ᐅᑫᒪᓇᐠ ᐅᒋ ᑫᓂᐧᐢᐠ
ᑌᐸᐊᒧᐊᐧᑲᒋᓇᐠ ᑕᐸᒋᑕᑕᐧᐤ " ᐁᑯᒪ ᑲᑫ ᒪᒥᐢᑯᑕᐠ ᐸ3ᐳ3 ᐯᑯᐦ ᐅᑕ
ᐤ ᐊᔭᑕᐤ ᐅᓂᑲᓂᐢᑕᒪᑫᐅᐊᐧᐠ ᑕᑌᐯᔭᒧᑕᐧᐤ ᑐᐢᑲᐤᐊᐧᐯᐢᑕᑐᑕᐧᐤ ᐁ
ᐊᓂ ᐅᐃ ᐊᑎᐟ ᑫᑲᐧᐩ ᑕᒪᒥᐢᑯᑕᑲᐧᐤ ᑫᐢᐱᐠ ᑌᐸᐊᒧᐊᐧᑲᐠ ᑕᑫ ᐊᐸᒋᐃ
ᑯᐟ ᒪᑲ ᐯᑯ ᐅᔭᒋᐃᐧᐊᐧᐠ ᐁᑯᑕ ᑕᐸᐟᑎᐢᑕᐧᐤ ᑕᒪᓭᓇᐃᑫᐃᑕᐧᐤ ᒪᒋᑲ
ᑲᑕᐁᐧᑫᑲᐧᐩ ᑌᑯᔭᐢᑌᐤ ᒪᒋᑲ ᒣᐢᑕᐃ ᑫᑲᐧᐩ ᑲᐃᐧ ᓇᓇᐸᒋᑕᐠ ᐊᐧ
ᐃᐧᐢᐠ ᐁᑯᒪ ᑲᐯ ᑯᐠᑲᑌᑲᐧᐤ ᐊᒋᑕᒪᑫᐅᓇ ᒣᑐᓂ ᐃᐧᐢᓭᑫᑌᑌᐢᑲᑲᐧᐠ
ᑌᐸᐊᒧᐊᐧᑲᓇᐠ ᒣᑲᐧ− ᐅᒪ ᐁᑯᐦ ᐸᑲᒋ ᐃᐢᐸᔭᑭ ᒣᒋᐟ ᐁᔭᓇᐊᐧᐠ ᑕᐳᓇ
ᐃᑌᐁᐅᐊᐧᐠ "ᐁᑲᐧ ᓂᔭᓇᐠ ᐅᔭ ᐅᐦᒋ ᐁᑯᒪ ᐅᑕ ᑲᑫ ᐃᐧᒋᐃᐃᐧᔭ ᑲᑫᒪ
ᓭᑕᔭᐠ ᐊᑎᐟ ᑫᑲᐧᐩ ᑳᒧᐢᑫᓇᒫᐠ ᐊᓄ− ᑕᐯᐢᑯ− ᐁᑯᓂ ᐅᐃ ᐊᑎᐧᐅ
ᑫᒪᓇᐠ ᐅᐢᒋ ᑲᑫ ᒪᒪᑕᐅᐃᐧᑕᑕᐧᐤ ᐯᑭᐢᑭᐧᐃᐧᓇ ᑕᐳᐳ ᑲᑫ ᐃᑎᐧᐢᑕᒧᐊᒋᑲᑌ
ᑲᐧᐤ ᒪᒋᑲ ᐁᑯᒪ ᐯᔭᐠ ᑕᑯᐢᑫᐃᐧᐠ ᒣᑲᐧ− ᓂᔭᑯᑕᓇᐠ ᐁᑯᒪ ᒪᓭᓇᐃᑲᐠ
ᑯᔭᐢᑕᔭᐠ ᒪᒋᑲ ᐁᑯᓂᐠ ᑲᐃᐧ ᐯᑭᐢᑭᐧᐢᑕᒪᑫᑕᐧᐤ ᑕᓂᐢᑐᑕᒪᐧᐠ ᐁᑲᐧ ᑫᑲᐧ
ᐩ ᑫᒋᓇ ᑫᑎᐧᒪᑲᐠ ᐯᑭᐢᑭᐧᐃᐧᐠ ᓂᒪ ᓂᓴᐧᓴᐠ ᐁᑯᒪᒣᓇ ᑲᒪᓭᑕᔭᐠ ᑕᑭᐧ
ᓂᐢᑕᓇᒧᐊᔭᑲᐧᐤ ᐁᔭᒧᐊᐧᐠ ᑕᐳᓭ ᑫᒋᓇ ᐁᐃᑕᑭᑌᑲᐧᐤ ᐊᒋᑕᒪᑫᐅᓇ ᑕᐳᓭᑫᒋ
ᓇ ᐁᓭ ᐃᑎᐧᑕᒧᐊᐧᑕᒥᐠ ᐁᑯᒪ ᑲᑲᑭ ᓂᒋᑲᒪᑫᔭᐠ ᓂᐢᑕᑕ ᑲᔭᐢᐯᒋ
ᑕᐳᓭ ᑲᑫᐯ ᐃᑕᑲᑕᑲᐠ ᐁᑯᓂ ᐅᐃ ᒣᒣᐟ ᒪᓭᓇᐃᑲᐠᓇ ᐯᑭᐢᑭᐧᐤᐃᐧᓇ
ᑲᐯ ᒪᐤᐊᐧᓭᑯᓇᒪᐠ ᒣᐢᑕᐃ ᑲᐯ ᓂᒋᑲᒪᑯᔭᐠ ᒪᒋᑲ ᐁᑯᑕ ᑲᐯ ᐸᓭᑯᓇᒪᐠ
ᐁᑯᒪ ᒪᓭᓇᐃᑲᐠ ᒪᒪᐤᐃᐧ ᓂᐊᐧᐢᑭᐩ ᑲᒧᒋᑕᔭᐠ ᐁᑯᒪ ᐁᓇᑐᓇᒪᐠ ᑕᐳ
ᓭᑫᒋᓇ ᐁᐃᑕᐢᑌᑲᐧᐤ ᐊᒋᑕᒪᑫᐅᓇ ᐁᑯᒪ ᐅᑕ ᐅᑫᒪᐤ ᑌᐸᐊᐢᑲᐠ ᐊᐢ
ᐳ3ᑕ ᑌᐸᐊᒧᐊᐧᑲᐠ ᐊᐢᐯᔭᒧᐊᐧᒋᑲᐠ ᓇᓇᐳ ᑲᑫᓭᐱᐧᐸᔭᑕᑕᐧᐤ ᐁᑯ
ᒪ ᑕ3 ᐃᐧᐢᑕ ᓂᔭ ᑲᑫ ᓂᑲᐠᓇᐯᐃᑲᐤᔭᐠ ᐁᑯᒪ ᒪᒋᑲ ᓂᑫᒪᒪᓭᓇᐃᑫ
ᐊᐅᐊᐧᐠ ᐅᓇᑲᒋᑕᐅᐃᐧᔭᒧᐊᐧᐠ ᑕᒧᐢᑫᓇᑲᐧᐤ ᐁᑯᒪ ᒪᒋᑲ ᑲᑫᔭᐤ ᐯᑭᐢ

ᑭᐧᐃᐧᐣ ᐁᑫ ᒪᓄᐊᐧᓯᑯᓇᒥᐠ ᐁᑯᑕ ᐁᑲᐧ ᑲᑫ ᐅᓯᐢᑕᓯᐣ ᐁᑯᒪ ᒪᓯᓇᐃ
ᑲᐣ ᑕᒥᐢᑲᓄᐊᐧᓂᐟᒍᐃᐧᓯᐣ ᐁᑲᐧ ᐅᒋᒋᐸᔪ ᐅᑕᐤ ᑕᓇᓇᐢᑯᒪᑲᐧᐤ ᑕᑐ
ᑲᑫ ᓂᐢᑯᑲᒪᑫᑕᐧᐤ ᐁᑯᒪ ᒪᓯᓇᐃᑲᐣ ᑯᓯᐢᑕᐠ ᑕᑐ ᑫᑲᐧᐩ ᑳᒪᒥᐢᑯᒋᑲᑌᐠ
ᓂᑳᐣ ᐁᑯᒪ ᒥᐢᑕᐃ ᓴᑭᐢᑲᑯᐃᓇᐠ ᐁᑯᓂᐠ ᐅᑭ ᑌᐸᐊᒍᐊᐧᑲᐣ ᐊᐢᐯᔭ
ᒍᐊᐧᑭᑲᐣᑯᓂᐠ ᐅᐦᒋ

ᐃᑲᐧ ᒣᐢᑕᐃ ᓂᓇᓇᐢᑯᒪᓇᑯᓂᐠ ᐁᑯᓂᐠ ᐅᑭ ᓂᓴᐧᓯᐠ ᐅᐦᒋ ᐅᑫᒪᓄᐊᐧᐠ ᐅᑫᒪᓇᐠ
ᐅᐦᒋ ᑳᑌᐯᔭᒍᑕᐧᐤ ᒋᓂᓯᓄᐊᐧ ᑲᐸᑫᑌᓇᑕᐧᐤ ᒪᒋᑲ ᑲᑫ ᐊᐸᒋᐊᔭᐠ ᐁᑯᓂᐊ
ᒍᐨ ᑫᑲᐧᐩ ᑲᒍᐢᑭᐣᑳᑌᑲᐧᐤ ᐁᑯᒪ ᒪᓯᓇᐃᑲᐣ ᑯᓯᐢᑕᒪᑫᐠ " ᐁᑲᐧ ᒣᐢᑕᐃᓂ
ᑕᑕᒣᐃᑯᓇᓇᐠ ᐁᑯᓂᐠ ᐅᑭ ᐅᑌ ᐅᐦᒋ ᐅᓂᑲᓇᐳᐊᐧᐠ ᐁᔦᓂᐤ ᐊᐢᑫᔭ ᑲᑌ
ᐯᔦᑕᒍᑲᓯᐠ ᑲᐸᐟᓇᒪᑫᑕᐧᐤ ᐁᑲᐧ ᒣᓇ ᐯᔭᐠ ᐅᑕᑐᐢᑫᔭᑲᐣᒍᐊᐧᐊᐧ ᐁᐸ
ᑫᓇᑕᐧᐤ ᐸᓂᓯᑲᒪᑯᔭᐠ ᐁᑯᒪ ᓇᓇᑐᓇᒫᐠ ᑫᑲᐧᐩ ᑲᐧᐣ ᑌᑎᕽ ᐁᓴᔦᑲᓯᐤ
ᐁᑲᐧ ᒣᓇ ᐁᑯᑕ ᓂᑕᑎᒣᔦᑯᓇᓇᐠ ᐅᐯᑭᐢᑯᐃᐧᓂᔪ ᑕᐸᒋᑕᐅᐊᐧᓯᐣ ᒪᓯᓇᐃᑲᓂᐠ ᑲ
ᑫ ᒪᓯᓇᐊᐠ " ᐁᑲᐧ ᒣᓇ ᓂᑲᓇᓇᐢᑯᒪᓇᓇᐠ ᐁᑯᓂᐠ ᐅᑭ ᐅᑌ ᐅᑐᐢᑲᐧᓂᐠ ᐅ
ᒋ ᐅᐊᐧᐸᑌᐃᐃᐧᐊᐧᐠ ᓂᐢᑕᑕ ᐯᒋ ᐁᔦᓂᐤ ᐯᒪᒋᐊᐧᑲᓇ ᑳᒪᓄᐊᐧᒋᑕᑕᐧᐤ ᐁᑲᐧᒣ
ᓇ ᑲᐸᑲᑌᓇᒪᑯᔭᑲᐧᐤ ᐃᐧᑕᐊᐧᐤ ᐁᒣᑯᔭᑲᐧᐤ ᑲᐧᐣ ᑌᑎᕽ ᐅᑲᒋᒍᐃᐧᐣᓂᔪ ᑲᐸᒋᑕᐤ
ᐊᐧᔭᐠ " ᐁᑲᐧ ᐁᑯᒪ ᓂᑲᒪᒥᐢᑯᑌᐣ ᑫᒋᓇ ᓇᒍᔭ ᑫᔭᐢᑯᐃᐧᐣ ᐁᑯᒪ ᑕᑐ ᑫᑲᐧᐩᑲ
ᔦᒍᒋᑲᑌᐠ ᐅᑕ ᒪᓯᓇᐃᑲᓀᐠ ᒣᒣᐟ ᑕᑐ ᑲᑫ ᒪᑕᓯᑐᑕᑕᐧᐤ ᑕᐃᐧᒋᑕᑯᑕᐧᐤ ᐅ
ᑐᑌᔦᑕᒍᐃᐧᐣᒍᐊᐧᐤ ᐅᑕ ᑲᐸᒋᑕᐅᐃᐧᐟ ᑕᕽ ᑲᓂᓱᑲᒍᐊᐧᑕᐤ ᐁᑲᐧ ᒣᓇ ᐁᑯ
ᓂᐠ ᐅᑭ ᑫᓯᐊᔭ ᑲᑫ ᒪᑕᓯᑐᑕᑕᐧᐤ ᐁᑯᑕ ᓇᓇᐢᑯᒪᓄᐊᐧᐠ ᐁᑯᓂᐠ ᐅᑭ ᐅᐦᒋ
ᑌᐸᐊᒍᐊᐧᑲᐣ ᐊᐢᐯᔦᒍᐊᐧᒋᑳᐣᑯᓂᐠ ᐅᐦᒋ ᐅᓂᑲᓂᐢᑕᒪᑫᐤᐊᐧᐠ ᓇᒍᔭ ᑫᒋᓇ
ᑕᑫ ᐃᑎᐠ ᐅᔭᐅᐊᐧᐤ ᓇᔦᐢᑕᐤ ᐅᑐᑌᔦᑕᒪᓄᒍᐊᐧᐤ ᑲᑫᔭᐤ ᑲᑫ ᐊᐸᒋᒋᑳᑌᔦᐠ

ᐁᑲᐧᐊᐧ ᐅᐢᐸᐧᑲᐣ ᑳᐊᐧᓴ ᑳᒣᑕᐃᐟ ᐁᑯᑕ ᐁᑭᐧᓯᐠ
ᑫᒋ ᐯᑭᐢᑭᐧᐃᐧᐣ ᐁᐊᐸᑕᐠ

Part One

The Treaty-Making Process

Chapter One

Canada's Northwest Indian Policy in the 1870s: Traditional Premises and Necessary Innovations*

by
John Leonard Taylor

In 1870, the Government of Canada assumed sovereignty over the
"Northwest" of the fur trade. That portion of the territory lying between the
mountains on the west, the Great Lakes on the east, the United States
boundary, and the Saskatchewan River system was considered ripe for
settlement and development. If this was to be undertaken without the danger
of the Indian wars experienced in the United States, then the Indians of the
region would have to be placated.

The traditional means of doing so in British North America had been
through treaties providing compensation in return for land surrender. In
whatever way they understood them, the western Indians themselves were
anxious to have treaties. Consequently, between 1871 and 1877, treaties
numbered from one to seven were concluded between the government and the
Indians of the proposed settlement areas. In the government view, the Indians
had agreed upon land surrender and the maintenance of peace. In return, the
government was to provide the Indian people with a small cash annuity,
reserves of land, schools, agricultural assistance, and hunting and fishing
supplies. The precise terms varied from treaty to treaty.[1]

---

* This paper was originally prepared for the National Museum of Man Symposium on Approaches to Native
History in Canada, 2-4 October 1975.

---

[1] The complete texts of the treaties are most readily available in Alexander Morris, *The Treaties of Canada
with the Indians of Manitoba and the North-West Territories* (1880; reprint ed., Toronto: Coles Publishing
Co., 1971). They are also to be found for the individual years in Canada, *Sessional Papers*, and together
with the texts of earlier treaties and surrenders, in Canada, *Indian Treaties and Surrenders from 1680 to
1902*, 3 vols. (1891; reprint ed., Toronto: Coles Publishing Co., 1971). The texts of individual treaties are
supplied on request by the Department of Indian Affairs and Northern Development, Ottawa.

These seven numbered treaties laid the foundation of the Dominion's Indian policy in the Northwest. In fact, during that decade the treaties were almost the only instrument and expression of that policy. Based on the premises and methods of the traditional British North American Indian policy, they were nevertheless innovative in some respects. This only becomes apparent when the treaty-making decade is examined in some detail.

This has been difficult to do because no detailed or well-researched account of the subject has been produced. Some printed primary sources have been readily available. The official record appeared in successive annual issues of the *Sessional Papers*. In 1880, Alexander Morris, who had been chief negotiator for four of the seven treaties, brought out his book entitled *The Treaties of Canada with the Indians of Manitoba and the North-West Territories*. Much of his material duplicates that in the *Sessional Papers*, but it does include some additional accounts of treaty negotiations and some of his own views. The sketchy secondary accounts in existence have been based on these two sources.[2]

Stanley's chapter on the treaties in his now forty-year-old book, *The Birth of Western Canada*,[3] remains the most thoroughly researched and most detailed account of the subject in print. His purpose in this book, however, was not to expound on the treaties, but to explain the causes of the Northwest Rebellion. His chapter entitled "The Indian Problem: The Treaties" is merely a prologue to his major thesis. His theory is that, within the context of a culture clash, some Indians joined the Métis in rebellion because of maladministration by the Indian Department. He does not find the causes of Indian discontent in the treaties themselves, but in the period that followed. Stanley challenged only half of the conventional wisdom—the quality of the Indian administration. He left the treaties and the treaty-making process largely intact.

The conclusions which emerge from the official records and the secondary literature are (1) that Canada's Indian policy in the Northwest was a further application of the traditional British North American policy which had evolved from British eighteenth-century practice and had come to fruition in Upper Canada; (2) that this policy was deliberate, wise, and benevolent.

Any attempt to question the validity of these conclusions must take into account the manuscript sources which were not used by the authors of the

---

[2] Alexander Begg, *The Great Canadian North-West* (Montreal: 1881); Alexander Begg, *History of the North-West*, vol. 2 (Toronto, 1894); A.G. Harper, "Canada's Indian Administration: The Treaty System," *América Indígena* 7, no. 2 (April 1947); David Laird, *Our Indian Treaties* (Winnipeg: Manitoba Free Press, 1905); E.H. Oliver, "Saskatchewan and Alberta: General History," in *Canada and Its Provinces*, ed. A. Shortt and A. G. Doughty (Toronto, 1914); D. C. Scott, "Indian Affairs, 1867-1912," in *Canada and Its Provinces*, ed. A. Shortt and A.G. Doughty (Toronto, 1913).

[3] George F.G. Stanley, *The Birth of Western Canada: A History of the Riel Rebellions* (Toronto: University of Toronto Press, 1960).

existing literature. These sources include the papers and records of major participants: Sir John A. Macdonald Papers, A.G. Archibald Papers, Alexander Morris Papers, Records of the Indian Affairs Branch, and Records of the R.C.M.P.[4]

As far as it goes, there is no reason to doubt the soundness of the first conclusion derived from the existing accounts. Ministers and government officials gave every indication that they intended to adhere to traditional practices as closely as possible. They believed that treaties faithfully observed had been responsible for a successful and peaceful relationship with the Indian people of Canada in contrast to the Indian wars in the United States. Since the Indians themselves seemed anxious to have treaties, the government wished to continue the traditional policy of treaty making.

Not only was treaty making the first premise of traditional policy, but there was precedent in old Canada for every significant item which came to be included in the western treaties. Some earlier eastern treaties had provided for reserves and annuities. The Robinson Treaties of 1850 had also included hunting and fishing rights. Agriculture and education had received official encouragement from the Indian Branch, while hunting and fishing supplies were amongst the earliest items supplied to Indians. All of this could be described as traditional Indian policy and practice. What was new in the Northwest was the inclusion of all these items in the treaty terms as obligations upon the Crown.

These features of the treaties gave a plausible ring to the impression of considered purpose, wisdom, and benevolence behind the government's actions as conveyed in the secondary literature. There the treaties are presented as creations of the government. The Indian contribution was confined to "intransigence" and the making of "extravagant demands." This view is not supported by a closer examination of the evidence. A good case can be made that the Indians, and not the government, were responsible for introducing most of the important treaty terms.

Treaties One and Two were both concluded during August 1871 and contained identical terms. The government's initial offer to the Indians consisted only of reserves and a small cash gratuity and annuity. A draft treaty was sent from Ottawa to the commissioners before they negotiated Treaty One. Ken Tyler found it amongst the *A.G. Archibald Papers*, and discovered that it included only those provisions along with a prohibition of alcoholic beverages. Yet what emerged from the negotiations at Lower Fort Garry was a treaty providing not only for these items, but also for schools and farm animals, implements and supplies. These additions appear to have been proposed by the Indians, since the commissioners had no instructions to offer

---

[4] Sir John A. Macdonald Papers, Records of the Indian Affairs Branch (RG10), and Records of the R.C.M.P. (RG18) are in the Public Archives of Canada, Ottawa; A.G. Archibald Papers and Alexander Morris Papers are in the Public Archives of Manitoba, Winnipeg.

them. This view is further supported by the fact that the agricultural aid was not included in the treaty text, but in the form of "outside promises" which were reduced to writing by the commissioners in a memorandum.[5] This memorandum only became a formal part of the treaties in 1875.

The government displayed no intention of offering so much in subsequent treaties. Prior to the negotiation of Treaty Three with the Saulteaux, only annuities and the initial gratuity were discussed in correspondence which passed between Alexander Morris, the treaty commissioner, and the minister, Alexander Campbell.[6] The Saulteaux, however, had demands of their own to make. They had drawn up a list as early as January 1869. It included agricultural aid as well as hunting and fishing supplies. They managed to have these items included in the text of their treaty.

Like Treaties One and Two, Treaty Three carried the marks of its dual origins. In both instances, the Indian parties had added to the government's traditional terms some necessary innovations. To the Indians, these additional treaty terms were necessary because of their fear and anxiety about their own survival. They were necessary innovations to the government because without them they would have had even more difficulty getting treaties, if they had been able to get them at all.

None of the secondary literature contains any recognition of this Indian contribution. Some of it notes that there were difficulties getting treaties in some places, but where reasons were given for these difficulties, the official sources are quoted to the effect that the Indians made "extravagant demands." This is the major reason given for the failure to make the first treaty with the Lakeland Saulteaux between Lake Superior and Red River. Treaty One was made at the Red River Settlement instead. The government concluded Treaty Three with the Saulteaux only after four unsuccessful attempts had been made. Nor was Treaty One concluded easily. Treaties Four and Six also involved difficult negotiations because of extravagant Indian demands, according to the commissioners. Some of those extravagant demands were in fact the provisions for schools, agricultural assistance, and help in making the transition to a new life, which give the treaties the appearance of a forward-looking plan for the economic and social well-being of the Indian people.

Once it is realized that those treaty provisions that best support a claim for deliberation, wisdom, and benevolence came from the Indian side, it is evident that no plan meriting the description "wise and benevolent" was ever produced by the government. In fact, no plan at all was ever produced. The picture is one of a government seeking to forestall potential trouble from

---

[5] The Indian parties to the treaty disputed that the memorandum contained all that had been promised them.

[6] Morris, *Treaties*, p. 48.

the Indian inhabitants occupying the site of its prospective development project, and attempting to do so at the least cost.

In spite of government intentions, the Indians were able to obtain more than they were originally offered. Credit must be given to the treaty commissioners, who showed some understanding of the problems and exercised enough flexibility to meet Indian suggestions part way. Nevertheless, it is evident that the Indians themselves had displayed an awareness of their situation and had taken the initiative in suggesting the means of coping with it.

Chapter Two

Two Views on the Meaning of Treaties Six and Seven

by
John Leonard Taylor

To mark the importance of the Indian treaties of the 1870s, the Government of Canada had a medal struck for distribution to the chiefs. The reverse side of this medal carries the image of a treaty commissioner grasping the hand of an Indian. The clasped hands and the buried hatchet suggest that a common understanding had been reached between red man and white. The one definite conclusion that will be advanced in this paper is a denial that a common understanding had been reached on fundamental issues involved in the treaties. More tenuous are the attempts to specify in what ways the views of the two parties diverged.

Attention will be confined to the crucial issue of surrender of territorial rights. The treaty texts present the government view. We do not know to what extent the meaning of the treaty texts was communicated to the Indians. Written accounts of the treaty negotiations concentrate almost entirely on what the Indian parties would receive, barely mentioning what was to be given up by them. We know even less about the Indian understanding. Nevertheless, the purpose of this paper is to present what we do know on the subject from the written or archival sources, and to compare that with the understanding held by Indian elders today as presented in their oral testimony.

This essay consists of three sections. The first provides some general geographical and historical background to the treaty making. This is followed by a description of the treaty negotiations derived from archival sources. The final section contrasts the impressions derived from these sources with the views contained in the oral testimony of present-day Indian elders.

The area covered by Indian Treaties Six and Seven includes the central portion of the Province of Saskatchewan and the southern half of the Province of Alberta. This country is prairie in the south and parkland and forest to the north. The two branches of the Saskatchewan River flowing through it collect the waters of many smaller rivers. East of Prince Albert, these two branches unite, flowing ultimately into Lake Winnipeg.

Before this region was taken over by the Dominion of Canada in 1870,[1] it was populated principally by the Saulteaux, Cree, Blackfoot, Blood, Peigan, Assiniboine, and Sarcee nations. In addition, about five hundred Sioux had moved north from Minnesota in 1863, and had become permanent residents of the area that later was to be Manitoba and Saskatchewan. The Saulteaux (Ojibwa) and Cree were a varied and numerous people, who also inhabited territory far to the east of the region dealt with here. The Ojibwa territory followed the contours of the Great Lakes to Georgian Bay, while that of the Cree adjoined it to the north and extended east of Hudson and James Bays. These two Indian nations had spread from their eastern districts, gradually pushing further west until some bands had moved into the prairie and parkland regions and adopted the way of life of the buffalo hunters.

The two major ways of life amongst the Indians in this region were those of the prairie and the woodland. The former was based on buffalo hunting almost exclusively. It depended on the horse and a quasi-military organization of the bands. This made the Prairie Indians particularly formidable as potential enemies. The Woodland Indians were scattered in smaller groups in pursuit of forest-dwelling game, including fur-bearing animals and fish. They were less dependent on any one animal than were the buffalo hunters. The Saulteaux and Cree nations contained both woodland and prairie bands, while all of the other Indian nations of the region were buffalo hunters, with only minor exceptions.

From the eighteenth century onwards, the territory inhabited by these people had been penetrated by the French and British fur traders. Its fur resources had been tapped even earlier by the Hudson's Bay Company. The Company had been formed in 1670 by Royal Charter and had established posts at the mouths of the large rivers flowing into Hudson Bay. Through the use of Indian middlemen, the effect of the fur trade had been felt far beyond the bay even before the first inland post of the Company was founded in 1774. This post was built in response to the Montreal-based traders who had reached the "Northwest," as it was called, via the St. Lawrence-Great Lakes canoe route.

The European fur traders were a mere handful in the midst of an Indian population that numbered in the tens of thousands. Since no European women were brought out, alliances were made with Indian women, which resulted in

---

Editor's Note: Although this paper was written while the author was employed by the Indian Claims Commission, the views expressed are entirely his own and are not necessarily those of the Commissioner.

---

[1] The Hudson's Bay Company claimed ownership to the territory under the terms of a royal charter granted in 1670. In 1870, the Company sold its territorial rights to the Dominion of Canada.

a population of mixed-blood, or Métis, people. By 1870, they had become a numerous group with a consciousness of themselves as a ''new nation.''

Indian life had been slowly, but significantly, transformed in the two centuries prior to 1870. Even those who did not participate directly in the fur trade obtained European goods from Indian middlemen, while those Indians who did participate, blending a subsistence living with the pursuit of furs for trade, became particularly dependent upon European goods: guns, ammunition, traps, hardware of all sorts, and manufactured cloth. One Indian, while expressing antipathy towards the Hudson's Bay Company, said that the Indians would die if the Company went away.[2]

Beyond the subsistence activities of hunting, fishing, and gathering, the fur trade provided the major economic base for the Indian and Métis population of the Northwest. Many of these people were indirectly or directly involved in the trade, whether as trappers, buffalo hunters, tripmen,[3] or traders on their own account. The prairie region had long been the food basket of the fur trade. Dried buffalo meat (pemmican) was a staple food on the trail or in the trading post. As a fur region, the Prairies were insignificant. Prairie trading posts like Carlton were more valuable as collection centres for pemmican than for the furs traded there.

During the second half of the nineteenth century, the pace of change in the Northwest quickened. More efficient and intensive trapping and hunting techniques were reducing game generally, so that the Indians and Métis became worried about their food supply. Both subsistence and participation in the fur trade as trappers or suppliers of pemmican were threatened.

The seemingly endless supply of buffalo, especially, was showing signs of diminishing. Pressure on the buffalo for pemmican was no doubt partly responsible. The greatest factor in the disappearance of the buffalo, as for change generally, however, was settlement in the United States, which preceded that north of the boundary by at least a quarter century. The combination of American settlement and hunting was the major factor in the steady diminution of the buffalo herds. The trade in buffalo robes played a large part in the destruction. This trade was extended from Benton, Montana, to Fort Edmonton in the later 1860s.

Events in the United States provided an example of what settlement could mean to Indians. Destruction of game, loss of territory, disease, and wars with American troops made the period a desperate one for the Indians of the western United States. Kinship united many of the tribes along the international boundary and gave many British Indians an awareness of these circumstances. They could hardly have welcomed similar occurrences in

---

[2] Alexander Morris, *The Treaties of Canada with the Indians of Manitoba and the North-West Territories* (1880; reprint ed., Toronto: Coles Publishing Co., 1971), p. 111.

[3] These people manned the York boats, canoes, and Red River carts. Some men were employed as labourers in a variety of capacities.

their own territory. Yet penetration of American traders and gold seekers raised the question of the region's future. American frontiersmen would be unlikely to respect the sanctity of Indian country or of the trading preserve of a British fur company.

While these events in the United States were having their effect in the Northwest, other occurrences were taking place in the east which were to become even more significant to western Indians. In 1867, three colonies of British North America united to form the Dominion of Canada. Compared to its present size, the new Dominion was geographically very small. From the beginning, however, its founders had plans for expansion. They looked upon the Northwest as the logical region for Canadian territorial growth.

Many reports had been received in Canada about the prospects for agricultural settlement in the Northwest. Although they were not all entirely favourable, there seemed sufficient likelihood that the land and resources of the region could support a vigorous population. Confederation of the British North American colonies, political acquisition of the Northwest, and a railway could secure to the Canadian business community the two-way trade of a new region ripe for development. Some of these Canadian businessmen and the politicians who supported their views had an even wider vision of a new political and commercial union from the Atlantic to the Pacific. If the Crown colony of British Columbia was to be included in the Dominion, it would be essential to acquire first the Hudson's Bay Company lands which separated that remote colony from the other British North American colonies in the east.

The motives of those who sponsored Confederation and acquisition of the Northwest were commercial and political. The drive towards the northwest was inspired by the potential land for settlement and resources for exploitation, and the hoped-for trade which such settlement and resource exploitation could be expected to generate. Those who would undertake the work of settlement and development in the Northwest would be drawn from the older colonies, from overseas, or from the United States.

No one anticipated that the native Indians or the Métis would take much part in this work. At best, they might survive the changes by learning to farm in imitation of the agricultural immigrants who could be expected to pour into the country. The success or failure of the project would not depend on the native people, but would be determined by the resources of the country itself and by the kind of immigrants who could be attracted there.

Yet the Indians could not be entirely ignored. They were numerous relative to the few Europeans then in the country. Although little was known about the northwestern tribes, the protracted and expensive Indian wars of the United States were well known north of the boundary. If for no other reason than that the Indians could seriously hamper its plans for the Northwest, the new Dominion would have to take them into account. Once

Northwest acquisition became a reality, an Indian policy for the region would have to be worked out.

The only policy the government had was an inheritance from the British and British North American past. The British, like the French, had encountered Indians everywhere they had gone in North America. Each European nation had made alliances with some tribes and fought wars against others. They conducted diplomacy and trade with the Indians. Just before the Seven Years' War, the British appointed Indian superintendents to conduct relations with the pro-British tribes. After the war, Great Britain emerged as sole European master of the eastern portion of the continent. At that time, the Proclamation of 1763 set out some of the basic principles of British Indian policy. Both Crown title and aboriginal right in the soil were implied, while it was reserved to the Crown alone to acquire Indian land by extinguishing aboriginal title at a general assembly of the Indians concerned. Private citizens were forbidden to do so.

Indian policy continued to be military in motivation and nature through the American Revolution and afterwards until 1830. By this time, Indians were no longer looked upon as potential allies or enemies, but as uncivilized or semi-civilized natives in need of protection from the vices of civilization and aid in acquiring its virtues. These included settlement in a fixed place and some means of earning a living. In society as it was, this almost always meant learning to farm. Conversion to Christianity and the acquisition of the rudiments of an English education were also desirable goals. As a result, various schemes were tried to accomplish these ends. These were largely influenced by the wave of religious and humanitarian enthusiasm which was motivating reform both in Britain and throughout the Empire.

In Upper Canada particularly, an aboriginal right in the soil continued to be recognized, although no attempt at definition was made. Whenever land surrenders became necessary, they were accomplished through treaties between the Crown and a general assembly of the Indians affected. While the earlier Upper Canadian treaties provided compensation only in the form of a once-for-all payment in goods, later treaties included annuities. In addition, reserves were sometimes set aside as homes for Indian bands.

In 1850, W.B. Robinson negotiated two treaties on behalf of the United Province of Canada with the Indians of Lakes Huron and Superior. Alexander Morris wrote of these Robinson treaties as "forerunners of the future treaties." According to him, the main features of the Robinson treaties were annuities, reserves, and liberty to fish and hunt on the unceded domain of the Crown.[4] These treaties were the first to contain all three provisions.

These were the elements of the Indian policy inherited by the new Dominion of Canada in 1867. In an addresss to the Queen that year praying

---

[4] Morris, *Treaties*, p. 16.

for the admission into the Dominion of the Hudson's Bay Company's territories, the two Houses of the Canadian Parliament assured Her Majesty that ''the claims of the Indian tribes to compensation for lands required for purposes of settlement will be considered and settled in conformity with the equitable principles which have uniformly governed the British Crown in its dealings with the aborigines.''[5] The intention to continue in the tradition of the established policy thus expressed was incorporated into the Order in Council admitting Rupert's Land and the Northwestern Territory into the Dominion.[6]

In private correspondence, members of the government admitted their ignorance of the new territory and its people. They did know that they were facing a new and different Indian situation from that pertaining in old Canada. They knew that it would not be sufficient simply to extend the activities of the Indian Branch to the Northwest as had been done for the Maritime provinces. An administration for the western tribes would have to await agreements between those peoples and government respecting their future relationship. In making these agreements, there seems never to have been much doubt that the government would follow the general principles of the traditional Indian policy.

After incorporating the Northwest into the Dominion in 1870, the Government of Canada did begin to negotiate treaties with the Indian inhabitants of the region. The first two were made in what is now the southern portion of the Province of Manitoba extending slightly into the present Province of Saskatchewan. It appears that the government intended giving no more to the Indians of this western country than Robinson had given on the Upper Lakes twenty-one years earlier. Only annuities and reserves were offered. Even hunting and fishing rights were not included in these treaties. The treaty commissioner told the Indians verbally that they could continue to hunt and fish over their old territory until it was taken up for other purposes.

After several days of negotiations, Treaty One was concluded. It contained some terms which had not been part of the government's original offer.[7] A school was to be maintained on each reserve. Intoxicating liquors were banned from reserves. Even with these additions, the written treaty did not contain everything discussed and agreed upon at the negotiations. Besides omitting hunting and fishing from the formal terms, specified items of agricultural aid had been negotiated, but were not written into the treaty either. Confusion over precisely what had been agreed upon occurred immediately after the treaty was made. Disagreement occurred not only

---

[5] *Revised Statutes of Canada 1970*, Appendices, p. 264.

[6] Ibid., p. 260.

[7] See draft treaty in A.G. Archibald Papers, Public Archives of Manitoba, Winnipeg. A.G. Archibald was lieutenant-governor of Manitoba and *ex-officio* of the Northwest Territories. Together with Wemyss Simpson, Indian commissioner, he negotiated Treaties One and Two in August 1871.

between the commissioners and the Indians, but amongst the commissioners themselves. The latter finally set down on paper a version acceptable to themselves of what agricultural aid they believed had been agreed upon with the Indians.[8] Although not all of the Indians were satisfied with this written version of the "outside promises," the commissioners' memorandum was made part of Treaties One and Two by Order in Council four years after the treaty itself had been made.

Since the archival evidence makes it clear that the government had intended giving only reserves and annuities, the provisions for schools and agricultural aid must have been introduced into the negotiations by the Indians. Some of them, those at St. Peter's, for example, were already familiar with schools and with farming. They may also have been influenced by American Indians in making these demands. It is highly to the credit of the first Indians in western Canada to make treaty with the Dominion that they took the initiative in making these proposals.

Meanwhile, Treaty Three was concluded with the Saulteaux in the lake and forest region west of Lake Superior and east of the Red River. It had been intended to make the first treaty with these people, since their country lay on the route west from old Canada, but the first four attempts to do so had failed. The Saulteaux would not accept the terms offered. As a result of their repeated refusals, their treaty was not successfully concluded until 1873. It included all the provisions of the first two treaties, as well as providing for an annual expenditure of fifteen hundred dollars on hunting and fishing supplies. In addition, the annuity was raised from three dollars to five, and the size of reserves from 160 acres per family of five to one square mile. All of these provisions were written into the treaty text, including the hunting and fishing clause and the specific items of agricultural aid. Treaties Four and Five, negotiated in 1874 and 1875, were similar in their terms.[9]

While the government intended eventually to make treaties across the whole prairie region to the mountains, the Cabinet decided in the summer of 1873 not to do so at once, but to proceed only as the territory was required for settlement or other purposes. While this policy may have met the government's requirements, it did not take into account those of the western Indians. They were reported to be disturbed about their future. W.J. Christie, the senior Hudson's Bay Company officer at Fort Edmonton, transmitted to Lieutenant-Governor Archibald at Winnipeg a message from the Cree chief, Sweet-Grass. Christie's covering letter is dated 13 April 1871. Sweet-Grass complained:

---

[8] Morris, *Treaties*, pp. 126-28.

[9] One notable difference in Treaty Five was the reduction in the size of reserves to 160 acres per family of five (as in Treaties One and Two), and in some cases to 100 acres.

We heard our lands were sold and we did not like it; we don't want to sell our lands; it is our property, and no one has a right to sell them.

Our country is getting ruined of fur-bearing animals, hitherto our sole support, and now we are poor and want help—we want you to pity us. We want cattle, tools, agricultural implements, and assistance in everything when we come to settle—our country is no longer able to support us.[10]

Treaty making began that summer in Manitoba, but did not cover the territory as far west as that inhabited by Sweet-Grass and his people. Government action was frequently speeded up by prodding from Alexander Morris, who succeeded Archibald as lieutenant-governor in December 1872. He sent to Ottawa a steady stream of reports and letters from persons in a position to know the Indian situation in the Northwest, together with views of his own. He continually informed the government of Indian dissatisfaction over the speed with which the authorities were dealing with them. In spite of all the information received, the government still hesitated. In the summer of 1875, so Morris informed Laird, the Cree stopped the Geological Survey at the elbow of the North Saskatchewan. After a great deal of telegraphing to the minister of the Interior, Morris finally got permission to promise a treaty to the Cree of the Saskatchewan country for the following year.

On 27 July 1876, Morris left Fort Garry to negotiate the treaty. He was accompanied by his fellow commissioner, W.J. Christie, formerly of the Hudson's Bay Company, and a secretary, Dr. Jackes, M.D. The third commissioner, the Honourable James McKay,[11] was to meet them at Fort Carlton where the treaty would first be made. For the first time, the North West Mounted Police were to provide an escort for the treaty commissioners.[12]

On arrival at Fort Carlton, Morris was met by Mistawasis (Big Child) and Ahtukukoop (Starblanket), the two head chiefs of the Carlton Cree. The main body of the Indians assembled on 18 August. Morris described the scene:

On my arrival, the Union Jack was hoisted, and the Indians at once began to assemble, beating drums, discharging fire-arms, singing and dancing. In about half an hour they were ready to advance and meet me. This they did in a semicircle, having men on horseback galloping in circles, shouting, singing and discharging fire-arms.

They then performed the dance of the "pipe-stem," the stem was elevated to the · north, south, west and east, a ceremonial dance was then performed by the Chiefs and head men, the Indian men and women shouting the while.

---

[10] Morris, *Treaties*, pp. 170-71.

[11] James McKay was a Métis and spoke Cree. The title "Honourable" derived from his membership on the Executive Council of Manitoba. Consequently, he was well known to Morris. He had also participated in making every other treaty in the Northwest except Treaty Four.

[12] Christie and Dickieson travelled with a Mounted Police escort to pay annuities to the bands of Treaty Four during the summer of 1875. Carlton, however, was the first treaty negotiation to be attended by the Mounted Police.

Courtesy Manitoba Archives and Glenbow-Alberta Institute

Drawing of Fort Carlton

> They then slowly advanced, the horsemen again preceding them on their approach to my tent. I advanced to meet them, accompanied by Messrs. Christie and McKay, when the pipe was presented to us and stroked by our hands.
> After the stroking had been completed, the Indians sat down in front of the council tent, satisfied that in accordance with their custom we had accepted the friendship of the Cree nation.[13]

In this statement, Morris underestimated the importance to the Indians of the pipe-stem ceremony. It signified more than an offer of friendship, although that was certainly included.[14] The pipe-stem ceremony was a sacred act undertaken before conducting any matter of importance. In the presence of the pipe, "only *the truth* must be used and any commitment made in its presence must be kept."[15]

From the point of view of the government officials, the ceremonial was merely a picturesque preliminary favoured by Indian custom. To them, the binding act of making treaty was the signing of the document at the close of negotiations. This was the mode of affirming agreements among Europeans. On the other hand, " . . . the only means used by the Indians to finalize an agreement or to ensure a final commitment was by the use of the pipe."[16]

Morris continued his account of the proceedings:

> I then addressed the Indians in suitable terms, explaining that I had been sent by the Queen, in compliance with their own wishes and the written promise I had given them last year, that a messenger would be sent to them.[17]

Two interpreters accompanied the government party. The Indians had also brought their own interpreter, a man named Peter Erasmus. These men rendered the commissioner's address into Cree. Morris stressed the friendship that had always existed between the British and the Indians. He told them that the Indians in the East were happy and contented. The Queen's councillors saw that the Indians' means of living were passing away from them and therefore sent men to speak to them and to tell them that their children must be educated and taught to raise food from the soil.

> We are not here as traders, I do not come as to buy or sell horses or goods, I come to you, children of the Queen, to try to help you; when I say yes, I mean it, and when I say no, I mean it too.
> I want you to think of my words, I want to tell you that what we talk about is very important. What I trust and hope we will do is not for to-day or to-morrow only; what I will promise, and what I believe and hope you will take, is to last as long as that sun shines and yonder river flows.[18]

---

13 Morris, *Treaties*, pp. 182-83.
14 See appendix two.
15 Ibid.
16 Ibid.
17 Morris, *Treaties*, p. 183.
18 Ibid., pp. 201-2.

The relationship of trust and friendship implied in these words of Morris preceded the negotiation of specific terms. They set whatever terms might be arranged within a general context of care and concern on the part of the Queen for the welfare of her Indian people. On the Indian side, the atmosphere of alliance and friendship had already been expressed through the pipe-stem ceremony. Whatever specific provisions might be put in the treaty, they could hardly be inconsistent with the spirit in which both Indians and Her Majesty's representative had come together on this solemn occasion. One Indian elder of the present day expressed it this way:

> That is why they were agreeable to treaty because the promises were so good. The government official was always making reference to a woman (Queen) who had sent them. The Indians sympathized with the woman, the Queen, through her representatives. That is why it was not difficult to give up the land. [19]

Only after setting the discussions within a context of friendship and care were specific treaty terms proposed. They were similar to those of the first five treaties. Peter Erasmus related that on the second day of meeting Morris asked for the Indians' views on these terms. Nevertheless, he added that he could go no further than he had the previous day.

> Pound Maker who was not a chief at that time but just a brave, spoke up and said, ''The governor mentions how much land is to be given to us. He says 640 acres, one mile square for each family, he will give us.'' And in a loud voice he shouted, ''This is our land! It isn't a piece of pemmican to be cut off and given in little pieces back to us. It is ours and we will take what we want.''
>
> A strong wave of approval came back from the seated Indians at his statement. Some braves in the last row rose to their feet, waved their hands and arms, shouting, ''Yes! Yes!'' in Cree. Apparently these were Pound Maker's followers. It was some time before the main chiefs could restore order. [20]

Erasmus claimed that Morris was visibly shaken by this episode which portended difficulty in gaining acceptance of the government's treaty terms. Morris replied that unless certain lands were set aside for the sole use of the Indians, the country would be flooded with white settlers who would crowd the Indians out as they had elsewhere. This reply dealt with only one of Poundmaker's points, the principle of reserves. It by-passed the questions of their size and of the Indians' role in determining the conditions of their own future. Mistawasis brought that day's proceedings to a close by suggesting that the commissioner's words should be thought out quietly.

The Indians did not hold a council the next day (Sunday). The people were given the day to talk things over amongst themselves. The Indian council was called for Monday and the full assembly with the commissioner for Tuesday.

---

[19] See Chapter five, ''Interviews with Elders,'' Lazarus Roan, Smallboy Camp, 30 March 1974.

[20] Peter Erasmus, *Buffalo Days and Nights* (Calgary: Glenbow-Alberta Institute, 1976), p. 244.

The only source of information for the Indian council is Peter Erasmus. He had begun as interpreter for the Indians. Shortly after negotiations began, he was also taken into the pay of the treaty commission, while remaining the Indians' interpreter. He became convinced by the second day of meeting that the proposed treaty terms would be in the Indians' best interests. This is the probable meaning of his statement that " . . . my sympathies transferred to the Governor's side." He claimed that Mistawasis and Ahtukukoop were also convinced of the fairness and justice of the terms. Opposition to the treaty terms appeared to be led by Poundmaker and two other men, identified only as the Badger and "a Chipeway."

The views of the two chiefs, Mistawasis and Ahtukukoop, were those that prevailed in the council. The major argument of the former was that Indians were beginning to experience hardship from the diminution of the buffalo and that this situation was likely to worsen rather than improve. He saw a new way of life offered to them in the treaty and asked those who opposed signing the treaty, "Have you anything better to offer our people?" He did not acknowledge directly the point made by Poundmaker that the proposed terms were inadequate to provide a new way of life and that they should insist on better terms. He offered a counter argument, however, in saying that even if all the tribes were to act together, their numbers were too small to make their demands heard.

Ahtukukoop spoke in the same way. The buffalo were going, and without them the Indian would die unless he could find another way. "For my part, I think that the Queen mother has offered us a new way and I have faith in the things my brother Mistawasis has told you. . . . Surely we Indians can learn the ways of living that made the White man strong . . . "[21]

The majority of the other chiefs and councillors appeared to be in agreement with Ahtukukoop and Mistawasis. The latter adjourned the council in saying that there would be an opportunity to ask questions and that the interpreter would write down the things that the council thought should be in the treaty.

The Indians met the commissioners again the following day (Tuesday, 22 August). The chief concern of those who addressed the commissioners was the food problem. Morris seemed to understand their situation.

> The whole day was occupied with this discussion on the food question, and it was the turning point with regard to the treaty. . . . they were not exacting, but they were very apprehensive of their future, and thankful, as one of them put it, "a new life was dawning upon them."[22]

In spite of the differences that had appeared in Monday's council between supporters and opponents of the proposed treaty, all the Indian

---

[21] Ibid.
[22] Morris, *Treaties*, p. 185.

spokesmen asked for better terms. The essential difference between them was in the lengths to which they were prepared to go. The more intransigent would have united in the last resort in a refusal to sign the treaty. The majority were prepared to acquiesce after making every effort possible to get better terms, short of an actual refusal of the treaty. Tuesday's speakers prepared the way for the presentation of the Indians' proposals for better terms.

The conference continued on 23 August, with the interpreter, Peter Erasmus, reading a list of the changes they wished to make in the commissioners' offer.

They asked for an ox and a cow each family; an increase in the agricultural implements; provisions for the poor, unfortunate, blind and lame; to be provided with missionaries and school teachers; the exclusion of fire water in the whole Saskatchewan; a further increase in agricultural implements as the band advanced in civilization; freedom to cut timber on Crown lands; liberty to change the site of the reserves before the survey; free passages over Government bridges or scows; other animals, a horse, harness and wagon, and cooking stove for each chief; a free supply of medicines; a hand mill to each band; and lastly, that in case of war they should not be liable to serve.[23]

After assuring himself that these demands were indeed those of the whole people, Morris made his reply. He expressed his pleasure at their request for missionaries, but explained that for this they must look to the churches and noted the presence of missionaries at the conference. He did agree to make some additions to the number of cattle and farm implements in order to encourage them to settle. Three entirely novel terms were also added. To aid them while cultivating after they had settled on the reserves, provisions were to be supplied to the extent of one thousand dollars per annum, "but for three years only, as after that time they should be able to support themselves."[24] Another new clause in this treaty provided for a grant of assistance "in the event hereafter of the Indians comprised within this treaty being overtaken by any pestilence, or by a general famine." The third additional clause provided that a medicine chest should be kept at the house of each Indian agent. These three new clauses and the increased level of agricultural aid had all been added at the request of the Indians.

Morris gave his assent to them while making the point that what was offered was a gift, since they still had their old way of life. His apparent understanding of the Indian fears regarding the buffalo was not evident in this statement.

Ahtukukoop called on the people for their assent and they gave it by shouting and holding up their hands. At this point, Poundmaker rose and said that he did not see how they could feed and clothe their children with what

---

[23] Ibid.
[24] Ibid., p. 186.

was promised. He explained that he did not know how to build a house or cultivate the ground. Another Indian made further requests in the name of Red Pheasant,[25] but when Morris charged the latter with bad faith for assenting to the terms and then demanding more, Red Pheasant said that the spokesman did not speak for him at all. The principal chiefs then stated that they accepted the terms as offered by Morris.

At some time previous to the negotiations, the proposed treaty had been written in a fine hand on six separate sheets of parchment. Now the three new clauses and additional farming aid had to be added to this text. Erasmus noted that ''these special provisions were added into the draft of the treaty before the signing began.''[26] The extra farming supplies agreed upon were written between the lines in a different hand. The places in the text where these items were inserted were marked by arrows. New sheets were drawn up containing the three additional terms. These were placed before the signature page on which the last few lines of the treaty's concluding paragraph remained in the original penmanship.

Erasmus remarked that the reading of the treaty took a great deal of time and the services of all the interpreters. ''Mistawasis had called me aside and told me to keep watch on the wording and see that it included everything that had been promised; however the other chiefs appeared satisfied that the Governor would carry out his promises to the letter. I was able to assure Mistawasis that everything promised had been included in the writing. He was satisfied and his name was the first in the signing.''

The terms offered at Carlton were similar to those of the previous treaties; an immediate, cash gratuity and an annuity of five dollars per head, reserves of one square mile per family of five, schools, a hunting guarantee along with an annual allotment of supplies, and specified farming aid. In addition, each chief and councillor would receive a suitable suit of clothing every three years, and each chief a flag and medal and also a horse, harness, and wagon.

The Fort Carlton bands signed Treaty Six on 23 August 1876. Five days later, Morris took the adhesion of the Duck Lake Band, which had not participated in the negotiations. Chief Beardy addressed Morris. ''He said some things were too little. He was anxious about the buffalo.'' Beardy said that he wanted assistance when he was utterly unable to help himself, but Morris reiterated what he had told the main body, that the government could not support or feed the Indians, and that all it could do was help them cultivate the soil. If a general famine ensued, the government would come to their aid. Meanwhile, the governor general and the Council of the Northwest Territories would examine the feasibility of a law to help preserve the

---

[25] Ibid., p. 242. Red Pheasant described himself as a Battle River Indian.
[26] Erasmus, *Buffalo Days and Nights*, p. 253.

buffalo. Having received these assurances, three chiefs and their headmen signed the treaty.[27]

The commissioners then left for Fort Pitt, the second place of meeting appointed for Treaty Six negotiations. These began on 7 September. Again, the Mounted Police, under Inspectors Walker and Jarvis, provided the escort. ''The Indians approached with much pomp and ceremony, following the lead of 'Sweet-Grass.''' Morris called this man ''the principal Chief of the Plain Crees.''

A ceremony similar to that which had taken place at Carlton was conducted. Morris then addressed the Indians.

> I told them what we had done at Carlton, and offered them the same terms, which I would explain fully if they wished it. . . . On the 8th the Indians asked for more time to deliberate, which was granted, as we learned that some of them desired to make exorbitant demands, and we wished to let them understand through the avenues by which we had access to them that these would be fruitless.[28]

On 9 September, the Indians were still in council, but at length approached the commissioners. Morris asked them to speak to him. After some time, Sweet-Grass did so. His address was an acceptance of the government's terms, although his words as reported by Morris seemed a plea for co-operation in protecting the Indians from extinction. ''When I hold your hand and touch your heart, let us be as one; use your utmost to help me and help my children so that they may prosper.''

Morris reported that the people assented to the speech of Sweet-Grass ''by loud ejaculations.''[29] He expressed his satisfaction with what he termed their unanimous approval of the treaty terms. The chiefs and headmen of the bands gathered at Fort Pitt, then signed the same treaty as had been negotiated at Carlton.

One chief, Big Bear, came to see Morris after the signing. He said that he spoke for the bands which were out on the prairie hunting. He made the request that the commissioner should save him from what he most dreaded, that the rope should be about his neck. Morris replied that the Queen's law provided that murderers should be hanged and that only bad men needed to fear it. Big Bear repeated his request, but it was again denied. He also wanted the buffalo preserved and was pleased that something was to be done about it. He said that he could not sign the treaty because his people were not present, but promised to tell them what he had heard and to return next year. Morris claimed that Big Bear gave assurances that he accepted the treaty as if he had

---

[27] Morris, *Treaties*, p. 188.

[28] Ibid., p. 190.

[29] Ibid., p. 237.

Sweet-Grass

Courtesy Provincial Archives of Alberta, E. Brown Collection

Pakan or James Seenum, chief who signed Treaty Six

signed it and would return the next year with all his people to meet the commissioners and sign it.[30]

Treaties had now been negotiated with Indians throughout the prairie region except for those in what is now southern Alberta. These were the Blackfoot, Blood, and Peigan, and their allies, the Sarcee. The Mountain Assiniboine or Stonies in the foothills of the Rockies were also outside any treaty.

Unlike the Saulteaux, Cree, and Prairie Assiniboine, these people were not on the main travel route through the Northwest. They had had less to do with traders until the American traders moved north in the 1860s and 1870s. They were traditional enemies of the Cree and Prairie Assiniboine, and probably resented the close connection between those nations and the Hudson's Bay Company, especially the supplying of arms and ammunition to them.

While the Blackfoot people had remained largely outside the major British fur trade network, their isolation was broken by the American traders from the south. It then became only a question of which orbit would draw them in, the American or the Canadian. The arrival of the Mounted Police in the summer of 1874 was a significant event in Blackfoot history. The police were followed by settlers. These events placed the Blackfoot in a position similar to that of the other Indians of the Northwest. Henceforth, their territory, too, was regarded as a region for settlement. The prospect of increased settlement in their territory gave some importance to a treaty from the government's point of view.

The Blackfoot, too, no doubt saw their own position differently than they had prior to 1870. In that year, their numbers were much reduced by smallpox. Whiskey, which had been a major item in the American buffalo robe trade, had further weakened them. The Mounted Police had stopped the trade in whiskey, but their arrival, followed by that of the first settlers, must have aroused concern for their future position. The danger that the buffalo would disappear was becoming more evident each year. Late in 1876, their food supply was further threatened by the arrival on the edge of their territory of five thousand Sioux, refugees from the United States. All of these factors were likely to have disposed the Blackfoot towards making a treaty, whether or not they were actively proposing one.

Morris strongly recommended against further delay. He pointed out that missionaries and others in the region had agreed that it was important to make a treaty in order to preserve "the present friendly disposition of these Tribes." This disposition might be changed by the settlement of white people "who are already flocking into Fort McLeod and other portions of this Territory."[31] Morris advised the minister of the Interior that a Roman

---

[30] Ibid., p. 242. In fact, Big Bear did not sign the treaty until 1882.
[31] Canada, *Sessional Papers*, 1878, no. 10, XVI; see also Morris, *Treaties*, pp. 245-49.

Courtesy Provincial Archives of Alberta, E. Brown Collection

Big Bear

Bobtail, Cree chief who signed an adhesion to Treaty Six

Catholic priest, Father Scollen, who had lived amongst both Cree and Blackfoot, and the Methodist missionary, John McDougall, of the Mountain Assiniboine, had both strongly suggested that a treaty be made with the Blackfoot the following year. He had asked for statements of their views in writing and enclosed these for the minister.[32]

The government accepted this advice and preparations were made to negotiate the last of the treaties of that period. When it was concluded, the government would consider Indian rights in the entire prairie region and eastward to the Great Lakes watershed to have been extinguished, and the whole territory open for the kind of development which had been the purpose behind Dominion acquisition of the Northwest.

Although Morris had urged western treaties throughout his entire term of office, he was not to preside over the negotiation of the final one. Immediately after the signing of Treaty Six, the Northwest Territories Act of 1875 was put into effect to provide a separate government for the Territories. Morris was relieved of the governorship there, while remaining lieutenant-governor of Manitoba and of Keewatin. David Laird, whose Cabinet post as minister of the Interior was given to David Mills, was sent out to become the new lieutenant-governor of the Territories.[33] Laird was also appointed Indian commissioner or chief superintendent in that jurisdiction. As such, he would be responsible for the Indian administration and bore chief responsibility under the minister for the negotiation of Treaty Seven.

James McLeod, who became commissioner of the Mounted Police in 1876, in succession to French, was also appointed an Indian commissioner in order that he might serve with Laird in negotiating the treaty. This appointment reflected the important role of the Mounted Police in relation to the Indians of the southwestern region in contrast to their position in the Saskatchewan country where they had barely begun to establish themselves by 1876. In the making of Treaty Six that summer, they had merely acted as an escort for the commissioners, and many of the Indians who came to Fort Carlton and Fort Pitt may have been seeing the scarlet-coated horsemen for the first time. The police had been much more visible in the Blackfoot territory, the main centre of their operations, and had established genuine rapport with the Indians, who gave them great credit for keeping out the whiskey traders. McLeod had earned the respect of the local chiefs and enjoyed a good relationship with them. His position as an Indian commissioner was expected to assist in inducing the Blackfoot to sign a treaty on terms that the government was prepared to offer.

---

[32] Morris to minister of the Interior, 24 October 1876, Alexander Morris Papers, Public Archives of Manitoba, Winnipeg. The missionaries' reports are included also.

[33] Laird reached Swan River, N.W.T., the temporary seat of government, on 11 November 1876, and took the oaths of office there on 27 November.

Courtesy Carling-O'Keefe Breweries of Canada and Glenbow-Alberta Institute

Painting of Blackfoot Crossing

Laird and McLeod travelled to the Blackfoot Crossing of the Bow River, where the treaty negotiations had been appointed to begin on Monday, 17 September. Although the commissioners reached the Crossing and were prepared to begin that day, not all the Indians had arrived. Nevertheless, the formalities were commenced with those who were present.[34]

The proceedings began very much as they had at previous treaty makings. The chiefs were introduced to the commissioners and then Laird addressed the assembled Indians. Because they were not all present, Laird said that he would not hurry the negotiations, but would wait until Wednesday to give the others time to arrive.

Although the principal Blood chiefs had not yet arrived, negotiations began again on the Wednesday with a speech by Laird. To the extent that the available text of Laird's address can be trusted,[35] he appears to have placed the proposed treaty terms within a similar context to that used by Morris at Carlton.

> The Great Spirit has made the white man and the red man brothers, and we should take each other by the hand. The Great Mother loves all her children, white man and red man alike; she wishes to do them all good. . . . But in a very few years the buffalo will probably be all destroyed, and for this reason the Queen wishes to help you to live in the future in some other way. She wishes you to allow her white children to come and live on your land and raise cattle, and should you agree to this she will assist you to raise cattle and grain, and thus give you the means of living when the buffalo are no more.

Laird then outlined the terms being offered. He described them as similar to those accepted the previous year by the Cree in Treaty Six. They would not be expected to give an answer at that time, but on the following day.

The next day, the proposed terms were further explained. According to Laird, Eagle Tail, head chief of the Peigan, was satisfied with them, while the chiefs of the Assiniboine "unreservedly expressed their willingness to

---

[34] Hugh Dempsey, *Crowfoot* (Norman, Okla.: University of Oklahoma Press, 1972), pp. 93-94. Hugh Dempsey explains that the Blackfoot chief, Crowfoot, had refused to attend the negotiations in a white man's fort (Fort McLeod) and insisted that the negotiations be conducted further north in his own area. For that reason, the site had been changed to Blackfoot Crossing. This angered the chiefs of the Blood and the North Peigan, who pointed out that Ford McLeod was central to all the tribes. When told that a further change would not be made, several Blood chiefs refused to attend. The status of Crowfoot also caused confusion and resentment. "One of the underlying causes of the dissension was the false position in which the Mounted Police and other officials placed Crowfoot in regard to the negotiations. Crowfoot was considered by them to be the head chief of the whole nation and the undisputed leader not only of the Blackfeet but also of the Bloods and the Peigans. Such a thought was entirely foreign to the Blackfeet, with the result that chiefs with equal or greater influence than Crowfoot felt they were being ignored."

[35] Morris, *Treaties*, p. 250. Morris, who includes the address in his book, commented, "I now append . . . a report of the speeches of the Commissioners and Indians, extracted from a report in the *Globe* newspaper, dated October 4th, 1877, which, though not authentic, I believe, gives a general view of what passed during the negotiations."

accept the terms offered."[36] Yet a Blood chief[37] made a speech in which he both praised the Mounted Police for the benefits they had brought the Indians, and claimed compensation for the wood they had used to the extent of fifty follars to each chief and thirty dollars to all others. Laird feared that this suggestion might be considered to have been accepted by the commissioners were he not to deny it promptly. Accordingly, he did so, telling the Blood chief that any payment to be made in the matter referred to should come from the Indians for the services of the police. "Here the Indians indulged in a general hearty laugh at this proposition."[38]

Crowfoot said on Thursday that he would not speak until the next day. On Friday, it was rumoured that the Indians were divided, not an unusual situation at treaty negotiations nor one that should occasion surprise. Laird commented, however, that the opposition could not have been very strong, since the treaty was accepted by the chiefs that day. Crowfoot asked for some further explanations. When the commissioners asked the Indians to give their views, Crowfoot spoke first. "His remarks were few, but he expressed his gratitude for the Mounted Police being sent to them and signified his intention to accept the treaty."[39] The other chiefs all assented in the same fashion, according to Laird, so that it was arranged to have the treaty signed on the following day (Saturday).

Hugh Dempsey, using information gathered in interviews in 1939 and 1957, provides a somewhat different interpretation of the negotiations. He claims that Eagle Calf was the only Blackfoot chief in favour of accepting the treaty as it was discussed in council on the Wednesday evening. Eagle Calf's position was that white settlers were coming anyway, so that they might as well receive some compensation. Crowfoot wanted the opinions of the chiefs of the other Blackfoot tribes, especially Red Crow, head chief of the Blood, before taking a stand himself. Consequently, he delayed the negotiations until the Blood arrived. This would explain why he declined to speak on the Thursday. Old Sun, another Blackfoot chief, similarly declined. Only Medicine Calf gave his speech that day and it was a counter proposal to the treaty. Dempsey noted that by the end of that day, the only chief who appeared to openly favour the treaty was the Stoney, Bearspaw. "The Blackfeet had been silent and the few Bloods present had been opposed."[40]

---

[36] Canada, *Sessional Papers*, 1878, no. 10, XI.

[37] Dempsey, *Crowfoot*, p. 99. Dempsey identifies him as Medicine Calf, more commonly known as Button Chief, and calls him "War Chief of the Bloods." Laird described him as a "minor Blood chief."

[38] Morris, *Treaties*, p. 271. In his official report, Laird described this occurrence differently. "Hereupon 'Crowfoot' and the other Chiefs laughed heartily at the Blood orator of the day," (Canada, *Sessional Papers*, 1878, no. 10, XXXIX). Dempsey challenged the interpretation put on this incident by Laird. He stated that the treaty minutes, as printed in the *Manitoba Daily Free Press* of 8 November 1877, read "the Indians indulged in a general hearty laugh at this proposition," that is, at the suggestion of Laird.

[39] Canada, *Sessional Papers*, 1878, no. 10, XI.

[40] Dempsey, *Crowfoot*, p. 100.

Courtesy Glenbow-Alberta Institute

Crowfoot

Courtesy Provincial Archives of Alberta, E. Brown Collection

Red Crow

On the Thursday evening, the Blood arrived in camp. Red Crow and Crowfoot conferred together. "There is no record of what went on that night."[41] Although some of the Blood war chiefs were opposed, Red Crow obtained approval of the treaty from his council. But he told Crowfoot on the Friday morning that, because he had been present for the full negotiations, the final decision would be left to him. Crowfoot was heavily influenced by the benefits the Mounted Police had brought to his people and by his trust in McLeod. Although he did not want settlement and change, he, too, feared it was coming anyway. "That would be the time they would need to rely on the white man for help."[42] When Crowfoot made his acceptance speech that afternoon, the chiefs of the other tribes agreed to sign, too.

Crowfoot's views were particularly influential because his first loyalty was to his people, while at the same time he enjoyed the confidence of the white men. Dempsey credits Crowfoot, McLeod, and the Mounted Police generally for the fact that a treaty was obtained. According to his account, it was a much closer decision than Laird's report represents it to have been. Sir Cecil Denny, an officer of the Mounted Police who was present at the negotiations, also indicated that the Indians had not been as favourably inclined towards a treaty as Laird's version suggests. "More than once it looked as if all chance of concluding a treaty would have to be abandoned, the Indians threatening to leave the ground."[43]

Having gained the verbal acceptance of the Indians, Laird spent the rest of Friday preparing the draft treaty. In order to save time in full assembly, McLeod meanwhile discussed reserves with the various chiefs. The choice of reserves proceeded so smoothly, according to Laird, that it became possible to name the places chosen in the treaty, as had been done in Treaty One. A common reserve was assigned to the Blood, Sarcee, and Blackfoot at Blackfoot Crossing. This arrangement may have obscured real differences, since in later years the Blood and Sarcee requested their own reserves in different parts of the country.[44]

The treaty was signed in the usual way on Saturday, 22 September. The following Monday, an assembly was held to affix the signatures of some minor chiefs who had not remained to sign on the Saturday. On this occasion, an additional formality was included. "The Chiefs were then asked to stand up in a body, their names were read over and the Indians once more asked to say whether they were their recognized chiefs."[45] After a little confusion over the position of one chief, the issue was settled satisfactorily.

---

[41] Ibid., p. 101.

[42] Ibid., p. 98.

[43] Sir Cecil E. Denny, *The Law Marches West*, 2nd ed. (Toronto: J.M. Dent and Sons (Canada), 1972), p. 109.

[44] Dempsey, *Crowfoot*, p. 104-11.

[45] Canada, *Sessional Papers*, 1878, no. 10, XI.

Courtesy Provincial Archives of Alberta, H. Pollard Collection

Crow Eagle, Peigan chief who signed Treaty Seven

Courtesy of Glenbow-Alberta Institute

Bull Head, Sarcee chief who signed Treaty Seven

Courtesy Glenbow-Alberta Institute

Chiniquay, Stony chief who signed Treaty Seven

Laird and McLeod were then able to give the chiefs their flags, uniforms, and medals, following which the Mounted Police made the payments to the Indians. The presentations and payments were made separately to the Assiniboine, who were encamped two miles further up the river. On the invitation of the chiefs, the commissioners went on Wednesday to the council tent, where an interpreter, speaking on behalf of the Indians, expressed their gratitude to the commissioners ''for the kind manner in which they conducted the negotiations, to me [Laird] personally for having come so far to meet them, and to Lieutenant-Colonel McLeod for all that he and the Mounted Police had done for them since their arrival in the country.''[46] The commissioners in reply assured the Indians that they would not regret having agreed to the treaty.

The terms of Treaty Seven did not differ in any fundamental way from those of previous treaties. Nothing was included about intoxicants, but a general prohibition existed through the Territories anyway, and the police were now present and attempting enforcement. Two items which had appeared for the first time in Treaty Six were not repeated, the provisions for aid in case of famine or pestilence and for a medicine chest to be kept by the agent. The Treaty Seven chiefs were to be given Winchester rifles instead of horses and wagons, while agricultural aid emphasized cattle rearing rather than field crops.[47] With these exceptions, the familiar terms of previous treaties reappeared in almost the same language.

Did the Indian people and the government have a similar understanding about the meaning of a treaty? The commissioners' understanding and that of the government are well described in the written text of the treaties. ''The Plain and Wood Cree Tribes of Indians, and all other the Indians [*sic*] inhabiting the district hereinafter described and defined, do hereby cede, release, surrender and yield up to the Government of the Dominion of Canada for Her Majesty the Queen and her successors forever, all their rights, titles and privileges whatsoever, to the lands included within the following limits . . . '' After describing the territory to which the treaty was deemed to apply, the treaty text contains a comprehensive clause which amply provides for any defectiveness in the description. ''And also all their rights, titles and privileges whatsoever, to all other lands, wherever situated, in the North-West Territories, or in any other Province or portion of Her Majesty's Dominions, situated and being within the Dominion of Canada.''[48]

---

[46] Ibid., XII.

[47] The terms allowed for two alternatives. The Blackfoot, Blood, Peigan, and Sarcee were expected to undertake cattle rearing by preference and the Assiniboine to choose the cultivation of field crops. Consequently, more cattle were allowed to the former, in place of implements, such as ploughs and harrows. The quantity of ploughs and harrows allowed to those choosing them followed the terms of Treaty Six rather than the less generous provisions of the earlier treaties.

[48] Morris, *Treaties*, p. 352.

In return for the surrender of the Indian title to their territory, the bands adhering to a particular treaty were to receive specified items of compensation separately negotiated for each treaty. The government view of a treaty was that of an instrument of land surrender with provisions for a *quid pro quo* in terms of annuities, reserves of land, and other traditional items.

It is more difficult to ascertain the Indian understanding of the significance of the treaties. It is obvious from the words and actions of some Prairie Indians prior to 1876 that they saw a connection between non-Indian use of their territory and a treaty to provide compensation for such use. They seemed willing, even anxious, to enter into negotiations with representatives of the Queen's government to determine the nature and amount of the compensation to be given to them. But did they understand that a land surrender would be required of them, or more fundamentally, what surrendering land meant?

There is no evidence that any preparation of the Indian people for making a treaty preceded the negotiations themselves. No one ever appears to have gone out from the government to explain the nature and purposes of the treaty beforehand. Once the decision was taken to make treaty with a particular group of people, it was usually done as speedily as possible. The Indians concerned were often given very little advance notice that they were to gather at a certain time and place to meet with the commissioners. They were assembled and within a few days were expected to give assent to propositions which we now know would be momentous for their future. This was the pattern followed in making Treaties Six and Seven.

The Reverend George McDougall was commissioned to tell the Indians of the Saskatchewan only that the government would make a treaty with them during the summer of 1876. He was not instructed to make any explanations. Following his death during the winter of 1875-76, his son, the Reverend John McDougall, tried to prepare some of the Indian people for the treaty negotiations. "We could assure them on general principles but as to details we did not know ourselves." The general principles seemed to be very general indeed. "However, we [another missionary, Henry Bird Steinhauer, was with him] did extol British justice and we emphasized the need of faith in God."[49] There is no indication that McDougall attempted to explain the meaning of a land surrender or that any other missionary did so.

Similarly there is no recorded evidence that the commissioners attempted at the treaty negotiations to explain what they meant by a surrender. They did refer to the danger that settlers would come in and possibly take all of the Indians' land. The treaty, however, was presented as a protection against this eventuality. Reference to settlers and other newcomers was usually made in connection with the idea of keeping the peace and not

---

[49] John McDougall, *Opening the Great West*, with an Introduction by Hugh A. Dempsey and J. Ernest Nix (Calgary: Glenbow-Alberta Institute, 1970), p. 42.

molesting these people. The Indians were to allow them to share the land and resources. This concept would not have been unfamiliar to Indians of the time.[50] The lack of emphasis in the negotiations on the surrender by the Indians of their territory is in sharp contrast to the prominence and explicit detail of the surrender clauses of the treaty texts.

The text of the treaty required them to "cede, release, surrender and yield up to the Government of the Dominion of Canada . . . all their rights, titles and privileges whatsoever" to their lands. These words, read to the assembled Indian people at the close of the negotiations, were at variance with the emphases made during the discussions. There, land cession had been ignored, while the focus had been on what the Indians would receive.

What, then, did the Indians think they were giving up? The archival evidence provides only small clues. Morris records the question of one chief in Treaty Three who asked, "Should we discover any metal that was of use, could we have the privilege of putting our own price on it?" To which Morris replied,

> If any important minerals are discovered on any of their reserves the minerals will be sold for their benefit with their consent, but not on any other land that discoveries may take place upon; as regards other discoveries, of course, the Indian is like any other man. He can sell his information if he can find a purchaser.[51]

The Fort Francis chief told Morris, "In this river, where food used to be plentiful for our subsistence, I perceive it is getting scarce. We wish that the river should be left as it was formed from the beginning—that nothing be broken." Morris replied, "This is a subject that I cannot promise." He was seconded by his assistant, Simon J. Dawson, who said, "Anything that we are likely to do at present will not interfere with the fishing, but no one can tell what the future may require, and we cannot enter into any engagement."[52] In both Treaties Three and Seven, individuals asked payment for pre-treaty use of wood and timber. The archival evidence creates a strong impression that at the negotiations of Treaties One and Three the Indians wanted to retain control over most of their territory. To what extent they understood that by signing the treaties they were totally relinquishing any control except for their reserves is unknown. This point was certainly not made evident at the negotiations.

The archival evidence leaves many questions unanswered about the Indian understanding of the treaties. It is mostly official or semi-official in nature and Euro-Canadian in origin. Whatever Indian material it does contain reaches us at one remove. Has any information been passed down by Indian

---

[50] Selby Smyth had implied this idea in his report to Morris when he said that the Saskatchewan Indians "decline permitting their country to be made use of by Government officials until the treaty becomes a fact" (Smyth to Morris, 6 August 1875, Alexander Morris Papers, Public Archives of Manitoba, Winnipeg).

[51] Morris, *Treaties*, p. 70.

[52] Ibid., pp. 73-74.

people themselves which might help us to discover what understanding their ancestors possessed of the meaning of the treaties?

In an attempt to find out what Indians understood by the treaties, some native organizations have interviewed older people who could be expected to have some information from parents or grandparents. One body of such material was made available for purposes of this paper by the Treaty and Aboriginal Rights Research (T.A.R.R.) wing of the Indian Association of Alberta. Considerable numbers of elders throughout the province were interviewed in their own language over the last few years and their testimony recorded. It was later translated into English and typed.

Since the treaties were made a century ago, none of the interviewees were eyewitnesses, except in the case of Treaty Eight, made in 1899 and 1900. The use of evidence that is not first-hand testimony poses problems which cannot be solved by an examination of the evidential material alone. Does the interviewees' testimony represent an oral tradition from the time of the treaty making, or does it originate from some more recent time? This question can perhaps be partly answered by research into Indian-government relations during the past one hundred years and into the history of the Indian associations and other political activity. A thorough evaluation of the testimony would require further research. All that can be attempted here is to outline the general answers to the questions raised as derived from the oral testimony and to see how they compare with the archival material.

Information obtained through the oral testimony in the Treaty Six region concentrated on the questions of what the Indians gave up or did not give up and what they were to receive in return. The understanding which runs through all of the testimony is that the Indians gave up limited rights in the land, namely, the surface rights. This was explained as being land required for farming. It is most often expressed in terms of depth, informants varying on the actual depth, from six inches to two feet.

In a summary of the interviews with elders, Lynn Hickey has an explanation based on language:

> The almost universal occurrence in the Treaty 6 area of the idea that only the surface of the land was sold may stem from a linguistic problem. The fact that all interviews so far are from Cree speakers may lend support to the idea that the word "land" may not translate into Cree with the same meaning as it does in English. There is evidence that "land" is usually used with various prefixes which must be added in order to specify more precise meanings. Thus, if the prefix indicating "surface" land were used to explain what settlers needed for farming, Cree-speakers may have understood they were being asked for something entirely different from "land" with some other prefix attached. Since we cannot know which Cree word for "land" was used in translating at Treaty 6 negotiations, and since Cree requires great precision in the use of prefixes, there are innumerable possibilities for misunderstandings to have occurred simply over this one issue.[53]

---

[53] Lynn Hickey, "Summary of Elders' Interviews" (paper prepared for the Indian Association of Alberta).

There is no archival evidence that any overt distinction was made at the treaty negotiations between surface and subsurface rights. The closest any of it comes to the subject is the question raised by the Treaty Three chief about minerals. While the archival evidence is simply silent on the point, it is universally mentioned in the Treaty Six oral testimony. Most of that testimony expresses the view that subsurface rights were not surrendered. Some interviewees stated that Morris actually said he was only buying the surface or enough for farming and indicated by a gesture how deep this was. In contrast, some few interviewees said that the distinction between surface and subsurface rights was not mentioned.

In spite of this variation over the actual historical event, there is unanimity over the interpretation. The elders do not believe that the Indians surrendered the subsurface rights. They believe that their ancestors understood the treaty as providing for a limited surrender or sharing of territorial rights. Expected settlement was agricultural. Farmers used only the surface of the earth. The Indians had agreed not to molest settlers who came to farm. When non-Indians began to dig into the subsurface for minerals, oil, and natural gas, it seemed to them a breach of the treaty agreement on what it was they had surrendered.

Similarly, commercial use of timber, game, and fish by non-Indians was seen by some as a breach of the treaty. There was universal agreement amongst the interviewees that the animals, birds, and fish were not surrendered. Some explained that these things would not have been given up because they were needed in order to live. With regard to timber, there was a split between those who believed that it had been surrendered and those who did not. Amongst those who dealt with water (lakes and rivers) and the mountains, all said that they had not been given up. Some mentioned the spiritual significance of the mountains and said that Indians would never have surrendered them. Many of the informants said that water and mountains had not been mentioned at the treaty negotiations. This answer is more likely to mean that they were not given up than the reverse. They see the treaty negotiations in terms of certain things being requested by the commissioners. Only those specific items were surrendered.

This view is a complete contradiction of the literal meaning of the treaty text, but it is the understanding of the elders. There are evidently two divergent views on the meaning of Treaty Six. One of the elders explained the difference in this way. "When they [the treaty commissioners] took the papers back to Ottawa, they made them so that the government could claim all of Canada. They did not ask permission here to do that. So now Canada is owned by the white man as a whole."[54] Whatever historical basis there might or might not be for this allegation, the important point about it is that it is an

---

[54] See chapter five, "Interviews with Elders," John Buffalo, Ermineskin Reserve, 18 April 1975.

attempt to explain the existence of widely divergent views concerning what had been agreed upon at the treaty negotiations.

A notable difference in the Treaty Seven testimony from that given in Treaty Six is that none of the informants saw the treaty as an instrument of land surrender at all. It is most characteristically viewed as a peace treaty. "On the Peace Treaty, Tall White Man [David Laird] never mentioned land deal when he promised to pay twelve dollars every year as long as the sun shines and rivers flow."[55] "Tall White Man spoke and every time he spoke, he said, 'This is the Queen's word. Now we sit together to have treaty. We will have no more fighting—and we will all live in peace.'"[56]

Some attempts were made to explain how the land was related to the treaty. One interpreter explained that "they wanted to share the land so they loaned the land out."[57] An elder represented the governor general (Indian Commissioner Laird?) telling Crowfoot, "If we both agree to make peace or treaty this day, I will run your vast land because you do not know how to develop a land and I know how to operate the country. . . . I come not to take it away from you."[58] "The Indians had felt that they could go on living the way they used to. It was not until they were put on reserves that they realized they could no longer live the way they used to."[59]

With regard to what Indians were to receive, there is a difference of emphasis between the people of Treaty Six and those of Treaty Seven. If some rights are being sold or surrendered, then it seems reasonable that the sellers should receive some consideration in return. The Treaty Six people believed they were giving up the surface rights or allowing the use of the land to agricultural settlers. The archival evidence records that a greater effort was made by them to get better terms. In their view, the treaty benefits were, in part at least, compensation for what they were giving up or sharing. Yet, even there the belief was strong that the Queen had made a treaty to protect and care for her Indian subjects. The Treaty Seven people have an even stronger belief in this purpose of the treaty.

With the evidence available at present, all that could be attempted in this paper was to demonstrate the existence of a divergence of views between the representatives of government and the Indians, and to make some attempt to describe and compare these views. Unfortunately, we are dependent on inference from inadequate evidence for much of the Indian viewpoint.[60] It

---

[55] T.A.R.R. Interview with Elders Program, interview with Joe Chief Body, Blood Reserve, 12 November 1973.

[56] Ibid., interview with Charlie Coming Singer, Blood Reserve, 30 October 1973.

[57] T.A.R.R. Workshop, 10-11 April 1974, oral report by Allan Wolfleg.

[58] Stoney Cultural Education Program, interview with George Ear, Stoney Reserve, date not recorded.

[59] See chapter five, "Interviews with Elders." Annie Buffalo, Peigan Reserve, 12 March 1975.

[60] There is a need for research into the understanding held by Prairie Indian peoples on subjects related to land and resources. If this can be done, comparison can then be made with the entrepreneurial viewpoint which prevailed in nineteenth-century Canada.

appears that government and Indians began from different assumptions, and that there was little attempt on the part of the government either to understand the Indian viewpoint or to convey its own to the Indian people. Under these circumstances, it is hardly surprising that Indian interpretations of the treaties do not conform to those of the government, or that there are some variations in the viewpoints of Indian people themselves on the meaning of their treaties.

Chapter Three

The Spirit and Terms of Treaty Eight

by
Richard Daniel

> *You may be assured that my Government of Canada recognizes the importance of full compliance with the spirit and terms of your Treaties.*
> *Queen Elizabeth II**

As its title suggests, this paper is concerned with much more than a narrow reading of the written terms of Treaty Eight of 1899. If, as the above quote from Queen Elizabeth suggests, the Government of Canada intends to respect the spirit in which its representatives and the Indian people reached an agreement on their future relations eighty years ago, then we must attempt to define that "spirit" as closely as possible. The first thing that must be understood in this regard is that the written document that was supposedly assented to by the government and the Indians in 1899 and 1900 is of very limited value in indicating the spirit of the agreements. To begin with, it was written in legalistic language and presented to illiterate people unfamiliar with legal agreements based on written documents. Although the document was apparently read and translated to the Indian people, this was only a small part of the exchange between the parties, not only during the treaty meetings, but in the months of preparation for those meetings. We must look at the entire negotiating process to determine the commitments made by both parties.

However, aside from the "outside promises" that were made by both parties and not necessarily included in the written document, by "spirit of the treaty," Indian people understand much more. We must attempt, therefore, to go beyond the very incomplete evidence of what was actually said at the negotiations to make a serious effort to understand what both sides may have intended by their respective commitments. On the government side, this paper will look at internal government correspondence in the period leading up to the treaty as well as correspondence with those outside the government. On the Indian side, we will look at historical and anthropological material as well as the oral tradition within Indian communities, which has preserved their understanding of the treaty. The result, hopefully, will be a much more

---

* Calgary, 5 July 1973.

accurate and realistic representation of the agreements than that provided by the treaty document alone.

INDIAN LIFE AND THE FUR TRADE BEFORE THE TREATY

The Treaty Eight area includes most of northern Alberta, that portion of northeastern British Columbia lying to the east of the Rocky Mountains, a portion of the Northwest Territories lying generally to the south of Hay River and Great Slave Lake, and the extreme northwestern corner of Saskatchewan to the north of Clearwater River and west of Cree River. It lies within the boreal forest region of Canada, approximately coincides with the southern half of the Mackenzie River basin, and is drained primarily by the Athabasca, Peace, and Hay Rivers. The most significant variation in the geography of the area occurs in the region from Lesser Slave Lake through the Peace River block and in the vicinity of the town of Fort Vermilion, where patches of parkland have made possible the most extensive farming district that far north on the continent. The extreme northeast corner, north of Lake Athabasca, is characterized by the rock and open woodland of the Canadian Shield. The climate is somewhat more harsh than that of the grassland and parkland areas to the south. Whereas the average frost-free period of the southern prairies is from 80 to 120 days, in most of northern Alberta it is only 60 to 70 days, and even in the vicinity of Lesser Slave Lake and the Peace River block, it is only 80 to 90 days.[1]

When Treaty Eight was negotiated in 1899, the government found Indians of two major language groups living on the land to be included under the treaty. These were Crees and Athapaskans or Dené (including Chipewyans, Beavers, Slaveys, Dogribs, and Yellowknives). Cree-speaking people were living in various locations throughout what is now northern Alberta. Chipewyans were living in the eastern part of the treaty area, primarily in the vicinity of Lake Athabasca, north of the lake into what is now the Northwest Territories, and south along the Athabasca River. Beaver Indians were living in the western part of the treaty area in what is now British Columbia and along the Peace River in Alberta. Slaveys, Dogribs, and Yellowknives were living in the northern part of the area.

The life of Indians of the boreal forest always differed markedly from that of the Plains Indians to the south, as this region was characterized by a harsh climate and cyclical fluctuations of plant and animal life.[2] Prior to the fur trade era, their economy consisted of hunting, fishing, and gathering, with variations to suit local resources. For example, the Chipewyans were

---

[1] Thornes R. Weir, ed., and Geoffrey Matthews, cartographer, *Atlas of the Prairie Provinces* (Toronto: Oxford University Press, 1971), pp. 1-5.

[2] Anthony D. Fisher, "The Cree of Canada: Some Ecological and Evolutionary Considerations," in *Cultural Ecology: Readings on the Canadian Indians and Eskimos*, ed. Bruce Cox (Toronto: McClelland and Stewart, 1973), pp. 126-39.

primarily caribou hunters and fishermen, while the Slavey were heavily reliant on moose. Both groups gathered birds' eggs and berries and hunted small game. All of these food resources were subject to fluctuations in supply, and it was necessary for the Indians to manage their use of resources in such a way as to take advantage of these fluctuations and to avoid over-use of particular resources which were in short supply.

According to Vanstone, each band had a specific territory which it customarily exploited, although the boundaries were flexible.

> Evidence indicates that during the aboriginal period, resources within the territories of the various Athapaskan groups were available to all who needed them. When there was no game in a particular area, the people who had been hunting there felt perfectly free to move into an area being exploited by neighbors, and there appears to have been no resentment on the part of those who shared their resources. It should be emphasized, however, that this kind of sharing among subgroups was usually confined within the larger boundaries of a single group. Even these boundaries were doubtless flexible.[3]

Resources were not only shared with members of a band, but to some extent with outsiders as well. Even non-Indians were accepted, provided that they behaved decently and did not threaten the Indian way of life.[4] This easy acceptance of outsiders allowed the fur trade to establish posts throughout the area with no initial hostility. However, as will be noted in later sections of this paper, other incursions of whites into Indian land were seen as threats to the Indian people and were resisted.

The fur trade had made some inroads into what is now northern Alberta as early as 1717 when some Athapaskan bands were travelling on foot to the Hudson's Bay Company post at Fort Churchill from beyond Lake Athabasca.[5] However, after that date the Crees increasingly took over the role of middlemen in the trade with these distant bands. Exploiting their military supremacy gained through access to the guns of the fur traders, the Crees rapidly spread into formerly Chipewyan territory south and west of Lake Athabasca.[6] Their monopoly over trade with the distant bands also gave the Crees a strong position in determining the terms of trade with the Hudson's Bay Company, which had no alternative access to these furs.[7]

After 1763, strong competition between free traders and the Hudson's Bay Company prompted both to move their posts further and further into the western hinterland in a struggle for control of the trade with inland bands.

---

[3] James Vanstone, *Athapaskan Adaptations: Hunters and Fishermen of the Subarctic Forests* (Chicago: Aldine Publishing Co., 1974), p. 44.

[4] Paulette et al., Supreme Court of the North West Territories (1973), testimony of June Helm, pp. 77 and 94.

[5] Arthur J. Ray, *Indians in the Fur Trade: Their Role as Trappers, Hunters and Middlemen in the Lands Southwest of Hudson's Bay, 1660-1860* (Toronto: University of Toronto Press, 1974), p. 59.

[6] Ibid., pp. 19-21.

[7] Ibid., pp. 61-70.

Peter Pond established the first post on the Athabasca River in 1778.[8] Five years later, Pond and many of the most prominent free traders joined in the formation of the North West Company, which was to be the major competitor to the Hudson's Bay Company until the two companies merged in 1821. Pond's post was moved to Fort Chipewyan in 1788 and expanded to become the most important North West Company post in the north.[9] Within four years, the North West Company also had established posts near the present sites of Fort McMurray and Peace River,[10] and by 1805 had important posts at Dunvegan and Fort St. John, both on the Peace River,[11] and at Lesser Slave Lake.[12]

Coincident with the expansion of trading posts on the Athabasca and Peace Rivers was the spread of smallpox to many of the bands of the area, with drastic results. Samuel Hearn estimated that 90 per cent of some Chipewyan bands had been killed by the disease in 1781,[13] and at approximately the same time, deaths in the Fort McMurray region were so numerous that the North West Company abandoned its post there.[14]

By the end of the eighteenth century, the North West Company and the Hudson's Bay Company had established posts to trade directly with the Chipewyans on the Athabasca River and with the Beaver Indians on the Peace River. Ray suggests that the consequent decline of the Crees' position as middlemen and their relative lack of trapping skills were largely responsible for the substantial Cree migration to the buffalo ranges to the south.[15]

In the decade prior to the merger of the two fur trade giants in 1821, the rich fur district of Athabasca became the site of the most intense competition between the companies. The Indians were able to exploit this competition to obtain favourable terms of trade, but by 1821, the fur resources of the region had been seriously depleted.[16]

This period of establishment and development of the fur trade in the study area prior to 1821 was apparently accomplished with no resistance from Indian tribes, but with some intertribal conflict over territory. Fur traders were able to establish themselves in new areas only by recognizing and appreciating the Indians' patterns of resource use and their view of the fur

---

[8] Ernest Voorhis, *Historic Forts and Trading Posts of the French Regime and of the English Fur Trading Companies* (Ottawa: Department of the Interior, 1930), p. 34.

[9] Ibid., p. 52.

[10] Ibid., pp. 69 and 107.

[11] C.A. Dawson and R.W. Murchie, *The Settlement of the Peace River Country: A Study of a Pioneer Area* (Toronto: Macmillan Co. of Canada, 1934), p. 16.

[12] William Peter Baergen, "The Fur Trade at Lesser Slave Lake, 1815-1831" (M.A. diss., University of Alberta, 1967), p. 25.

[13] Vanstone, *Athapaskan Adaptations*, p. 93.

[14] Henry John Moberly and William Bleasdale Cameron, *When Fur Was King* (London and Toronto: J.M. Dent and Sons (Canada), 1929), p. 142.

[15] Ray, *Indians in Fur Trade*, pp. 98-102.

[16] Ibid., pp. 117-23 and 141-44.

trade. The fur trade had to adapt to Indian culture as much as Indians had to adapt to the fur trade. Foster notes that the ceremonies of trade reflected a basically reciprocal arrangement—a compact between the trading company and the band, in which each had the right to make certain demands of the other.[17] For example, it was the practice of the Hudson's Bay Company to provide free medical attention to Indians and to care for those who were unable to hunt due to age or infirmity. The most serious conflicts between traders and Indians occurred not as a result of expansion of the trade, but rather as a result of its contraction; several posts were closed and operations were streamlined after the merger of 1821.[18]

The merger of the trading companies under the name of the Hudson's Bay Company initiated a period of thirty-eight years in which the new company enjoyed exclusive rights to trade with the Indians of the Northwest. However, this monopoly in Rupert's Land was only maintained by carrying on a fierce struggle with competitors in the surrounding regions in order to prevent them from encroaching upon the monopoly area. Competition was particularly strong in Upper and Lower Canada, British Columbia, and the Manitoba–North Dakota area.[19] In these areas as well as on the western plains where the trade had shifted from furs to provisions of food for the northern trading operations, alcohol remained an essential item of trade for the Company.[20] In the more northerly forested regions, however, monopoly brought about substantial changes in the nature of the fur trade. The Hudson's Bay Company sharply curtailed the use of alcohol,[21] and in addition, was able to change the terms of trade to the disadvantage of the Indians.[22] However, the Company was partially successful in inducing the Indians to practice conservation and to reduce the level of fur harvest that had threatened the resource base and the fur trade during the years of competition.[23]

In 1848, the fur trade monopoly was being threatened by free traders, particularly in the vicinity of the Red River settlement. The free traders won a decisive victory when a Fort Garry court set a Métis free without penalty, despite his conviction for violating the Company's monopoly. The local

---

[17] See chapter seven, "Indian-White Relations in the Prairie West during the Fur Trade Period—A Compact?"

[18] Harold Adams Innis, *The Fur Trade in Canada: An Introduction to Canadian Economic History* (Toronto: University of Toronto Press, 1962). p. 288; see also Voorhis, *Historic Forts and Posts*, p. 63.

[19] John S. Galbraith, *The Hudson's Bay Company as an Imperial Factor, 1821-1869* (Toronto: University of Toronto Press, 1957), pp. 8-13.

[20] Ray, *Indians in Fur Trade*, p. 198; Moberley and Cameron, *When Fur Was King*, pp. 30-31.

[21] Ray, *Indians in Fur Trade*, pp. 197-98.

[22] Innis, *Fur Trade in Canada*, pp. 287-88 and 318-19.

[23] Ray, *Indians in Fur Trade*, pp. 201-3.

citizens rushed out of the trial shouting "Le commerce est libre! Le commerce est libre!"[24]

In the 1850s, a more serious threat to the monopoly than that of the free traders became apparent—a coalition of editors, farmers, and politicians in Canada was becoming increasingly vociferous in its insistence that the lands of the West were fertile and should be annexed by Canada.[25] Exaggerated claims of the exploitation of the Indians by the Hudson's Bay Company were advanced to discredit the Company and to undermine its charter. A British House of Commons committee, established in 1857 to examine the Company's rights, vindicated the Company of the extreme charges regarding its treatment of Indians. Its hearings made it apparent that the fundamental conflict was not between the Indians and the Hudson's Bay Company, but between the interest of the fur trade and the interests of settlement.[26] Although the charter would not be surrendered for another twelve years, settlement was clearly inevitable and the leadership of the Company began to make preparations for a successful transition to the new order.[27] Whether its partners in the fur trade, the Indians, would be as successful in the transition was doubtful.

Through the fur trade, the Indians of the study area were able to benefit from development of their material culture while retaining substantial control over the terms of trade, the nature of their interactions with the traders, and their access to natural resources. Thus, although they became increasingly dependent upon trade goods and the services of the trading companies, they never lost the option of returning, to a greater or lesser degree, to a life based on hunting, fishing, and trapping for subsistence rather than trade. In fact, for most of them, continued reliance on traditional pursuits was a necessary supplement to the fur trade economy.

Prior to substantial agricultural settlement on the Prairies, the Indians of the Northwest enjoyed a virtual monopoly over the harvesting of wildlife resources. The extension of trading posts into the Interior, along with the decline of the Indian middlemen and the monopolization of trading, reduced the effectiveness of this monopoly on resources, but could not entirely destroy it. The ability of the trading companies to exert greater control over the trade was limited, even under conditions of a trading monopoly, by the difficulty of inducing the Indians to exert themselves much beyond the level of effort required to provide for basic necessities, and by the Indians' ability to provide most of those necessities from the land if the terms of trade became too oppressive. The material basis for traditional cultures remained largely

---

[24] George F. G. Stanley, *The Birth of Western Canada: A History of the Riel Rebellions* (Toronto: University of Toronto Press, 1960), p. 47.

[25] Galbraith, *Hudson's Bay Company*, pp. 335-36.

[26] Ibid., pp. 341-42.

[27] Ibid., pp. 355-428.

intact despite the availability of economic and cultural development. It might be argued that despite the continued existence of a subsistence alternative, the cultural changes induced by the fur trade rendered the Indian people incapable of choosing such an alternative, and that consequently their dependence on the fur trade was total. However, as previously noted, the social and cultural relations between traders and Indians were more often characterized by an interdependence based on equality and reciprocity than on domination.

There is some evidence from studies of the cultural ecology of northeastern Algonkians that the fur trade brought about substantial changes in the patterns of resource use and tenure among Indians of the boreal forest regions. Leacock argues that the fur trade was responsible for a movement away from communal harvesting of resources and communal ownership of land towards harvesting by individuals and family units, a clearer definition of territorial rights, and eventually the beginnings of a concept of individual land ownership.[28] Integration into an economy based on production for exchange rather than for use draws attention away from ownership of the products of the land towards ownership of the land itself.

More recent work by Rolf Knight indicates that the fur trade did not provide sufficient conditions for the development of a clear-cut system of family territoriality, and that, except where the fur trade provided a reliable survival security, communal ownership remained important.[29] At most fur trade posts, such security was not available.

> Leacock holds that as Indian groups become more integrated into the fur trade, they become less limited by and more independent of the environment. But if we look at a trapping-trade situation from a trapper's-eye view, we see that not only do the various animal populations continue to fluctuate, but a whole host of new factors, fluctuating and only partly predictable, enter. Prices of pelts change from year to year and possibly between the time the trapper leaves the post and the time when he returns with the pelts. The availability of credit varies. The acceptable condition of pelts changes. Posts open, expand, decline and close, requiring changes in routes or relocation of trapping areas. Transport routes and costs change, changing the price of commodities at different posts. Though the development of the fur trade did undoubtedly offer new opportunities and goods which allowed a much more effective utilization of the environment, a potentially higher standard of living, it did not necessarily create a stabilization of income and a subsistence security base against economic fluctuations.[30]

---

[28] Eleanor Burke Leacock, "The Montagnais 'Hunting Territory' and the Fur Trade" (Ph.D. diss., Columbia University, 1952), pp. 74-78.

[29] Rolf Knight, "A Re-examination of Hunting, Trapping and Territoriality Among the Northeastern Algonkian Indians," in *Man, Culture and Animals: The Role of Animals in Human Ecological Adjustments*, ed. Anthony Leeds and A.P. Vayda (Washington, D.C.: American Association for the Advancement of Science, 1965), p. 41.

[30] Ibid., p. 36.

Not only did the fur trade not require complete subordination of Indian culture and social organization to European standards, in most areas it actually required a substantial continuity with the cultural ecology of pre-contact societies.

Although most of these detailed studies of cultural ecology are concerned with Algonkians of the boreal forests of northeastern Canada, it would seem that Knight's work in particular is applicable to the conditions that existed among Crees (Algonkians) and Dené (Athapascans) of the study area during the nineteenth century. Cree bands tended to rely upon a system of intensively hunting and trapping an area until depleted, then moving to a new area and allowing the former area to regenerate. This system would not allow the development of a concept of exclusive ownership of land.[31]

The Dené tended to be more sedentary than the Crees. Vanstone notes that the fur trade did lead the Dené to place greater emphasis on individualism while some co-operative activities declined in importance, " . . . but the sharing of big game and other important resources in the environment, a deeply rooted concept in traditional Athapaskan culture, has continued to be significant."[32]

The fur trade as it existed prior to settlement in the Northwest brought substantial changes to the cultures and social organizations of the Indians of the study area. It would appear, however, that unlike other metropolitan interests that were to assert control over this hinterland, the fur trade was not characterized by conflict with Indian people. It allowed, and even required, the independence, development, and continuity of Indian culture and patterns of resource use and tenure. European alternatives in language, religion, economics, and social organization became increasingly familiar to the Indians, but were only selectively adopted. Furthermore, these alternatives were successfully integrated with developing Indian economies and cultures more often than they were the source of serious conflict.[33]

Although anthropological and historical research on the aboriginal and fur trade ecology of the study area is not extensive, the foregoing review of the literature does provide the basis for a tentative analysis of how the Indian people might have perceived the treaty in relation to recent changes in their environment and in relation to their cultural ecology at the time. The recent work by Ray and Foster on the fur trade in what are now the Prairie provinces

---

[31] Bennett McCardle, "The Rules of the Game: the Development of Government Controls over Indian Hunting and Trapping in Treaty 8 (Alberta) to 1930" (paper prepared for the Treaty and Aboriginal Rights Research of the Indian Association of Alberta, May 1976), p. 155.

[32] Vanstone, *Athapaskan Adaptations*, p. 101.

[33] See John J. Honigmann, "The Fur Trade as a Developmental Stage in Northern Algonkian Culture History" (paper delivered at First Conference on Algonkian Studies, St. Pierre de Wakefield, Alta., 13-15 September 1968). Honigmann refers to the fur trade era as the "Florescent Period" in his analysis of developmental stages of Northern Algonkian culture history. In this period, " . . . the newly derived cultural elements and certain persisting or reinterpreted aboriginal traits became integrated into an intricate new cultural organization that proved highly satisfying to the people themselves" (p. 2).

has tended to discredit many popular conceptions about the Indian's role in the trade. In particular, the view that the Indian people, acting out of ignorance of the fur trade economy, bartered away rich furs for trinkets and alcohol is not supported by their research. Instead, a picture emerges of a people who welcomed the substantial material benefits of the trade, adopted European culture on a very selective basis, and retained virtually unrestricted access to natural resources.

Prior to the treaty, the Indians had no direct experience of land as a commodity to be bought and sold. They were dependent on wildlife and fish and did have considerable experience, through the fur trade, of rights to control, buy, and sell animals. If, through the treaty negotiations, they sought to protect their way of life and their access to natural resources, we assume that these aims would have been expressed primarily as a demand for control of wildlife resources rather than in terms of land rights under Canadian law.

With reference to newcomers, we assume that the Indians would have sought to insure that they behaved decently and lived in peace, rather than attempt to exclude them, which in any event, would have been a hopeless task considering the linguistic and cultural diversity of the Indian population.

Finally, the Indians were undoubtedly aware, to some extent, that the Hudson's Bay Company represented a declining power and the Queen an ascending power in their country. Social services formerly provided by the Company and the missions were gradually becoming a government responsibility, and the rumours of treaty would have further emphasized this transfer, particularly because a few of the Indians of the Lesser Slave Lake area had migrated from the Edmonton area and would have been aware of the significance of a treaty in this regard. The treaty may have been seen as an opportunity to ensure that the government's generosity would be at least equivalent to that of the Company and the missions.

GOVERNMENT MOTIVES FOR THE TREATY

When the Indian treaties of the "fertile belt" were signed in the 1870s, the Canadian government knew little about the land lying to the north of this belt or about the native people of the area. However, between 1870 and 1899, missionaries, traders, and government geologists and geographers supplied the government with a wealth of information and opinions, often conflicting, about the potential for settlement of the area, the natural resources, and the condition of the Indian population.

Although there were undoubtedly periods of famine in the Athabasca and Mackenzie districts throughout the nineteenth century, the Canadian government did not become fully aware of the extent of the hardships until after the Hudson's Bay Company had surrendered its charter to Rupert's Land in 1870 and the Dominion of Canada assumed jurisdiction over the area. The

Department of Indian Affairs and the prime minister then began to receive petitions from missionaries and the Hudson's Bay Company employees for government relief for the Indians. Both the Company and the missionaries felt that they should no longer be responsible for providing relief now that the territory had been transferred to the Dominion. The Company, faced with not only the loss of its monopoly of the fur trade but also with falling fur prices in the 1880s, was particularly resentful of expectations that it would continue to finance relief to the Indians.[34] At the same time, missionaries like Vital Grandin, Catholic bishop of St. Albert, persistently wrote to the prime minister and the lieutenant governor of the Northwest Territories with descriptions of starvation and pleas for government aid. The government response was to disclaim any responsibility for Indians with whom no treaty had been signed,[35] and to hold rigidly to the policy of postponing treaty negotiations until the land was required for settlement.

The petitions did have the effect of prompting some people in the federal government to consider the advantage of signing a treaty before the land was actually required for settlement. In 1883, the superintendent general of Indian Affairs advised the prime minister:

> The undersigned was informed from several quarters while in the Northwest that very much uneasiness exists among the Indians in the unceded part of the Territories at parties making explorations into their country in connections with railroads, etc., without any Treaty being made with them; and it was reported to him by persons well acquainted with these Indians that they are most anxious to enter into Treaty relations with the Government and that it is in the interest of humanity very desirable that the Government should render them assistance, as their condition at many points is very wretched. The Indians in the unceded portions of the Territories are not numerous; but at the same time they could of course do great injury to any railway or any public work which might be constructed in their country, unless the Government had a previous understanding with them relative to the same.[36]

However, Prime Minister Macdonald held to the view "that the making of a treaty may be postponed for some years, or until there is a likelihood of the country being requested for settlement purposes."[37]

Difficult conditions in 1887 and 1888 prompted a new round of vigorous appeals from the Company and the missionaries for government supplies, and accounts of starvation began to appear in prominent newspapers. During the winter of 1887–88, there were reports that Indians in Fort St. John were killing their horses for food, that one of the Hudson's Bay Company's cattle

---

[34] René Fumoleau, *As Long as This Land Shall Last: A History of Treaty 8 and Treaty 11, 1870-1939* (Toronto: McClelland and Stewart, n.d.), p. 31.

[35] Correspondence, 27 September 1880, Record Group 10, Public Archives of Canada, Ottawa, 3708: 19502-1.

[36] Superintendent general to prime minister, 5 November 1883, Record Group 10, Public Archives of Canada, Ottawa, 4006: 241209-1.

[37] Prime minister to superintendent general, 27 May 1884, ibid.

had been killed, and that more might be killed unless the government aided the Indians and also brought law to the area.[38]

There appeared to be a developing public opinion in favour of assistance, regardless of whether or not a treaty had been signed, as expressed in the *Calgary Tribune*, 5 February 1887:

> If the matter is looked at squarely, it is surely a fearful thing that any community under Canadian rule should perish for lack of assistance that it is possible to render. It is not a duty that we owe to the Indians as much as one that we owe to ourselves and to humanity in general. Not only is the Country under a moral obligation to render assistance to these people but it would be good policy to do so. Sometime soon a treaty bill will have to be made with them as a preliminary to the opening of their splendid country and were timely assistance to be rendered to them now in their time of need it would pave the way for a good feeling when the treaty came to be made that would not be to the disadvantage of the Country.[39]

In 1888, the federal government took its first significant step towards providing relief by making available $7,000 to the Hudson's Bay Company for provisions for destitute Indians in all of the "unorganized territory." Similarly in 1889, Parliament voted an annual grant of $500 to the Roman Catholic bishop of the Mackenzie for the purpose of distributing twine and fish hooks to the Indians. In the field of education, the government had been providing some assistance to the Grey Nuns' school at Fort Chipewyan since 1880.[40]

The policy of providing government relief through the Hudson's Bay Company was controversial within the Department of Indian Affairs because the Company was getting undeserved credit from government assistance; also, as the costs of this program escalated each year, some became suspicious that the Company was using the grant to supply its own hunters.

The need for assistance in times of hardship apparently had the effect of prompting some of the Indian population to give some consideration to the benefits that might be derived from a treaty. One trader in the Lesser Slave Lake area reported he had been asked by Chief Kinosayoo to inform the government that the Indians of the area had held a meeting on 1 January 1890 to consider applying for a treaty.

> A very few of those present were against the treaty, but a very large majority were in favour of it. After it was over many letters written in Cree characters were received from Indians who were unable to attend but who wished to have the treaty. The Indians of the upper part of Peace River are also anxious to have the treaty.[41]

---

[38] Peter Lunn, 31 January 1888, Record Group 10, Public Archives of Canada, Ottawa, 3708: 19502-1.

[39] *Calgary Tribune*, 5 February 1887, ibid.

[40] Morris Zaslow, *The Opening of the Canadian North, 1870-1914* (Toronto: McClelland and Stewart, 1971), p. 74.

[41] Record Group 10, Public Archives of Canada, Ottawa, 3708: 19502-1.

Conditions appear to have improved somewhat after 1890, as by 1897, the Indian commissioner of the Northwest Territories was reporting that appeals for assistance from non-treaty areas were "comparatively infrequent" and that the Indians were presently "in an independent condition."[42]

It is clear that conditions of starvation among the Indian population of the Peace River and Athabasca River areas were of very little, if any, importance in the government's decision to enter into a treaty. In fact, when Treaty Eight was finally signed, it did not include the Isle à la Crosse area from which there had been many reports of hardship and requests for a treaty, but did include most of the areas of known mineral wealth and agricultural value.

While the government was receiving these reports of the condition of the Indians of the "unorganized territories," it was also receiving reports from field personnel of the Department of the Interior and the Geological Survey Department which indicated that parts of these territories might be considerably more valuable than previously expected.

As early as 1793, the explorer Sir Alexander Mackenzie had mentioned that tar and oil could be found oozing from the banks of the Athabasca. Since that time, few explorers of the area failed to mention the tar sands or to speculate on its future potential. However, it was not until the late 1870s and the 1880s that government geologists and geographers began to take serious notice. In 1875–76, A.R.C. Selwyn and Professor Macoun of the Geological Survey of Canada reported that petroleum existed in the Athabasca region in almost inexhaustible quantities.[43] A more detailed report of the Athabasca region by Robert Bell of the Geological Survey of Canada in 1883 reported the existence of "petroleum bearing sandstone, petroleum-impregnated marl, flowing asphalt, petroleum strata, free petroleum, petroleum and asphalt." This report was given added weight by a survey of the Athabasca region in 1890 and 1891 by R.G. McConnell of the Geological Survey of Canada, who estimated that there were 4,700 million tons of tar in the region, as well as natural gas, bitumen, oil, and pitch.[44] A few years prior to this, McConnell had also found large quantities of petroleum in the vicinity of the Mackenzie River and Great Slave Lake and commented:

> . . . its situation north of the still unworked Athabasca and Peace River oil field will probably delay its development for some years to come, but this is only a question of time. The oil fields of Pennsylvania and at Baker already show signs of exhaustion,

---

[42] Ibid.

[43] Record Group 15, Public Archives of Canada, Ottawa, 509: 143882.

[44] Canada, "Report on a Portion of the District of Athabasca" (Ottawa: Queen's Printer, 1893).

and as they decline the oil field of northern Canada will have a corresponding rise in value.[45]

The optimism of the earlier geological reports by Selwyn, Macoun, and Bell prompted the formation in 1888 of a Senate committee to investigate the value of the entire territory lying north of the Saskatchewan watershed, between the Rocky Mountains and Hudson Bay.[46] The third report of this committee indicated that the Athabasca and Mackenzie valleys contained

> . . . the most extensive petroleum field in America, if not in the world. The uses of petroleum and consequently the demand for it by all nations are increasing at such a rapid ratio, that it is probable this great petroleum field will assume an enormous value in the near future and will rank among the chief assets comprised in the Crown Domain of the Dominion.[47]

Deposits of silver, copper, iron, asphaltum, and other minerals were also mentioned. The committee also made some very optimistic comments concerning the viability of agriculture on a grand scale throughout the North; however, these seem to have been part of the government propaganda of the time to convince potential settlers and businessmen that Canada had just as much room for future expansion and development as the United States, whose potential had recently been receiving widespread public notice. Government officials, on the other hand, paid more attention to the cautious reports from the field, which admitted of the possibility of farming in some of the river valleys, but were divided over whether or not the growing season on the prairies of the Peace River block was long enough.[48]

There can be little doubt that by about 1890 or 1891 the government had been convinced that the Peace, Athabasca, and Mackenzie regions contained great mineral wealth, but it is more difficult to estimate the rate at which they expected this wealth to be developed. As early as 1887, there were proposals for an extensive program of research on the oil territories of the Peace and Athabasca, which received the favourable consideration of the director of the Geological Survey of Canada.[49] In the same year, an application was made for a charter for a railroad from Churchill through the Athabasca Tar Sands and the Peace River district to the Pacific Coast, to be accompanied by a pipeline to carry petroleum.[50] At the same time, the *Edmonton Bulletin* was

---

[45] *Annual Report, Geological and Natural History Survey of Canada* (Montreal: William Foster and Brown Co., 1890), vol. 4, *1888-1889*, pp. 31D-32D.

[46] Fumoleau, *Land Shall Last*, p. 40.

[47] Canada, Senate, *Journal*, 1888, p. 163.

[48] Zaslow notes: "The question of whether or not the region was a good farming district still was unresolved; boosters generalized from the few successful farms along the Peace River Valley, critics from the disappointing results of the few farms on the plateau" (Zaslow, *Opening of North*, p. 92).

[49] Record Group 15, Public Archives of Canada, Ottawa, 509: 143882.

[50] Proposal of Mr. Diggles, 14 December 1887, Record Group 15, Public Archives of Canada, Ottawa, 552: 164187; see also proposal of Mr. Van Horne, William Pearce Papers, University of Alberta Archives, Edmonton, 24: 12-AO18. It is not certain whether these were two separate proposals.

suggesting that the only thing that was holding up the development of the Athabasca and Mackenzie oil fields was the lack of railway communication.[51]

It would seem that, in most of these optimistic plans for immediate development of the Athabasca Tar Sands, little consideration was given to the difficulties of extraction. It may have been assumed that where such huge quantities of tar sands existed there must also be large pools of conventional oil and gas which could be removed easily. Between 1894 and 1899, the Geological Survey of Canada conducted exploratory drilling "at the mouth of the Pelican River and other places in the north, to test whether the tar sands in depth carried higher grade oil. They were found to carry only heavy oil and large accumulations of gas were also discovered."[52]

Whether the government considered mineral development to be an immediate prospect or merely a future possibility, by 1891 there was sufficient importance attached to the mineral wealth of the North that serious plans were made for signing a treaty with the Indians in the summer of 1892. The Privy Council report authorizing the treaty clearly indicated that the government's primary motive was to extinguish the Indian title prior to the development of mineral resources and the construction of railways:

> On a report dated 7th of January, 1891, from the Superintendent General of Indian Affairs, stating that the discovery in the District of Athabasca and in the Mackenzie River Country, that immense quantities of petroleum exist within certain areas of these regions, as well as the belief that other minerals and substances of economic value, such as Sulfur, on the south coast of Great Slave Lake, and Salt, on the Mackenzie and Slave Rivers, are to be found therein, the development of which may add materially to the public wealth, and the further consideration that several railway projects, in connection with this portion of the Dominion, may be given effect to at no such remote date as might be supposed, appear to render it advisable that a treaty or treaties should be made with the Indians who claim those regions as their hunting grounds, with a view to the extinguishment of the Indian title in such portions of the same, as it may be considered in the interest of the public to open up for settlement. The Minister, after fully considering the matter, recommends that negotiations for a treaty be opened up during the ensuing season.[53]

The boundaries of this proposed treaty were somewhat different from those of the actual treaty of 1899 in that they excluded British Columbia, but included larger areas of the present Northwest Territories and Province of Saskatchewan.

There is little in Department of Indian Affairs files to indicate why these plans lay dormant from 1892 until 1897, when the treaty was again discussed.

---

[51] Fumoleau, *Land Shall Last*, p. 41.

[52] Alberta Resources Commission, "Statement of World Policy in Regard to Petroleum" (Edmonton: Alberta Provincial Library, 1934), vol. 1, p. 16.

[53] Privy Council report, 26 January 1891, Record Group 10, Public Archives of Canada, Ottawa, 3848: 75236-1.

On 3 July 1891, the superintendent general of Indian Affairs wrote that "before going any further in this matter, we had better wait to see whether the money will be voted or not."[54] Fumoleau suggests that the delay was due to the political instability that followed the death of Prime Minister Macdonald, and the fact that oil exploration proved to be slower than expected.[55]

During these intervening years (1891–1899), increasing interest was being shown in the Peace and Mackenzie regions, and the Department of Interior was receiving many requests for maps and geological information on the North. However, the department attempted to discourage prospectors because of possible conflicts with the Indians and the poor results expected for gold mining:

> . . . It has been thought advisable to discourage as far as possible any immigration into the districts around the Peace and Mackenzie Rivers and northern country generally. The inducement seems to be the presence of Gold; but probabilities are that the search for it will not be paying; they thereupon develop into hunters, traders and trappers and the result is already observable in the scarcity of game and if many more come in, the deplorable results will be even more evident in the starvation of the Indians.[56]

A report of 24 November 1893 by Dr. Dawson, a geologist, indicated that a prospector could not expect to make profits so far from railways, and

> he (the prospector) usually combines trading with prospecting, disturbs the Indian population without doing it any good and annoys the H.B.C., and the missionaries who are the only representatives of law and order.[57]

The deputy minister of Interior agreed with this view and adopted the policy of discouraging prospectors.

While the government was discouraging individual gold prospectors, it was continuing its prospecting for oil on Pelican River, apparently without concern for the fact that no treaty had been signed. A well was drilled at Pelican Rapids in 1894 with no success, and a second well there in 1897 produced considerable gas, but little oil. Tests for petroleum at Athabasca Landing in 1894 received widespread attention. The lieutenant governor of the Northwest Territories referred to the tests when he opened the legislature on 2 August 1894, and predicted that, if the tests proved successful, Edmonton would become the centre of "vast oil-refining industries" with markets in British Columbia, California, Japan, and China. The tests, however, were unsuccessful, and in a speech to the legislature on 29

---

[54] Hon. E. Dewdney to L. Vankoughnet, 3 July 1891, ibid.

[55] Fumoleau, *Land Shall Last*, p. 43.

[56] William Pearce, 19 March 1893, William Pearce Papers, University of Alberta Archives, Edmonton, 48: 14-F-9.

[57] Dawson, 24 November 1893, ibid.

September 1896, the lieutenant governor expressed disappointment, but indicated that further tests would be made.[58]

While the federal government continued to be interested in the mineral resources of Athabasca, advances in transportation were rapidly opening the territory to frontiersmen of various sorts. These developments combined with effects of the Klondyke gold rush to produce within the settler communities of the Prairies a strong interest in northern hinterlands. Any other motives for signing a treaty were soon overshadowed by developments that were led not by the federal government, but by the settlers and adventurers of the Northwest Territories.

By 1886, the Hudson's Bay Company had abandoned the old Methye Portage route to the Mackenzie River system in favour of a portage from Fort Pitt to Lac la Biche, and towards the end of the 1880s, a wagon road was completed from Edmonton to Athabasca Landing. Coupled with the establishment of steamships on the Athabasca and Mackenzie in 1882, these transportation advances brought increasing numbers of white trappers, settlers, and prospectors into the region.[59]

When gold was discovered in the Klondyke in 1896, miners started migrating towards the Yukon via the Pacific Coast. Because most of the miners and speculators were American and the Yukon was not yet settled by Canadians, the Canadian government became concerned about establishing and maintaining its sovereignty over this rich area. In 1896 and 1897, the North West Mounted Police sent men overland to the Yukon from Edmonton for the purpose of reporting on the feasibility of such an overland route. By this time, the Mounted Police already had twenty men stationed in the Yukon for the purpose of maintaining law and order and asserting Canadian control over the area, but this was their first attempt to reach the Yukon through the Peace River region. Inspector Moodie, in his report on the expedition, noted that the Indians of the Finlay district were half starved and seeking assistance, and characterized them as mischievous and vindictive. However, he impressed upon them "the fact that the white men had the right to go anywhere through the country and hunt, trap, fish or dig for gold, also that their only chance of obtaining help was to behave well."[60]

Until 1897, the Mounted Police had restricted their role in the District of Athabasca to maintaining outposts at three locations on the Athabasca River for the purpose of controlling trade (particularly the liquor trade) into the region. However, for several years they had been made aware of the Indians' deep and growing bitterness over the indiscriminate and illegal use of poison traps by white and half-breed trappers. According to one police report, the

---

[58] Hon. Charles Herbert Mackintosh, 2 August 1894 and 29 September 1896, Record Group 15, Public Archives of Canada, Ottawa, 710: 362488.

[59] Fumoleau, Land Shall Last, pp. 29-30.

[60] Canada, Parliament, Annual Report of the North West Mounted Police, 1898, pt 2, p. 10.

Indians felt it unjust "that people who are not owners of the country are allowed to rob them of their living."[61] Other reports suggested that the use of poison was unknown before the advent of white men,[62] and that the Indians were prepared to "do some shooting" unless something was done immediately to bring the situation under control.[63]

In order to enforce the prohibition of poison traps as well as to look into the problems of destructive forest fires and the liquor trade, the Mounted Police, beginning in January 1897, made annual winter patrols to Lake Athabasca, Great Slave Lake, and parts of the Peace River region. Most of this law enforcement (under the Northwest Territories Act) was directed against whites and half-breeds rather than Indians, and in fact the Indians were apparently pleased with the action taken to reduce the use of poison.[64] However, these patrols were also concerned with prohibiting Indians and non-Indians from hunting buffalo, in accordance with an "Act for the Preservation of Game in the Unorganized Portions of the Northwest Territories of Canada," which was passed on 3 July 1894 and came into force on 1 January 1896. It would appear that the buffalo regulations were the only regulations enforced against Indian people prior to Treaty Eight.

This extension of government administration to an area which had not been ceded by treaty was defended by D.H. MacDowell, a member of Parliament, on 30 April 1894:

> As to the legal right of the Government in prohibiting the Indians and Half-breeds catching fish out of season, or killing game out of season, I believe that by a recent decision of the Imperial Privy Council, which was given about 14 months ago, they have every legal right to do this; that there is no necessity for the government to make a Treaty with Indians, or anybody else; that the treaties made have been merely to bring about a peaceful, happy and speedy conclusion of the entry of whites into lands formerly occupied by Indians, but that the Privy Council have decided one for all that the whole North West of Canada belongs to Her Majesty, that it is her property, and that she has absolute rights to do whatever she wishes. And in consequence, if Her responsible advisors recommend Her to prohibit fishing and shooting out of season, even though treaty has (not) been made with the Indians, it is a perfectly justifiable and legal act.[65]

North West Mounted Police reports seem to indicate that in some cases Indians willingly complied with the buffalo regulations, while in other cases violations occurred and Indians were convicted.[66]

The real problems of law and order occurred in 1897 and 1898 with the Klondyke gold rush. The invasion of miners was unlike anything the North

---

[61] Ibid., 1897, p. 170.
[62] Ibid., 1896, pt 2, p. 96.
[63] Ibid., p. 105.
[64] Fumoleau, *Land Shall Last*, p. 53.
[65] Ibid.
[66] Ibid., pp. 53-54.

had seen and resulted in many conflicts with the Indian people. It is estimated that over two thousand Klondykers set out from Edmonton via every conceivable river route to the Yukon, but few reached their destination.[67] Charles Mair, a member of the 1899 Half-breed Commission, described the situation:

> The gold seekers plunged into the wilderness of Athabasca without hesitation, and without as much as 'by your leave' to the native. Some of these marauders, as was to be expected, exhibited a congenital contempt for the Indians' rights. At various places his horses were killed, his dogs shot, his bear-traps broken up. An outcry arose in consequence, which inevitably would have led to reprisals and bloodshed had not the Government stepped in and forestalled further trouble by a prompt recognition of the natives' title.[68]

Clearly, the activities of the Klondykers and of the white trappers had exploited the Indians' acceptance of strangers and had violated their sense of justice. The Indians may have welcomed any newcomers who "behaved" and who did not threaten their way of life, but these newcomers were not behaving decently and were threatening an already precarious existence. A sign of serious Indian resistance came in June 1898, when 500 Indians at Fort St. John refused to allow police and miners to pass through the area until a treaty was signed. They protested that some of their horses had been shot and that the influx of so many men would drive away fur-bearing animals.[69]

A gold rush is a very unpredictable phenomenon. It was difficult for the government of the day to estimate the number of miners who would venture north from Edmonton, because news of such gold finds could spread rapidly and out of all proportion to the actual profits being made by miners. Evidence that the government expected a rush of large proportion and of greater duration comes from the fact that in 1897 and 1898 it gave serious consideration to the construction of various overland routes to the Yukon. At first, the government did not want to encourage prospectors to take the difficult and largely unproven overland route, and in 1897 sent a detachment of Mounted Police to explore the route.[70] Meanwhile, it was under considerable pressure to develop the route, and several companies submitted applications for the construction contract, including one plan to establish station houses every ten to twelve miles.[71]

Most of the pressure for an overland route came from communities of the western Interior, which hoped to profit in the trade for supplies and gold with

---

[67] Zaslow, *Opening of North*, p. 107.

[68] Charles Mair, *Through the Mackenzie Basin: A Narrative of the Athabasca and Peace River Expedition of 1899* (Toronto: W. Briggs, 1908), pp. 23-24.

[69] *Ottawa Citizen*, 30 June 1898, Record Group 10, Public Archives of Canada, Ottawa, 3848: 75236-1.

[70] Clifford Sifton to Governor-General in Council, 26 November 1897, Record Group 15, Public Archives of Canada, Ottawa, 740: 438655.

[71] Record Group 15, Public Archives of Canada, Ottawa, 740: 439739 and 440304.

the Klondykers. Resolutions of support came from the London Board of Trade, Regina Town Council, City of Winnipeg, the Legislative Assembly of the Northwest Territories, the Town of Edmonton, and various individuals.[72] The resolution of the Legislative Assembly of the Northwest Territories on 11 November 1897 is typical of these resolutions and indicates the type of pressure being exerted:

> That WHEREAS the farmers, ranchers, manufacturers and merchants of the Dominion of Canada are losing almost the entire present trade of the gold fields in the Yukon and adjacent districts for want of an overland all Canadian route to that part of the North West Territories. AND WHEREAS, until an all Canadian overland route suitable for wagons (and telegraph line) is opened from east of the Rocky Mountains, this same state of affairs will continue to a greater or less degree. AND WHEREAS, it has been demonstrated that an easy and cheaply built route is available via Edmonton, Peace River, and on to the Pelly Banks, pronounced by authorities to be very rich in minerals, and which would also open up for settlement a fine agricultural and ranching district. RESOLVED, that, in the opinion of this HOUSE, it is desirable that the above mentioned route should be opened by the Dominion Government with the least possible delay.[73]

By the spring of 1899, the Northwest Territories government had constructed 350 miles of this route out of a $15,000 grant from the Dominion government.[74]

The Department of Indian Affairs first realized the importance of signing a treaty with Indians occupying the proposed overland route in November 1897 as a result of a report by James Walker, formerly of the North West Mounted Police, who warned:

> From all appearance there will be a rush of miners and others to the Yukon and the mineral regions of the Peace, Liard and other rivers in Athabasca during the next year ...others intend to establish stopping places, trading posts, transportation companies and to take up ranches and homesteads in fertile lands of the Peace River. . . . They (the Indians) will be more easily dealt with now than they would be when their country is overrun with prospectors and valuable mines be discovered.[75]

In December 1897, a similar report was received from the commissioner of the North West Mounted Police and was forwarded to the commissioner of Indian Affairs with a request that he should ''report fully in the matter in time to admit of provision being made at the next session of Parliament for the expense of making a treaty should the same be decided upon.''[76] The

---

[72] Ibid., 438655.

[73] Resolution of the Legislative Assembly of the Northwest Territories, 11 November 1897, Record Group 15, Public Archives of Canada, Ottawa, 740: 438655.

[74] Privy Council report, 16 May 1899, ibid.

[75] Walker to deputy superintendent general, 30 November 1897, Record Group 10, Public Archives of Canada, Ottawa, 3848: 75236-1.

[76] J.D. McLean to A.E. Forget, 18 December 1897, ibid.

commissioner agreed that a treaty should be made and Cabinet approval was granted on 27 June 1898.

Aside from conflicts between miners en route to the Yukon and the Indian people, the government was also concerned that the gold rush would open other areas of the North to both mining and agriculture. Throughout the 1890s, the Department of Interior had been discouraging settlement of the Peace River district, but it was apparent that the gold rush was forcing a change in that policy. In 1900, the deputy minister of Indian Affairs gave a detailed explanation of why Treaty Eight had been signed:

> Although there was no immediate prospect of any such invasion by settlement as threatened the fertile belt in Manitoba and the Northwest Territories and dictated the formation of treaties with the original owners of the soil, none the less occasional squatters had found their way at any rate into the Peace River district.
>
> While under ordinary circumstances the prospect of any considerable influx might have remained indefinitely remote, the discovery of gold in the Klondyke region quickly changed the aspect of the situation. Parties of white men in quest of a road to the gold fields began to traverse the country, and there was not only the possibility ahead of such travel being greatly increased, but that the district itself would soon become the field of prospectors who might at any time make some discovery which would be followed by a rush of miners to the spot. In any case the knowledge of the country obtained and diffused, if only by people passing through it, could hardly fail to attract attention to it as a field for settlement. For the successful pursuance of that humane and generous policy which has always characterized the Dominion in its dealings with the aboriginal inhabitants, it is of vital importance to gain their confidence at the outset, for the Indian character is such that, if suspicion or distrust once be aroused, the task of eradication is extremely difficult. For these reasons it was considered that the time was ripe for entering into treaty relations with the Indians of the district, and so setting at rest the feeling of uneasiness which was beginning to take hold of them, and laying the foundation for permanent, friendly and profitable relations between the races.[77]

There was still some scepticism about agriculture being viable, especially without railways, but the gold rush brought a number of adventurers who were unwilling to await government approval to pioneer. Any widespread settlement prior to treaty probably would have created many administrative and legal problems because the Dominion Lands Act of 1872 did not apply to territory where the Indian title had not been extinguished.[78] The longer the treaty was delayed, the more squatters' claims there would have been to deal with when the land did come under the act.

PRELUDE TO THE TREATY

The federal government had good reason to postpone the negotiation of treaties in the North until the actual settlement of particular areas or major

---

[77] Fumoleau, *Land Shall Last*, pp. 49-50.
[78] Paulette et al., Supreme Court of the Northwest Territories (1973), ''Caveator's Brief,'' p. 151.

development of natural resources seemed imminent. The treaties with the Prairie Indians had proven to be more costly than anticipated, and at the same time, far from successful in their aim of providing the Indians with the means to adapt to an agricultural economy. There were fears that a northern treaty might encourage Indians to abandon the difficult life of hunters and trappers in favour of dependence on government provisions.

Pre-treaty correspondence of the Department of Indian Affairs reflects a strong emphasis on the need for peace and friendship between the native people and settlers and miners. The Order in Council setting up the commission for Treaty Eight reflects this concern:

> On a report dated 30th November, 1898, from the Superintendent General of Indian Affairs . . . it was set forth that the commissioner of the North West Mounted Police had pointed out the desirability of steps being taken for the making of a treaty with the Indians occupying the proposed line of route from Edmonton to Pelly River; that he had intimated that these Indians, as well as the Beaver Indians of the Peace and Nelson Rivers, and the Sicamas and Nihamas Indians, were inclined to be turbulent and were liable to give trouble to isolated parties of miners or traders who might be regarded by the Indians as interfering with their vested rights; and that he had stated that the situation was made more difficult by the presence of numerous travellers who had come into the country and were scattered at various points between Lesser Slave Lake and Peace River.[79]

When it became apparent that the treaty could not be signed in 1898 as planned, but would have to wait until the summer of 1899, the government distributed public notices throughout the proposed treaty area, setting the dates for the meetings in the following year. This notice included the phrase, "...it is deemed advisable to include within the said treaty the extinguishment of their title to the lands. . . . "[80] Missionaries and members of the North West Mounted Police distributed the notice and answered questions to the best of their ability. As a result of their discussions with the Indians, missionaries began to report to the government that the Indians were inclined to refuse treaty and to oppose settlement, due to their fear that they would lose their hunting, fishing, and trapping rights.[81]

Part of the government's response to this resistance was to persuade Father Lacombe and other missionaries to help in the negotiations. The assistance they gave in persuading the Indians to accept the treaty is discussed in a later section of this chapter.

In addition to seeking Lacombe's aid, the government also saw the need for giving the Indians some assurances that they would not be greatly affected by the treaty. On 25 January 1899, in reply to a missionary who had been

---

[79] Canada, Department of Indian Affairs and Northern Development, *Treaty No. 8, Made June 21, 1899 and Adhesions, Reports, Etc.* (Ottawa: Queen's Printer, 1966), p. 3.

[80] Public notice, June 1898, Record Group 10, Public Archives of Canada, Ottawa, 3848: 75236-1.

[81] Fumoleau, *Land Shall Last*, pp. 65-66.

unable to answer certain questions from the Indians, the superintendent general of Indian Affairs, Clifford Sifton, wrote:

> The game and fishery laws will, of course, apply to the country; but as the manner and extent of their enforcement must necessarily depend upon conditions of settlement, etc., there is not likely to be any marked change on account of the making of treaty. There will be reserves set aside for the Indians and in doing so everything possible will be done to meet their wishes as to the selection of localities. There is no general prohibition in consequence of the treaty of the freedom of the Indian in roaming and hunting over the country. Of course when settlement advances there will be the restriction which necessarily follows, and it is to meet such contingencies that reserves are set aside.[82]

Sifton was indicating that the Indians of Treaty Eight would be subject to the same legal restrictions as Indians of previous treaties, but that the effect of these restrictions would be minimal, due to less white settlement. In reply to another inquiry, David Laird, lieutenant governor of the Territories and Treaty Eight commissioner, also indicated that restrictions would be necessary, not so much as a result of settlement as for conservation for the Indians' benefit:

> You may explain to them that the Queen or Great Mother while promising by her Commissioners to give them Reserves, which they can call their own, and upon which whitemen will not be allowed to settle without payment and the consent of the Indians before a Government officer, yet the Indians will be allowed to hunt and fish all over the country as they do now, subject to such laws as may be made for the protection of game and fish in the breeding season; and also so long as the Indians do not molest or interfere with settlers, miners or travellers. These restrictions and laws however are not peculiar to Treaty Indians; whitemen, half-breeds and Indians who do not take Treaty, will not be allowed by the Great Mother to disturb or hurt any of her children whatever be their colour. It should likewise be remembered that laws for preventing game from being destroyed in the breeding season are rather for the benefit of the Indians than of the whitemen, as the whitemen live more on farm products than on game.[83]

During this period between the summer of 1898, when the treaty notice came out, and the following summer, when the treaty was made, the Indians made it quite clear (through missionaries, traders, and policemen who acted as intermediaries) that they would not favour a treaty unless they were assured that their way of life would not be restricted. The government strove to correct the "misleading reports" that were circulating to the effect that if Indians took treaty they would lose their hunting, fishing, and trapping rights.

It would appear that at least one of the commissioners, J.A. McKenna, was still worried that opposition to reserves and the fear of losing their

---

[82] Sifton to Rev. Charles R. Weaver, 25 January 1899, Record Group 10, Public Archives of Canada, Ottawa, 3848: 75236-1
[83] Laird to W.H. Routledge, 3 February 1899, ibid.

hunting grounds could lead the Indians to reject the treaty. In a long memo of 17 April 1899 to the superintendent general, he made a final effort to have the reserve system scrapped on the grounds that Indians of the North lived as individuals and their hunting grounds would not be required for settlement:

> From the information which has come to hand it would appear that the Indians who we are to meet fear the making of a treaty will lead to their being grouped on reserves. Of course, grouping is not now contemplated; but there is the view that reserves for future use should be provided for in the treaty. I do not think this is necessary . . . it would appear that the Indians there act rather as individuals than as a nation. . . . They are adverse to living on reserves; and as that country is not one that will be settled extensively for agricultural purposes it is questionable whether it would be good policy to even suggest grouping them in the future. The reserve idea is inconsistent with the life of a hunter, and is only applicable to an agricultural country.[84]

This statement is significant not only in showing the origins of the "reserves in severalty" policy, but also in demonstrating that the government expected that the Indians would continue to make their living on the "unoccupied land" of the North. In the same memo, McKenna went so far as to suggest that less compensation was required for these lands than for previous treaty lands because "there is no urgent public need of its acquirement." He also proposed that annuities be abolished for this treaty.

What McKenna wanted was a "slimmed down" version of the usual treaty. The Indians would be giving up less, although their title would still be extinguished, and therefore the government should not have to assume the same responsibilities as in previous treaties.

This proposal appears to have been partially accepted by Sifton. In a letter of 12 May 1899 to Laird, McKenna, and Ross, he stated the government's position:

> The Government has considered the policy to be adopted and has concluded that it is best to proceed upon the usual lines of providing for the payment of annuities to the Indians, and money will be provided so as to enable the first payment of the annuity to be made as well as the gratuity. It is, of course, understood that an additional payment will be made to the Chiefs and headmen.
>
> As to reserves, it has been thought that the conditions of the North country may make it more desirable to depart from the old system, and if the Indians are agreeable to provide land in severalty for them to the extent of 160 acres to each, the land to be conveyed with a proviso as to non-alienation without the consent of the Governor General in Council. Of course, if the Indians prefer Reserves you are at liberty to undertake to set them aside. The terms of the treaty are left to your discretion with this stipulation that obligations to be assumed under it shall not be in excess of those assumed in treaties covering the North West Territories.[85]

---

[84] McKenna to superintendent general, 17 April 1899, ibid.
[85] Sifton to Laird, McKenna, and Ross, 12 May 1899, ibid.

Evidence of the Indians' reluctance to sign a treaty at least made the government aware of the difficulties that would be encountered in attempting to apply the standard "Prairie" treaty to the North. However, due to the department's lack of knowledge of the northern Indians or the extent of claims they were likely to put forward,[86] Sifton was content merely to propose the new policy of reserves in severalty and to leave the other terms of the treaty to the discretion of the commissioners, rather than attempt to formulate a radically different sort of treaty for the area prior to negotiations. In his analysis of these instructions from Sifton, Fumoleau has suggested that the discretionary powers meant only that Indians may be led to accept cheaper conditions than previously.[87] However, this directive to minimize obligations, if possible, appears to have been based on the assumption that the Indians of Treaty Eight were not being required to give up the use of most of their land as the Indians of previous treaties had been required to do.

The considerations that went into defining the boundaries of Treaty Eight were primarily: (1) insuring the inclusion of areas likely to be opened up by miners or settlers, or to be passed through by large numbers of miners and settlers; (2) minimizing expenses and obligations of the government; and (3) restricting the area to that which might be reached in one summer by the commissioners.

For these reasons, large areas of the present Northwest Territories (up to 63° latitude) which had been included in maps of the proposed treaty of 1891 were omitted in 1899, except for the area south of Great Slave Lake, which was the site of considerable mining interest. All of British Columbia lying east of the Rocky Mountains was added to the earlier proposal because it was on the route to the Klondyke, and the mountains were a natural dividing line between Indian bands.[88]

It is interesting to note that all maps and descriptions of the treaty area in the 1899 as well as in the 1891 proposals included the portion of the Rocky Mountains lying to the west of Treaty Six and stretching as far south as the northern boundary of Treaty Seven.[89] However, in the various discussions, there does not appear to have been any mention of why this area was included in Treaty Eight.

The public notice sent out in 1898 indicated that Fort Smith would be the most northerly meeting point for the negotiations. However, in May of 1899, Sifton informed the commissioner that "in view of the reported mining development in the Great Slave Lake region it is important that the treaty should be extended to embrace that country if at all possible." It was left to

---

[86] Sifton to Governor-General, 18 June 1898, ibid.

[87] Fumoleau, *Land Shall Last*, p. 62.

[88] A more detailed discussion of these points may be found in ibid., pp. 58-60.

[89] Record Group 10, Public Archives of Canada, Ottawa, 3848: 75236-1.

the commission finally to decide on the treaty area,[90] and it was not until after their first meeting at Lesser Slave Lake that it was decided to make "adhesions" at all of the other points rather than to negotiate several treaties.[91]

Finally, it was also decided that because many "half-breeds" lived a very similar life to that of the Indians and would desire to be treated as Indians, the commission would be empowered to offer the treaty to such half-breeds.[92] Delegated with this discretionary power over the terms and the area of the treaty, and carrying the knowledge that the Indians were reluctant to sign treaty, the commissioners opened negotiations with the Indians on 20 June 1899 at Lesser Slave Lake.

THE TREATY AT LESSER SLAVE LAKE

The Treaty Eight Commission was to travel throughout northern Alberta with the Half-breed Commission, which had been given a mandate to offer "scrip" in the form of land grants to Métis settlers after the treaty negotiations had been completed in each area. The first treaty negotiations were scheduled for 8 June near the present site of Grouard on Lesser Slave Lake. Due to bad weather conditions and problems in transportation, they did not arrive until 19 June, eleven days late. However, Commissioner Ross, who had arrived on about 6 June, assured the native people that the other commissioners and Father Lacombe were on their way. In the intervening days, Ross visited the assembled Indians to explain the purpose of the treaty,[93] and asked them to elect a chief and headmen to speak for them.[94] Kinosayoo was chosen chief and the four headmen were Moostoos, Felix Giroux, Weecheewaysis, and Charles Neesuetasis. Aside from these five from the Lesser Slave Lake area, one headman from Sturgeon Lake, "Captain," attended as an observer and signed the treaty, although his band was not present and did not sign an adhesion until the following summer.

Once the commissioners had arrived, the first meeting was arranged for the following day, 20 June. Charles Mair, secretary of the Half-breed

---

[90] Order in Council 1703, 27 June 1898, ibid., reads in part: "The Minister also considers that, as to the territory to be ceded, the Commissioners will likewise have to be given discretionary power, for its extent will depend upon the conditions which are found to exist as a consequence of the inroads of white population; but he is of the opinion that the territory to be treated for may in a general way be restricted to the provisional district of Athabasca, and such of the country adjacent thereto as the Commissioners may deem it expedient to include within the treaty."

[91] Canada, *Treaty No. 8*, pp. 6-7.

[92] Order in Council 1703, 27 June 1898.

[93] Canada, *Treaty No. 8*, p.5.

[94] See *Edmonton Bulletin*, 10 July 1899, Record Group 10, Public Archives of Canada, Ottawa, 3848: 75236-1; and Emile Jean-Baptiste Marie Grouard, *Souvenirs de mes soixante ans d'apostolat dans l'Athabasca-Mackenzie* (Lyons-Paris: Librairie catholique, 1923), p. 368. Grouard's account states that the Indians selected their leaders between the first and second meeting. Mair's account agrees with that of the *Edmonton Bulletin*.

Reprinted from Charles Mair, *Through the Mackenzie Basin: A Narrative of the Athabasca and Peace River Expedition of 1899* (Toronto: W. Briggs, 1908)

Kinosayoo at Treaty Eight negotiations, Lesser Slave Lake Settlement

Commission, made brief notes on the discussions and later published these as part of a book on the treaty expeditions.[95] A correspondent for the *Edmonton Bulletin* also wrote several articles on the meetings.[96] One of the earliest missionaries of the area, Bishop Grouard, also included brief references to the meetings in a book on his life in the North.[97] In addition to these incomplete records of the proceedings, there are several reports by the commissioners which do not attempt to reconstruct the dialogue, but do provide summaries of the agreements as they saw them. Other eyewitnesses signed affidavits concerning the meetings when a controversy arose over the treaty provisions in 1937.

However, all of these archival sources record the negotiations from the point of view of government officials, missionaries, traders, and other non-Indians, and in many cases clearly reflect the interests of the author. In order to balance this perspective with an Indian view of the treaty, we must rely upon oral evidence given by Indian elders in recent years. A few of these elders were eyewitnesses to the negotiations, and many others have received stories of the negotiations from their parents and grandparents who were direct participants.

The *Edmonton Bulletin* described the setting of the first meeting as follows:

> After the detachment of police had gone through their little manoevers they lined up in front of their large tent where the commision sat, presented arms and retired. The chief and his band then came forward and sat down in no particular rotation, but as indifferently as possible with this exception, the chief and councilmen to the front and minor lights to the rear. They were given a short spell to look the "great chiefs" over, which they did, and when their gaze wandered away to the hills . . . Commissioner Laird addressed them. He said among other things, that as "they were here for a peaceful meeting a piece of tobacco would be given each for a friendly smoke." The T & B was passed around and after they had all filled up their pipes the commissioner proceeded.[98]

William Okeymaw, an 87-year-old Cree from Sucker Creek tells us how the same scene appeared to him, a young boy at the time:

> I was about twelve years old. We travelled by foot and by boat. We crossed the river here in a boat, then we walked the rest of the way. When we arrived, the commissioners were already prepared. Alongside them were about twenty-two North West Mounted Police. I was frightened because I was only a child. I even held my dad's hand I was so scared. A long memory is one thing I have. I can recall many things of long ago. I can recall a huge tent at the time with many people all around it. They were from different places far and near, but they had travelled for that special

---

[95] Mair, *Through the Mackenzie Basin*.

[96] Two of these articles may be found in Record Group 10, Public Archives of Canada, Ottawa, 3848: 75236-1.

[97] Grouard, *Soixante ans d'apostolat*, pp. 357-74.

[98] *Edmonton Bulletin*, 10 July 1899, Record Group 10, Public Archives of Canada, Ottawa, 3848: 75236-1.

Courtesy R.C.M.P. Museum, Regina, and Glenbow–Alberta Institute

Treaty Eight Commissioners

Left to Right: Harrison Young, secretary; David Laird, commissioner; Pierre d'Eschambault, interpreter

day, the treaty. They discussed it for three days to find out how it would work best, how the Indian would make his living when he accepted treaty.[99]

The commissioners appointed Albert Tate and Samuel Cunningham as interpreters and told the meeting that Cunningham would represent the Indians and that the two men would check each others' work.[100] Also present were three Catholic missionaries (Father Lacombe, Bishop Grouard, and Father Falher) and three Anglican missionaries.

Laird, after introducing the members of his commission, spoke for about an hour. Mair gives the most complete account of his opening speech:

I have to say, on behalf of the Queen and the Government of Canada, that we have come to make you an offer. We have made treaties in former years with all the Indians of the prairie, and from there to Lake Superior. As white people are coming into your country, we have thought it well to tell you what is required of you. The Queen wants all white, half-breeds and Indians to be at peace with one another, and to shake hands when they meet. The Queen's laws must be obeyed all over the country, both by the whites and the Indians. It is not alone that we wish to prevent Indians from molesting the whites, it is also to prevent the whites from molesting or doing harm to the Indians. The Queen's soldiers are just as much for the protection of the Indians as for the white man.

The Commissioners made an appointment to meet you at a certain time, but on account of bad weather on river and lake, we are late, which we are sorry for, but are glad to meet so many of you here today.

We understand stories have been told you, that if you made a treaty with us you would become servants and slaves; but we wish you to understand that such is not the case, but that you will be just as free after signing a treaty as you are now. The treaty is a free offer; take it or not, just as you please. If you refuse it there is no harm done; we will not be bad friends on that account. One thing Indians must understand, that if they do not make a treaty they must obey the laws of the land—that will be just the same whether you make a treaty or not; the laws must be obeyed. The Queen's Government wishes to give the Indians here the same terms as it has given all the Indians all over the country, from the prairies to Lake Superior. Indians in other places, who took treaty years ago, are now better off than they were before. They grow grain and raise cattle like the white people. Their children have learned to read and write.

Now, I will give you an outline of the terms we offer you. If you agree, to take treaty, every one this year gets a present of $12.00. A family of five, man, wife and three children, will thus get $60.00; a family of eight, $96.00; and after this year, and for every year afterwards, $5.00 for each person forever. To such chiefs as you may select, and that the Government approves of, we will give $25.00 each year, and the counsellors $15.00 each. The chiefs also get a silver medal and a flag, such as you see now at our tent, right now as soon as the treaty is signed. Next year, as soon as we know how many chiefs there are, and every three years thereafter, each chief will get a suit of clothes, and every counsellor a suit, only not quite so good as that of the chief. Then, as the white men are coming in and settling in the country, and as the Queen wishes the Indians to have lands of their own, we will give one square mile, or 640 acres, to each family of five; but there will be no compulsion to force Indians to

---

[99] See chapter five, ''Interviews with Elders,'' William Okeymaw, Sucker Creek Reserve, 27 March 1975.
[100] See footnote 98.

go into a reserve. He who does not wish to go into a band can get 160 acres of land for himself, and the same for each member of his family. These reserves are holdings you can select when you please, subject to the approval of the Government, for you might select lands which might interfere with the rights or lands of settlers. The Government must be sure that the land which you select is in the right place. Then, again, as some of you may want to sow grain or potatoes, the Government will give you ploughs or harrows, hoes, etc., to enable you to do so, and every spring will furnish you with provisions to enable you to work and put in your crop. Again, if you do not wish to grow grain, but want to raise cattle, the Government will give you bulls and cows so that you may raise stock. If you do not wish to grow grain or raise cattle, the Government will furnish you with ammunition for your hunt, and with twine to catch fish. The Government will also provide schools to teach your children to read and write, and do other things like white men and their children. Schools will be established where there is a sufficient number of children. The Government will give the chiefs axes and tools to make houses to live in and be comfortable. Indians have been told that if they make a treaty they will not be allowed to hunt and fish as they do now. This is not true. Indians who take treaty will be just as free to hunt and fish all over as they now are.

In return for this the Government expects that the Indians will not interfere with or molest any miner, traveller or settler.

We expect you to be good friends with everyone, and shake hands with all you meet. If any whites molest you in any way, shoot your dogs or horses, or do you any harm, you have only to report the matter to the police, and they will see that justice is done to you. There may be some things we have not mentioned, but these can be mentioned later on. Commissioners Walker and Cote are here for the half-breeds, who later on, if treaty is made with you, will take down the names of half-breed and their children, and find out if they are entitled to scrip. The reason the Government does this is because the half-breeds have Indian blood in their veins, and have claims on that account. The government does not make treaty with them, as they live as whitemen do, so it gives them scrip to settle their claims, at once and forever. Half-breeds living like Indians have the chance to take the treaty instead, if they wish to do so. They have their choice, but only after the treaty is signed. If there is no treaty made, scrip cannot be given. After the treaty is signed, the Commissioners will take up half-breed claims.[101]

Laird concluded by briefly outlining the Métis scrip provisions and by indicating that at the end of the meeting everyone would get flour, bacon, tea, and tobacco as a free gift from the Queen whether a treaty was made or not. He summed up the governments's position: " . . . the Queen owns the country, but is willing to acknowledge the Indian's claims, and offers them terms as an offset to all of them"; and then he asked the Indians to speak.[102]

The Indians were hesitant about the terms set forth by Laird. Kinosayoo began:

You say we are brothers. I cannot understand how we are so. I live differently from you. I can only understand that Indians will benefit in a very small degree from your offer. You have told us you come in the Queen's name. We surely have also a right to

---

[101] Mair, *Through the Mackenzie Basin*, pp. 56-59.
[102] Ibid., p. 59.

say a little as far as that goes. [Here he paused to get an explanation of the provision of clothes every three years, then continued.] Do you not allow the Indians to make their own conditions, so that they may benefit as much as possible? Why I say this is that we to-day make arrangements that are to last as long as the sun shines and the water runs. Up to the present I have earned my own living and worked in my own way for the Queen. It is good. The Indian loves this way of living and his free life. When I understand you thoroughly I will know better what I shall do. Up to the present I have never seen the time when I could not work for the Queen, and also make my own living. I will consider carefully what you have said.[103]

Moostoos followed with a brief, favourable speech:

Often before now I have said I would carefully consider what you might say. You have called us brothers. Truly I am the younger, you the elder brother. Being the younger, if the younger asks the elder for something, he will grant his request the same as our mother the Queen. I am glad to hear what you have to say. Our country is getting broken up. I see the white man coming in, and I want to be friends. I see what he does, but it is best that we should be friends. I will not speak any more. There are many people here who may wish to speak.[104]

Others indicated that they were also hesitant and wanted more time to discuss the proposal:

Wahpeehayo [White Partridge]: I stand behind this man's back [pointing to Kinosayoo]. I want to tell the Commissioners there are two ways, the long and the short. I want to take the way that will last longest.[105]

The Captain, an old man from Sturgeon Lake, then indicated that, although he did not have his family with him, he would accept the government's offer on behalf of all the people in his part of the country:

I am old now. It is indirectly through the Queen that we have lived. She has supplied in a manner the sale shops through which we have lived. Others may think I am foolish for speaking as I do now. Let them think as they like. I accept. When I was young I was an able man and made my living independently. But now I am old and feeble and not able to do much.[106]

Commissioner Ross then rose to answer some of the points raised:

Kinosayoo has said that he cannot see how it will benefit you to take treaty. As all the rights you now have will not be interfered with, therefore anything you get in addition must be clear gain. The whiteman is bound to come in and open up the country, and we come before him to explain the relations that must exist between you, and thus prevent any trouble. You say you have heard what the Commissioners have said, and how you wish to live. We believe that men who have lived without help heretofore can do it better when the country is opened up. Any fur they catch is worth more. That

---

[103] Ibid., pp. 59-60.
[104] Ibid., p. 60. The *Edmonton Bulletin* report attributes the quoted speech to Wahpeehayo rather than Moostoos, and records that he went on to ask for hay grounds for his cattle and a pair of boots like Commissioner McKenna's.
[105] Ibid.
[106] Ibid., p. 61

Courtesy Provincial Archives of Alberta, E. Brown Collection

Moostoos

comes about from competition. You will notice that it takes more boats to bring in goods to buy your furs than it did formerly. We think that as the rivers and lakes of this country will be the principal highways, good boatmen, like yourselves, cannot fail to make a good living, and profit from the increase in traffic. We are much pleased that you have some cattle. It will be the duty of the Commissioners to recommend the Government, through the Superintendent-General of Indian Affairs, to give you cattle of a better breed. You say that you consider that you have a right to say something about the terms we offer you. We offer you certain terms, but you are not forced to take them. You ask if Indians are not allowed to make a bargain. You must understand there are always two to a bargain. We are glad you understand the treaty is forever. If the Indians do as they are asked we shall certainly keep all our promises. We are glad to know that you have got on without any one's help, but you must know times are hard, and furs scarcer than they used to be. Indians are fond of a free life, and we do not wish to interfere with it. When reserves are offered you there is no intention to make you live on them if you do not want to, but, in years to come, you may change your minds, and want these lands to live on. The half-breeds of Athabasca are being more liberally dealt with than in any other part of Canada. We hope you will discuss our offer and arrive at a decision as soon as possible. Others are now waiting for our arrival, and you, by deciding quickly, will assist us to get to them.[107]

This picture of a post-treaty life in which Indians would remain free and independent, but with government assistance to fall back on and the prospect of greater opportunities in the fur trade, seems to have been responsible for removing many of the Indians' doubts. Wehtigo, followed by several others, made short speeches accepting the treaty.[108]

Kinosayoo asked for and received assurances that the treaty would be good forever and that the government would be ''willing to give means to instruct children as long as the sun shines and water runs, so that our children will grow up ever increasing in knowledge.''[109]

Father Lacombe then spoke in Cree, urging the Indians to accept the treaty. He emphasized his knowledge of treaty benefits that had accrued to the Prairie Indians to the south and insisted that he would have no part in a treaty which was not in the Indians' best interests. ''Your forest and river life will not be changed by the Treaty, and you will have your annuities, as well, year by year, as long as the sun shines and the earth remains. Therefore I finish my speaking by saying, Accept.''[110]

Laird then asked people to indicate acceptance by standing, but before the interpreter had even finished explaining this, a native named ''Jerou'' (possibly Giroux) jumped up and threatened to club any man who failed to stand up. Everyone arose amid laughter and the meeting adjourned for the day.[111]

---

[107] Ibid., pp. 61-62.
[108] See footnote 98.
[109] Mair, *Through the Mackenzie Basin*, p. 62.
[110] Ibid., p. 63.
[111] See footnote 98.

That evening, the commission met to draw up the treaty document to be presented to the Indians the next day. It seems plausible that the wording of this draft was based on the wording of Treaty Seven (1877), which was the last previous Indian treaty and which Laird had been involved in negotiating. However, there are several differences between the written terms of Treaty Seven and Treaty Eight, and these differences appear to reflect, in part, a recognition that the Indians of the North might wish to continue traditional economic activities, such as hunting, fishing, and trapping, and to resist being restricted to reserve land.

Whereas Treaty Seven refers to the protection of the Indians' ''vocations of hunting'' and other Prairie treaties refer to ''hunting and fishing,'' Treaty Eight refers to the

> *right to pursue their usual vocations of hunting, trapping and fishing* throughout the tract surrendered as heretofore described, subject to such regulations as may from time to time be made by the Government of the country, acting under the authority of Her Majesty, and saving and excepting such tracts as may be required or taken up from time to time for settlement, mining, lumbering, trading or other purposes.[112]

And whereas previous treaties had provided reserves of one square mile for every family of five, Treaty Eight provided:

> reserves for such bands as desire reserves, the same not to exceed in all one square mile for each family of five for such number of families as may elect to reside on reserves, or in that proportion for larger or smaller families; and for such families or individual Indians as may prefer to live apart from band reserves, Her Majesty undertakes to provide land in severalty to the extent of 160 acres to each Indian.[113]

In the field of education, both Treaty Seven and Treaty Eight committed the government to pay the salaries of such teachers of Indian children as the government may deem advisable. However, unlike Treaty Seven, Treaty Eight does not require that a band take up reserve land before this provision is implemented. The official report of the commissioners indicates that over and above this clause of the treaty, certain verbal assurances of education rights were necessary:

> As to education, the Indians were assured that there was no need of any special stipulation, as it was the policy of the Government to provide in every part of the country, as far as circumstances would permit, for the education of Indian children, and that the law, which was as strong as a treaty, provided for non-interference with the religion of the Indians in schools maintained or assisted by the Government.[114]

Treaty Eight provided the same tools for each band as Treaty Seven, provided that the band took a reserve. The provisions for stock and implements were similar, although not identical for the two treaties. Treaty

---

[112] Canada, *Treaty No. 8*, p. 12.
[113] Ibid., pp. 12-13.
[114] Ibid., p. 6.

Eight provided that each band that selected a reserve and cultivated the soil would receive:

> . . . two hoes, one spade, one scythe and two hay forks for every family so settled, and for every three families one plough and one harrow, and to the Chief, for the use of his Band, two horses or a yoke of oxen, and for each Band potatoes, barley, oats and wheat (if such seed be suited to the locality of the reserve), to plant the land actually broken up, and provisions for one month in the spring for several years while planting such seeds; and to every family one cow, and every Chief one bull, and one mowing machine and one reaper for the use of his Band when it is ready for them; for such families as prefer to raise stock instead of cultivating the soil, every family of five persons, two cows, and every Chief two bulls and two mowing machines when ready for their use, and a like proportion for smaller or larger families. The aforesaid articles, machines and cattle to be given once for all for the encouragement of agriculture and stock raising; and for such Bands as prefer to continue hunting and fishing, as much ammunition and twine for making nets annually as will amount in value to one dollar per head of the families so engaged in hunting and fishing.[115]

It is worth noting that Treaty Seven, foreseeing that ammunition might in the future become comparatively unnecessary, provided that ammunition money could be used for other purposes. By contrast, in referring to the choice between farming implements, stock, and hunting and fishing provisions, the Treaty Eight commissioners concluded that farming by Indians was not likely, stock raising would likely be restricted to the Lesser Slave Lake and Peace River areas, and

> in the main the demand will be for ammunition and twine, as the great majority of the Indians will continue to hunt and fish for a livelihood . . . .it is safe to say that so long as the fur-bearing animals remain, the great bulk of the Indians will continue to hunt and to trap.[116].

Treaty Eight, like Treaty Seven, neglected to mention any provision for medicine and medical services. Nor did the written terms of Treaty Eight give any indication that the government would take over other social services previously provided by the Hudson's Bay Company and missionaries. However, again the report of the commissioners indicates that they made significant verbal commitments in these areas.

The second day of the negotiations (21 June 1899) at Lesser Slave Lake began with Laird reading the treaty which had been drafted the previous evening. Although the meeting the previous day apparently had concluded with a consensus on the terms of the treaty, once this document was read aloud, a number of Indians, particularly some of the young ones,[117] raised further objections and reservations about the terms. According to Mair's

---

[115] Ibid., pp. 13-14.

[116] Ibid., p. 7.

[117] David Laird to superintendent general, 23 June 1899, Record Group 10, Public Archives of Canada, Ottawa, 3848: 75236-1.

account, Kinosayoo and Moostoos assented to the terms, but the dissent among others appeared to present a serious threat to the signing of the treaty and was only overcome by a lengthy discussion.[118] Little of this discussion was recorded, but the report of the commissioners refers to some of the major concerns of the Indian people and the promises that were made to overcome them:

> Our chief difficulty was the apprehension that the hunting and fishing privileges were to be curtailed. The provision in the treaty under which ammunition and twine is to be furnished went far in the direction of quieting the fears of the Indians, for they admitted that it would be unreasonable to furnish the means of hunting and fishing if laws were to be enacted which would make hunting and fishing so restricted as to render it impossible to make a livelihood by such pursuits. But over and above the provision, we had to solemnly assure them that only such laws as to hunting and fishing as were in the interest of the Indians and were found necessary in order to protect the fish and fur-bearing animals would be made, and that they would be as free to hunt and fish after the treaty as they would be if they never entered into it .... the Indians were generally averse to being placed on reserves. It would have been impossible to have made a treaty if we had not assured them that there was no intention of confining them to reserves. We had to very clearly explain to them that the provisions for reserves and allotments of land were made for their protection, and to secure to them in perpetuity a fair portion of the land ceded, in the event of settlement advancing.[119]

Whatever the government's intentions might have been in giving these assurances, the Indians saw them as guarantees of freedom to hunt, fish, and trap throughout the area—an assurance that they would be able to continue their way of making a living if they chose.

Interviews with Indian elders in the Lesser Slave Lake area indicate that this understanding of the treaty as a guarantee of their traditional livelihood is still very strong and widespread. Some have understood the treaty as leaving the Indians with ownership of wildlife:

> He [the King] made a promise to the Indian when he first gave them reserves: "as long as I live, I will look after you, my people, in this manner, and better if you respect me. I will look after your children and your wild game. Game will not be bought. Share with one another equally, carefully, totally. When we have this, we will vote, then the Indian will own what game he chooses for his consumption and use." This is what was decided about the moose. Moose is our main source of livelihood on this earth. Not like the white man, the King; he lived mainly on bread, he said. But the Indian lived on fish, ducks, anything. The King asked the Indian what he wanted for a livelihood. The Indian chose hunting and fishing not to be limited. As long as he lived.[120]

---

[118] Mair, *Through the Mackenzie Basin*, p. 64.

[119] Canada, *Treaty No. 8*, pp. 6-7.

[120] T.A.R.R. Interview with Elders Program, interview with Samuel Giroux, location and date not recorded.

Frank Cardinal, sixty-eight years old, was told many stories of the treaty by his father and grandfather, who were both present at the Lesser Slave Lake negotiations, and has a similar understanding:

> The way I see things, when an Indian chose his wild game, he was not to make hay to feed them, to fatten them. He was not to provide shelter for them from the cold. The Indian chose live animals. White man will govern his domestic animals. . . . These are the white man's responsibilities, but the wild animal belongs to the Indian.[121]

In 1937, several people signed affidavits concerning Treaty Eight, including James K. Cornwall ("Peace River Jim") who, in the late nineteenth century and the first half of this century, was responsible for many of the transportation enterprises that opened the North. Cornwall shared the Indian elders' view of the treaty as guaranteeing to the Indians some sort of primary rights over fish and wildlife:

> 1. I was present when Treaty 8 was made at Lesser Slave Lake and Peace River Crossing.
>
> 2. The treaty, as presented by the Commissioners to the Indians for their approval and signatures, was apparently prepared elsewhere, as it did not contain many things that they held to be of vital importance to their future existence as hunters and trappers and fishermen, free from the competition of white man. They refused to sign the Treaty as read to them by the Chief Commissioner.
>
> 3. Long discussions took place between the Commissioners and the Indian Chiefs and headmen, with many prominent men of the various bands taking part. The discussion went on for days, the Commissioners had unfavorably impressed the Indians, due to their lack of knowledge of the bush Indians' mode of life, by quoting Indian conditions on the Prairie. Chief Moostoos (the Buffalo) disposed of the argument by telling the Chief Commissioner that "a Plains Indian turned loose in the bush would get lost and starve to death."
>
> 4. As the Commission's instructions from Ottawa required the Treaty to be signed first at Lesser Slave Lake before proceeding North, and as the white population living in the Indian Territory had been requested by the Government, prior to the coming of the Commission, to be prepared to deal with them as such, the whites had done everything in their power to assist the Commissioners, by using every honorable influence that was possible.
>
> 5. The Commissioners finally decided, after going into the whole matter, that what the Indians suggested was only fair and right but that they had no authority to write it into the Treaty. They felt sure the Government on behalf of the Crown and the Great White Mother would include their request and they made the following promises to the Indians:—
>
>   a. Nothing would be allowed to interfere with their way of making a living, as they were accustomed to and as their forefathers had done.
>
>   b. The old and destitute would always be taken care of, their future existence would be carefully studied and provided for, and every effort would be made to improve their living conditions.
>
>   c. They were guaranteed protection in their way of living as hunters and trappers, from white competition; they would not be prevented from hunting and fishing as

---

[121] Ibid., interview with Frank Cardinal, location and date not recorded.

they had always done, so as to enable them to earn their living and maintain their existence.

6. Much stress was laid on one point by the Indians, as follows: They would not sign under any circumstances, unless their right to hunt, trap and fish was guaranteed and it must be understood that these rights they would never surrender.

7. It was only after the Royal Commission had recognized that the demands of the Indians were legitimate, and had solemnly promised that such demands would be granted by the Crown, also after the Hudson's Bay Company officials and Free Traders, and the Missionaries, with their Bishops, who had the full confidence of the Indians, had given their word that they could rely fully on the promises made in the name of Queen Victoria, that the Indians accepted and signed the Treaty, which was to last as long as the grass grew, the river ran, and the sun shone—to an Indian this means FOREVER.[122]

There can be little doubt that the missionaries played an important role in convincing the Indians that the treaty was in their own interests. Jean-Marie Mustus, age seventy-eight, was given this account by his grandfather Moostoos, who signed the treaty:

Father Lacombe was also present and spoke a lot to the Indian people on how to live. My grandfather said that he took Father Lacombe's advice because he had travelled with him many times. His advice was to take the treaty because it would help him and the young generations in the future.[123]

Other elders, such as William Okeymaw, eighty-seven years old, who was present at the negotiations, question the motives of the missionaries:

Lacombe . . . was the one who was pushing the Indians: "Take the treaty, take the treaty." But now it is obvious why he was really encouraging the Indians: there was only one church at the time at Grouard. There would also be a school; so what he had in mind was to try to make the Indians accept the money. That is the reason for his encouragement.[124]

Some written material tends to support his cynical view of the role of the missionaries. Bishop Grouard, in his own account of the negotiations, indicated that he was very uneasy about the treaty until the Indians indicated that if given a choice as to the denomination of their schools, they would choose Roman Catholic. Grouard then no longer feared to encourage the Indians to accept the treaty.[125] This is not to suggest that the missionaries sought personal gains or advantages in the treaty, but they saw it as a source of assistance to foster their education system, and were concerned about its possible effects on the zealous interdenominational competition for the allegiance of the Indian people.

---

[122] Fumoleau, *Land Shall Last*, pp. 74-75.

[123] See chapter five, "Interviews with Elders," interview with Jean-Marie Mustus, Joussard, Alta., 26 March 1975.

[124] See footnote 99.

[125] Grouard, *Soixante ans d'apostolat*, p. 370.

However, the missionaries believed that they were also serving the Indians' interests by promoting the treaty. Father René Fumoleau, who has done considerable research on Treaty Eight, notes that some of the missionaries who participated in the negotiations later felt that they had been "used" by the government. One such indication is contained in a letter written by Constant Falher, O.M.I. (who was present at the negotiations at Lesser Slave and Wabasca) to Bishop Breynat:

> If in 1899 we had not prepared the Lesser Slave Lake people to accept a treaty with the Government; if Bishop Grouard had not advised the chiefs to sign the treaty, telling them there was nothing which was not to their advantage; the treaty would still be waiting to be signed today. When Bishop Grouard sent me to Wabasca (at the request of Mr. Laird) to prepare the people and calm them, (it was then said that they were more or less in a state of revolt) I carried with me the government promises and I was very surprised when later on I was shown the document supposedly signed by the Indian Chiefs at Grouard . . . and thereabouts. So many important things are missing . . . but we do remember these things, and we suffer.[126]

At the end of the second day of negotiations at Lesser Slave Lake, the treaty was signed by the three commissioners and six Indian leaders. Although the treaty is marked with "X" marks for the signatures of the Indians, the *Edmonton Bulletin* reported that the Indians merely touched the pen.[127] On the third day, the treaty money was distributed and the Half-breed Commission began its meetings.

THE TREATY ADHESIONS

Having dealt with the Indians of Lesser Slave Lake, it still remained for the commission to obtain the adhesions of all other bands in the proposed treaty area. The Indians of each local area undoubtedly considered these local meetings to be just as important, if not more so, than the Lesser Slave Lake meeting. However, the treaty commissioners expected that, once it had been learned that the Lesser Slave Lake treaty had been signed, there would be less difficulty in obtaining the adhesions of the others. For this reason, they left us little written record of the other nine meetings in 1899 and four meetings in 1900 that took place from Fort St. John to Fond du Lac and from Fort Resolution to Wabasca. The following account, therefore, contains only a bare outline of these meetings.

Because they were considerably behind schedule after the Lesser Slave Lake meetings, the commissioners decided to divide the treaty party in two in order to try to reach all the designated points before the end of the summer. Even so, they had to leave four of the locations for the following summer:

---

[126] Fumoleau, *Land Shall Last*, p. 67.
[127] See footnote 98.

Fort St. John, Sturgeon Lake, Upper Hay River (Slavey Band), and Fort Resolution.

David Laird led one of the treaty parties to Peace River Landing where on 1 July they took the adhesion of a Cree band led by Duncan Tustawits. The Indians here expressed the fear that by taking the treaty they would be subject to conscription into the British army, and they would only sign when assured that this was not the case.[128] There were also several members of the Beaver Band of Dunvegan present, including the chief, but they refused to sign because the rest of their band was at Dunvegan.[129]

While Laird's group was at Peace River Landing, the other treaty party, led by McKenna and Ross, was attempting to reach Fort St. John. However, before they got there, they received word that the Indians had run out of provisions and had dispersed in four bands to hunt.[130] On returning from Fort St. John, McKenna and Ross obtained the adhesion of the Beaver Indians of Dunvegan, led by Natooses, on 6 July.

Laird by then was on his way to Vermilion where on 8 July an adhesion was signed by Chief Ambrose Tête Noir and Pierrot Fournier of the Beaver Indians and Kuiskuiskowcapoohoo, headman of the Tall Cree Band. Thomas Roberts, eighty-two years old, of the Beaver Ranch Reserve gives us this story of the Fort Vermilion meeting:

> I was not present at the treaty signing, but my father and grandmother were there. They were a long time in coming to an agreement. The people had a choice of treaty or scrip. There was a white man named Wilson who was here a long time. He did not speak our language. He was the husband of Gris' sister, this man Wilson was the one who advised us to take the treaty.[131]

The man named "Wilson" would have been F.D. Wilson of the Hudson's Bay Company who signed as a witness to the adhesion. At Vermilion, as well as Fort Chipewyan and Smith's Landing, the Indians made an earnest appeal for the services of a doctor.[132]

Another group of sixty-six Crees was met further down the Peace River at Little Red River and was believed to be part of the Vermilion Cree Band. It was with the headman of this Little Red River group that some difficulty was encountered. According to Mair's report, the headman refused to sign because of a divine inspiration. However, Grouard's account gives us more detail. Apparently, the headman had pointed out that it was not himself who had made this country, but God who had made the sky and earth. Therefore,

---

[128] Grouard, *Soixante ans d'apostolat*, pp. 372-73.

[129] Mair, *Through the Mackenzie Basin*, p. 65; correspondence, 1 July 1899, Record Group 10, Public Archives of Canada, Ottawa, 3848: 75236-1.

[130] Canada, *Treaty No. 8*, p. 7.

[131] T.A.R.R. Interview with Elders Program, interview with Thomas Roberts, location and date not recorded.

[132] Canada, *Treaty No. 8*, p. 5.

Courtesy R.C.M.P. Museum, Regina, and Glenbow-Alberta Institute

David Laird explaining Treaty Eight at Fort Vermilion

if he were to receive the money which the government was offering, he would be guilty of theft for selling something that did not belong to him. Grouard explained to him that this money was a form of compensation; this explanation was accepted and the adhesion was signed.[133] Grouard attributed this "case of conscience" to the man's recent acceptance of Christianity, but the problem seems more indicative of the difficulty the commissioners must have faced in trying to explain what they meant by the surrender of land rights to people for whom land had great religious significance and little, if any, significance as a saleable commodity.

The next stop for Commissioners McKenna and Ross was Fort Chipewyan, and fortunately we have considerable evidence of this meeting on 13 July 1899. The Roman Catholic Mission diaries at Fort Chipewyan give this account:

> Two members of the Commission landed here at noon (13 July) and called a meeting of all the Indians for 3 p.m. The meeting took place in the Fort's yard. All the heads of families were present. Noticing that the missionaries were absent from the gathering, Mr. McKenna wrote and invited them to be present at the discussions, and all the Fathers went there.
>
> The Commissioner explained the Government's views and the advantages if offered to the people. The Chief of the Crees spoke up and expressed the conditions on which he would accept the Government's proposals: 1) Complete freedom to fish; 2) Complete freedom to hunt; 3) Complete freedom to trap; 4) As himself and his people are Catholics, he wants the children to be educated in Catholic Schools.
>
> In his turn the Chipewyan spokesman set the same conditions as the first speaker. The Commissioner acknowledged all the requests which both had voiced.
>
> Mr. Driver, in charge of the Fort [HBC] store, interpreted for the Crees, and Mr. Pierre Mercredi, his assistant, interpreted for the Chipewyans. Then the Treaty was read and signed by both Government representatives, and witnessed by the Fathers, and by the most eminent people of the locality. The Commissioners nominated a chief for the Chipewyans who so far had never had one. They officially recognized as such, the Chief of the Crees. Two councillors were given to each of the Chiefs, to replace them if need be. The Chief of the Chipewyans is Alexandre Laviolette. As it was already 9 p.m. and everybody was feeling tired due to this day's excessive temperature, treaty money was paid to the Chiefs only. All the other people would be paid the following day. At noon, the next day (14 July) everything was over and both Commissioners left for Fort Smith.[134]

Bishop Breynat summarized the Indians' position by writing that "Crees and Chipewyans refused to be treated like the Prairie Indians, and to be parked on reserves . . . .It was essential to them to retain complete freedom to move around."[135]

The official report of the commissioners praised Chief Alexandre Laviolette of Fort Chipewyan for "keenness of intellect and much practical

---

[133] Grouard, *Soixante ans d' apostolat*, p. 374.
[134] Fumoleau, *Land Shall Last*, pp. 77-78.
[135] Ibid., p. 78.

sense in pressing the claims of his band.'' Elsewhere, Commissioner Ross gave further indication of the difficulties he encountered at Fort Chipewyan:

> Here it was, that the Chief asked for a railway—the first time in the history of Canada that the red man demanded as a condition of cession that steel should be laid into his country. He evidently understood the transportation question, for a railway, he said, by bringing them into close connection with the market, would enhance the value of what they had to sell, and decrease the cost of what they had to buy. He had a striking object lesson the fact flour was $12. a sack at the Fort. These Chipewyans lost no time in flowery oratory, but came at once to business, and kept us, myself in particular, on tenterhooks for two hours. I never felt so relieved as when the rain of questions ended, and satisfied by our answers, they acquiesced in the cession.[136]

Indian elders of the Fort Chipewyan area maintain today that the treaty guaranteed their rights to hunt, fish, and trap without restriction.[137] Fumoleau, after reviewing the diaries and archives of missionaries of this area and finding little reference to content or the importance of the treaty discussions, concluded: ''It would seem that few people were concerned with the land ownership question, the real reason for the coming of these visitors.''[138]

From Fort Chipewyan, McKenna and Ross proceeded to Fort Smith (or Smith's Landing) where they met the Chipewyan band of Slave River on 17 July. There is little archival evidence of this meeting. However, evidence of Indian elders before Justice W.G. Morrow in 1973 indicates that the treaty was understood as a peace treaty, to insure that there would be no conflict between the Indians and incoming whites, and that no mention of land was made.[139]

McKenna and Ross had an additional reason to be uneasy about the meetings at Smith's Landing and Fort Chipewyan. While travelling in the North, they had learned that Parliament was considering extending beyond the following January the prohibition against killing buffalo in the area to the west of Lake Athabasca.

> But at neither points could we take the responsibility of telling the Indians that the prohibition was to be extended. The chief difficulty in dealing with the Indians in this country arose from the fact that they believed that the making of a treaty would lead to interference with their hunting upon which they must depend for a living. When we were asked about the Wood Buffalo prohibition we had to say that we had no instructions as to any change in the law. Our mission would likely have been a failure if we had opened up the question.[140]

---

[136] Mair, *Through the Mackenzie Basin*, pp. 65-66.

[137] This view of the elders is supported by Pierre Mercredi, one of the treaty interpreters, who made a statement in 1939 to the effect that the original treaty document which he translated did not contain any reference to the application of hunting regulations to Indians (see Fumoleau, *Land Shall Last*, p. 79). We have found no other archival evidence to suggest that the terms of the treaty were altered in this manner.

[138] Fumoleau, *Land Shall Last*, pp. 78-79.

[139] Paulette et al., Supreme Court of the Northwest Territories (1973), testimony of Chief François Paulette and Antoine Beaulier, pp. 154-57 and 311-18.

[140] McKenna, 26 July 1899, Record Group 10, Public Archives of Canada, Ottawa, 6732: 420-2.

After the negotiations in these two communities had been completed, McKenna and Ross learned that the prohibition had been extended. In their opinions, it was an ill-advised measure based on ignorance of the conditions of the North and certain to create resentment among the Indians as well as the missionaries and fur traders, who sided with the Indians on the question. One can only speculate as to what the outcome of the meetings might have been had the Indians been made aware of the intentions of Parliament.

Laird's treaty party left Fort Chipewyan on 18 July for Fond du Lac to meet the band of Chipewyan Indians there. The adhesion for this band indicates that it was signed on 25 July by Laurent Dzieddin and Toussaint, "headmen." However, the name of Maurice Piché (also known as Moberly), listed as "Chief of Band" was added on 27 July: "the number accepting treaty being larger than at first expected, a Chief was allowed."[141]

However, an account by Bishop Breynat indicates that there was considerably more behind this late signature by the chief:

> The Indians were wearied from already waiting so long after the scheduled date for the treaty and they eagerly went to the meeting. Chiefs and councillors were elected and accepted without any difficulty. The meeting took place a few steps from the mission. Right after the text of the proposed treaty had been read, translated and explained, the Honourable Laird knocked on my door.
>
> "Complete failure!" he said, "We must fold down our tents, pack our baggage and leave." He explained that as soon as the discussion started Chief Moberly . . . nearly got into a fight with the interpreter, good-natured Robillard. They had already taken off their vests, and the police had intervened. The chief had jumped into his canoe and left to the other side of the bay. "Evidently there is nothing we can do," added Laird pitifully, with tears in his eyes. He was a good old man with a sensitive heart. I offered him my sympathy: "Let me try," I said, "everything might turn out all right." Chief Moberly was the very best hunter of the entire tribe. How many times his gun had saved indigent people who without him would have died of starvation. He was also very conscious of his superiority and his pride would not tolerate any opposition. He feared that the treaty might restrain his freedom. His pride could only despise the yearly five-dollar bait offered to each of his tribesmen in return for the surrender of their rights, until then undisputed, and which, one must admit, rightly so—he held as incontestable.
>
> Robillard tried to placate him by explaining this and that—he only made him angrier. Thus the fight! I called for one of the elected councillors, Dzieddin ('the deaf') known for his good character, his great heart and his good judgement. I explained to him: "If Chief Moberly, a great hunter and a very proud man, can despise and reject the help offered by the government, many old people without any income and many orphans will appreciate receiving a five dollar annuity, along with free powder, bullets, fishnets, etc." I added, "Accept and sign the treaty on behalf of all those poor people. Anyway, even all of you together, all the Caribou Eaters, you cannot help it. You may accept the Treaty or not, but either way the Queen's Government will come, and set up its own organization in your country. The compensation offered by the Government may be quite small, but to refuse it would only deprive the poor people of much-needed help." Dzieddin was convinced by this

---

[141] Canada, *Treaty No. 8*, p. 16.

argument and he signed the treaty. Many Indians had previously always been needy. Now they started to leave the Hudson's Bay store and those of the free traders who had followed the treaty party, looking like wealthy people with supplies of tea, flour, sugar, gunpowder, etc. Some families had received as much as $150 or more. The better off people who sided with Chief Moberley were gradually drawn by the lure of an easy gain and came to receive their allowance. One of the Chief's best friends came to me for advice—"So many people have already accepted Treaty. Don't you think it would also be good for me to accept it?"

At last Chief Moberley himself came, with two or three of the last objectors. They went back, with happy hearts and a canoe loaded with goods. The first day's quarrel was completely forgotten. Good old Robillard, the interpreter, was laughing within himself when he shook hands with them in farewell.[142]

Breynat, like other missionaries of the area, felt that the Indians had nothing to gain by refusing the treaty because the government was offering "relatively liberal" terms and would assume control of the region—treaty or no treaty.[143]

Finally, in order to reach their last two stops on the 1899 excursion, McKenna and Ross split up, the former going to Fort McMurray on 4 August and the latter to Wabasca on 16 August.

William McDonald of the Fort McKay band was only two years old when his people took treaty at Fort McMurray, but he later heard stories of the meeting from the chief of the band:

The Indians were not willing. They were afraid because during that time there were no white people in this part of the country. The only non-Indians were from the Hudson's Bay. . . . When the commissioner was ready to pay the Indians, they called them together. They talked there all day long. The Indians were going to get paid. They were going to be treated properly. When you accept the treaty money, it will never end. . . . But the Indians still would not go along with that idea. They were afraid and suspicious. The Indians thought they would lose their land or get killed and wiped out. That is the reason they were not willing. The priest then spoke to the Indians telling them to accept the money, that there was no danger and that they were being assisted. The Indians were to become friends with everybody and unite.[144]

Mr. McDonald goes on to indicate that the people were finally convinced by the priest and by the promise of annual rations.

We have no archival evidence on the Wabasca meeting; however, today, elders of that area strongly emphasize that they were guaranteed complete freedom to hunt, fish, and trap.

J.A. Macrae, Indian commissioner, was left with the task of securing four more adhesions in 1900, with the Beavers of Fort St. John, the Crees of Sturgeon Lake, the Slavey Band of Upper Hay River, and the Dogribs, Yellowknives, Chipewyans, and Slaveys of Fort Resolution. His instructions

---

[142] Fumoleau, *Land Shall Last*, pp. 79-80.

[143] Ibid., p. 81.

[144] T.A.R.R. Interview with Elders Program, interview with William McDonald, Fort McKay, 9 February 1974.

had been to take adhesions at Fort St. John and Fort Resolution, because the 1899 expedition had not reached these distant points. However, the Crees of Sturgeon Lake and the Slaveys of Upper Hay River met him and asked to be included. Because they were obviously entitled, Macrae drew up adhesions for them.[145]

Macrae's report on the 1900 expedition indicates that he encountered the same concerns among the Indians as in 1899:

> As was reported by your commissioners last year, there is little disposition on the part of most of the northern Indians to settle down upon land or to ask to have reserves set apart. Dealing, under your instructions, with demands for land, two small provisional reserves were laid out at Lesser Slave Lake for Kinoosayo's band, and fifteen or sixteen applications were registered for land in severalty by Indians who have already, to some extent, taken to agriculture.
>
> It appears that this disinclination to adopt agriculture as a means of livelihood is not unwisely entertained, for the more congenial occupations of hunting and fishing are still open, and agriculture is not only arduous to those untrained to it, but in many districts it as yet remains untried. A consequence of this preference of old pursuits is that the government will not be called upon for years to make those expenditures which are entailed by the treaty when the Indians take to soil for subsistence.[146]

Macrae also reported that the Indians who had been present at the 1899 meeting requested extended explanations of the terms for those who had not understood. Not surprisingly, the hurried 1899 trip had left something less than a clear understanding in its wake.

A medical doctor accompanied Macrae, and his services were appreciated by the Indians.[147]

Macrae recognized that, even with this trip in 1900, the task of taking all Indians into treaty was incomplete. There still remained a number of Indians (Macrae estimated over five hundred) who lived at points distant from those visited and who had not been given the option of taking treaty or scrip. Notwithstanding this, Macrae concluded that "the Indian title . . . may be fairly regarded as extinguished."[148]

INDIAN PERCEPTIONS OF THE TREATY

In the preceding sections, we have assembled available archival evidence on the historical background to Treaty Eight and the negotiations themselves. Where appropriate, brief reference has been made to the oral tradition of Indian communities, which has transmitted an understanding of the spirit and terms of Treaty Eight to the Indian elders of today. The present section will look more closely at the views of the Indian elders, and will

---

[145] Canada, *Treaty No. 8*, p. 20.
[146] Ibid., p. 21.
[147] Ibid.
[148] Ibid.

attempt to explain divergence within the oral tradition, as well as between the archival evidence and the oral tradition. Our aim is to determine how the Indian people might have understood Treaty Eight in 1899. This is not to assume that the Indian understanding of recent years will be identical to that of 1899, but that the testimony of today's elders constitutes an essential source of evidence on the treaties.

Of all the subjects discussed by the elders in these interviews, hunting, fishing, and trapping rights emerge as the most significant. Overwhelmingly, the elders of the Treaty Eight area believed that the treaty promised that there would be no restriction on their right to hunt, fish, and trap. The most common responses were either a simple statement to the effect that they were guaranteed that there would be no restrictions, or that they would be allowed to continue their "livelihood." Any requirements, such as hunting or fishing licences, are seen as a violation of treaty rights.

Melanie Hamelin, seventy years old, heard from her grandfather that "there would not be any restrictions on the pursuit of their livelihood. There would not be any restrictions on their hunting or the animals they killed."[149]

Isador Willier, who was over one hundred years old when interviewed, said that the Indians were told that

> . . . The way you have been struggling for a livelihood—no one will ever stop that form of livelihood. If you should take treaty, this is the way you will make your livelihood. Moose, cariboo, and any other wild bush animals, no one will ever stop you from obtaining these animals anywhere . . . .You will always make your livelihood that way. If you should take treaty, . . . nothing will stop you from fishing and duck hunting . . . .[150]

Several interviews conceived these rights to mean that Indians would retain ownership of all fish and wildlife. A few interviews mention the limitation that Indians would not be able to hunt on the white man's land or to shoot at his farm animals or buildings.

Unfortunately, the interviews did not dwell on the distinction between commercial and non-commercial hunting, fishing, and trapping. However, the frequent reference to the right to continue their "livelihood" would suggest that the Indians understood that they would be able to pursue these activities on a commercial basis, as they had before the treaty. A few interviews imply that Indians can hunt only to supply family needs, but this may be a reflection of current legal realities rather than treaty promises.

On the basis of oral and archival evidence, it would seem that the treaty would not have been signed if the Indians had not been given assurances that they would be as free to hunt, fish, and trap after the treaty as before. They

---

[149] T.A.R.R. Interview with Elders Program, interview with Melanie Hamelin, location and date not recorded.

[150] Ibid., interview with Isadore Willier, location not recorded, 18 November 1972.

were given assurances that the government was interested only in conserving wildlife for their benefit. Some evidence, not entirely conclusive, suggests that they were promised that they would be protected from white competition. In other words, whether it took the form of ownership of wildlife or protection from white competition, these assurances constituted a recognition that hunting, fishing, and trapping as a way of life would remain an option for treaty Indians. If the treaty commissioners had looked upon these rights as mere temporary privileges pending widespread settlement or mining, they failed to make this clear in the negotiations. More likely they believed that any conflicts that might arise would be far in the future.

At the time of the negotiations, the commissioners found that the Indians' fear of losing their hunting, fishing, and trapping rights was partly overcome by reference to the provisions for ammunition and twine. The frequency with which these provisions are mentioned by the elders today is an indication of their importance. Many of the elders mention that they originally got twine with which to make nets, and one man pointed out that when the government later tried to regulate the mesh size of nets, they started issuing nets instead of thread.

Several Indian elders of that portion of the Treaty Eight area now within the Northwest Territories have testified before Justice W.G. Morrow that there was no mention of land surrender or the allotment of reserves during the treaty negotiations. The treaty was essentially a peace treaty, designed to insure peaceful relations between Indians and non-Indians.

However, most of the elders interviewed in Alberta seem to accept the land surrender as part of the treaty, although they have divergent views over the exact meaning of the surrender. Several indicate that minerals were never surrendered, that the white man only wanted enough land in depth to be able to farm. Others, while demonstrating a clear grasp of other treaty issues, admit to being in doubt about the surrender of land:

> That is something that always puzzles me when I think of it. It appears as though the commissioner wanted to claim the land, to own the land for the government. That is why they took that action. . . . At times the Indian people get angry about that. The white man never bought the land. If he had bought it, there would have been very large sums of money involved. . . . [151]

When asked whether the land was surrendered to the commissioners, Francis Bruno, sixty-five years old, responded;

> That I do not know if it was or not. I cannot answer that. But what I do understand is that we were to share the land with other people who were the white people. That was

---

[151] See chapter five, "Interviews with Elders," interview with Felix Gibot, Fort Chipewyan, 5 February 1974.

the purpose of the treaty, I think, since there were going to be more white people, to share the land with them.[152]

This diversity of views on land and resource rights is not surprising, judging by the lack of attention given it during the negotiations. The archival evidence demonstrates that there was surprisingly little effort to explain the implications of the treaty phrase "the said Indians do hereby cede, release, surrender and yield up . . . . all their rights, title and privileges whatsoever, to the lands," and so on. We can only speculate as to why this crucial issue of the control of land and resources was avoided, or passed over lightly, in the negotiations when it was obviously the intention of the government to extinguish aboriginal rights. It is likely that the commissioners felt that it was a mere formality from the government point of view. The government had already made some laws applicable in the area and fully intended to establish further control. From their point of view, they already owned the land; so the treaty was merely a means of extinguishing the vague aboriginal rights and placating the native people by offering the advantages of a treaty.

However, the Indian people undoubtedly held a very different view of the treaty and of land and resource tenure. Even if the commissioners had been fully aware of these different views, it is very doubtful that they could have cleared up the misunderstandings on their hurried trip through the North.

Dr. June Helm, testifying before Justice W.G. Morrow in 1973, made these comments on the difficulty of communicating the concept of land surrender:

> . . . How could anybody put in the Athapaskan language through a Métis interpreter to monolingual Athapaskan hearers the concept of relinquishing ownership of land, I don't know, of people who have never conceived of a bounded property which can be transferred from one group to another. I don't know how they would be able to comprehend the import translated from English into a language which does not have those concepts, and certainly in any sense that Anglo-Saxon jurisprudence would understand. So this is an anthropological opinion and it has continued to puzzle me how any of them could possibly have understood this. I don't think they could have. That is my judgement.[153]

This view is supported by the report of the Nelson Commission in 1959, which was set up to examine the unfulfilled provisions of Treaties Eight and Eleven, as they apply to the Indians of the Mackenzie District:

> It should be noted that although the Treaties were signed sixty and thirty-eight years ago respectively, very little change has been effected in the mode of life of the Indians of the Mackenzie District. Very few of the adults had received an elementary education and consequently were not able to appreciate the legal implications of the

---

[152] T.A.R.R. Interview with Elders Program, interview with Francis Bruno, location not recorded, 7 February 1974.

[153] Paulette et al, Supreme Court of Northwest Territories (1973), testimony of June Helm, pp. 33-34.

Treaties. Indeed some bands expressed the view that since they had the right to hunt, fish and trap over all of the land in the Northwest Territories, the land belonged to the Indians. The Commission found it impossible to make the Indians understand that it is possible to separate mineral rights or hunting rights from actual ownership of land.[154]

The report went on to suggest that reserves were of no value to the Indian people under the circumstances in which they lived.

If the Nelson Commission had difficulty explaining "land surrender" to Athapaskans in the Mackenzie District in 1959, it is difficult to imagine that Laird and his commission would have had an easy time explaining it to Athapaskans and Crees living the same sort of life in what is now northern Alberta in 1899. But the point is that they apparently made no great effort to explain the concept, either because of a desire to avoid controversy and get the job over with, or ignorance of the basis of the Indians' misunderstanding.

Some of the Cree people in the southern part of the treaty area may have been more familiar with the treaties of the Prairies and therefore more fearful of losing their land. However, the promises that reserves were not compulsory and that they could continue to hunt, fish, and trap would have reassured them.

The Indian people in 1899 fully understood that white men would be entering their land, taking homesteads, and farming, as well as prospecting and mining. Indians were to live in peace with the newcomers and give up those areas of land required. But most of the land would remain unoccupied by whites and available to Indians for hunting, fishing, and trapping. Beyond these agreements, however, there appears to have been a "failure of the meeting of minds" with regard to the sharing of natural resources, that is, surface rights outside of agricultural areas, timber, wildlife, minerals, and water. This failure allowed both sides to look favourably upon the treaty at the time, but left a legacy of confusion and bitterness for future generations of Indians who were asked to believe that their fathers and grandfathers had "sold" the land they walked on and the lakes they fished in.

The treaty provision for reserves and lands in severalty was seen by both sides as protection for those bands living in areas likely to be settled, and as an alternative economic base for those who might wish to engage in agriculture or stock raising. Indians in more isolated areas had no interest in obtaining reserves in 1899. The archival evidence which we have reviewed indicates that the reserves were offered by the commissioners and explained at some of the treaty negotiations, but were not really discussed by the Indian people. Interviews with Indian elders indicate that the Indian people were generally unaware of the exact written terms of the treaty concerning reserve land.

---

[154] Walter H. Nelson et al., "Report of the Commission Appointed to Investigate the Unfulfilled Provisions of Treaties 8 and 11 as They Apply to the Indians of the Mackenzie District 1959" (1959; reprint ed., Toronto: Indian-Eskimo Association of Canada, 1970), pp. 4-5.

In light of the comments by the commissioners to the effect that the Indians reacted negatively to the suggestions of reserves in 1899, it might seem surprising that most of the elders today have positive attitudes towards the reserves. Reserves are seen as places where Indians can make a living without interference from whites, and where Indians own everything, including mineral rights. Some elders speak of the years of frustration that they had to go through before the government granted them a reserve. However, it is likely that this change in attitude towards reserves was a result of white settlement in particular areas. As the Indians saw whites taking up land which they had traditionally occupied, they began to appreciate the security offered by the reserves. Furthermore, during periods of declining opportunities in the fur trade, an attempt at agriculture would have looked more appealing.

Several elders believe that their reserves are too small and one, William Okeymaw, insists that the treaty promised that more land would be provided if the reserves became overcrowded. None of the elders interviewed had a clear understanding of the reserve provisions of the written version of the treaty.

The written version of the treaty contains detailed promises of assistance in agriculture and stock raising, including the provision of tools, implements, seed, cattle, and provisions for one month each year, for several years while crops were being put in. In the negotiations, it may not have been explained that the allotment of cattle and implements was a "once-for-all" provision in the written document, rather than an ongoing commitment to economic development. It is clear from the interviews of elders that assistance in agriculture has always been seen as a treaty right. Many of the elders remember that promises were made concerning cattle, implements, and provisions during planting. There is no indication that the Indian people understood these promises to be on a "once-for-all" basis, but the interviews did not focus specifically on this issue. It seems that the various details of agricultural assistance were seen by the Indians as amounting to a general commitment to provide whatever assistance was necessary to help them get started in farming, if they so desired.

The right to an education was stressed in the treaty negotiations by Kinosayoo and others, and the government assured them that this would be provided for. At the time of the negotiations, the churches were expected to continue to play a major role in education in the North, and the Indians were assured that they would have complete freedom in choosing education under the religion of their choice, in government supported schools. Wally Willier, an elder from Wabasca, explains that Indians were promised "schools in the years to come. That is why we were given a choice, either to take a Catholic priest or a minister." It would seem that neither the written treaty nor the negotiations were very specific about the extent and nature of the education that Indians would be entitled to under the treaty. Similarly, Indian elders today see these rights in very general terms. Some elders refer to it as "learning to read," or "learning to farm," or getting "an education like the white man," which would enable them to "know the white man's way of living."

One of the clearest discrepancies between the written treaty and the Indian understanding of the treaty is in the area of health care and social services. The treaty document makes no provision for such assistance. The Indian people might have expected the government to assume rather broad obligations similar to those of the Hudson's Bay Company in this area. The report of the treaty commissioners indicates that the Indians asked for "assistance in seasons of distress," and "urged that the old and indigent who were no longer able to hunt and trap and were consequently often in distress should be cared for by the government. They requested that the medicines be furnished. At Vermilion, Chipewyan, and Smith's Landing, an earnest appeal was made for the services of a medical man."[155] In response, the government insisted that they would not maintain Indians in idleness, but that:

> . . . the Government was always ready to give relief in cases of actual destitution, and that in seasons of distress they would without any special stipulation in the treaty receive such assistance as it was usual to give in order to prevent starvation among Indians in any part of Canada; and we stated that the attention of the Government would be called to the need of some special provision being made to assisting the old and indigent who were unable to work and dependent on charity for the means of sustaining life. We promised that supplies of medicine would be put in the charge of persons selected by the Government at different points, and would be distributed free to those of the Indians who might require them. We explained that it would be practically impossible for the Government to arrange for regular medical attendance upon Indians so widely scattered over such an extensive territory. We assured them, however, that the Government would always be ready to avail itself of any opportunity of affording medical service just as it provided that the physician attached to the Commission should give free attendance to all Indians who he might find in need of treatment as he passed through the country.[156]

The Indian people apparently understood this as a general commitment to provide health care. Today the elders say that Indians should have doctors, medicine, hospital care, and medical aid free of charge as a treaty right. What is important in the treaty is not the specific promises that were made, but the fact that the government agreed to provide health care and social services to the extent that was feasible. It was not the understanding of the Indian people that they would be restricted forever to what was available in 1899. Some of the elders specifically remember the promises of care for the aged.

Treaty Eight followed the practice of previous treaties in paying a gratuity and an annuity the first year—in this case, a seven dollars gratuity

---

[155] Canada, *Treaty No. 8*, p. 5.
[156] Ibid., pp. 5-6.

and a five dollars annuity per person. In subsequent years, of course, only the annuity was paid. Perhaps the nature of these payments was not made clear, because today many elders are puzzled by the fact that their payments were cut back from twelve to five dollars after the first year, and some see it as a trick to get the treaty signed, by offering large initial payments.

Clearly, to the Indian people the treaty was much more complex than a surrender of land in exchange for annuities and certain social services. It was, rather, an agreement on how the natural resources would be shared between the Indians, the Métis, and the non-native newcomers. Furthermore, it was an agreement on the extent to which Indian people would receive benefits of the non-native society with whom they were to share the land.

A review of the written terms of Treaty Eight and the available evidence of the context and content of the negotiations must lead to the conclusion that an agreement was only made possible by the existence of a large measure of trust between the parties and by the absence of reasonable alternatives to such an agreement. The treaty was not so much a precise legal definition of Indian rights under Canadian law as a compact or set of fundamental principles that would form the basis for all future relations between the Indian prople and the government.

For the Indian people, the assurances of the government's good intentions and its commitment to justice were of great significance, particularly when such assurances were given by those whom they had come to rely upon to bridge the enormous cultural gap between themselves and the white society—the missionaries and fur traders who lived in their country. Having had an example of the effects of an uncontrolled and lawless frontier expansion in the gold rush phenomenon, the Indians would have been well disposed to believe that a force strong enough to bring order and justice to such an environment was potentially an ally. Where the effects of white settlers and travellers had been less obvious, as perhaps was the case at Fond du Lac, the treaty may have appeared to have been more like an ultimatum, offering few benefits beyond a small quantity of money and rations.

Despite their previous ignorance of the North and the living conditions of northern Indians, the treaty commissioners had been impressed with the fact that the way of life there was radically different from that on the Prairies and would require substantially different government policy from that applied to the Prairie Indians. However, with the treaty successfully negotiated, the affairs of these Indians would now come under the jurisdiction of a small and distant federal bureaucracy, and for many years to come, a very small field staff.

Undoubtedly, the civil servants responsible for administering Indian policy assumed that substantial intervention in the affairs of northern Indians was neither required by the extent of social change in the area nor demanded by the Indians. The intrusion by miners, settlers, trappers, and others was still not on a large enough scale to require more than an affirmation of the government's intentions to apply the laws of the land to native and non-native alike. The condition of the native population only required that the government assume greater responsibility for their health, education, and welfare. Hunting, fishing, and trapping would continue to be the basis for the native economy for the foreseeable future, and the adoption of agriculture or other economic alternatives would not require the government's urgent attention as it had immediately following the Prairie treaties. Even the expense of reserve surveys could be spread out over many years as there were few areas of the North under immediate pressures of settlement.

Although the difficulty of drawing the attention of this distant bureaucracy to the problems of the northern Indians would become a serious detriment to the prospects of their economic and social progress, of equal significance was the growing political power of the settlers of the Prairies. This new power was represented by the movement towards increased legislative autonomy, which culminated in the establishment of the Provinces of Alberta and Saskatchewan in 1905, and the relinquishment of control over natural resources by the federal government in 1930. Increasingly, the treaty rights of Indians would be in direct conflict with the efforts of settlers, primarily through their provincial governments, to exploit the natural resources of the area. Under such circumstances, the unique conditions of northern Indians would receive little attention.

Part Two

Alberta Interpretations
of the Treaties

Chapter Four

T.A.R.R. Interview with Elders Program

by
Lynn Hickey, Richard L. Lightning, and Gordon Lee

THE PROGRAM (Lynn Hickey)

Over the past four years, T.A.R.R. has conducted interviews with Indian elders all over the Province of Alberta in an attempt to pin down what might be termed as an Indian understanding of treaty. The basic idea behind this effort is that most of our information on the treaties has come from written sources which either ultimately are derived from the government or other parties who had some interest in getting treaties signed. Thus, such sources may be presenting a one-sided view of the treaties, especially since Indian people often seem to have very different opinions on what the treaties mean.

Information from the Indian side is necessarily in oral, rather than written, form as it consists of stories that have been handed down by people who were actually present at the negotiations. Historians and anthropologists have pointed out some of the dangers inherent in the use of such oral testimony for the purposes of historical reconstruction.[1] Our purpose here, however, is simply to present what Indian people in Alberta feel their treaties were all about. Most people do not know "the Indian view" of the treaties, yet this view is very important for understanding Indian attitudes and actions with regard to the wider society, as well as Indian-white relationships in general.

We have gone about our task by questioning elders in all three of the treaty areas in the province as to what they have been told about the treaties. Since Treaties Six and Seven were signed in 1876 and 1877, the elders in

---

[1] For example, the standard reference work on the subject, Jan Vansina, *Oral Tradition, A Study in Historical Methodology*, trans. H.M. Wright (London: Routledge and Kegan Paul, 1965), makes the point that often historical tales are distorted so as to defend public interests. However, it is debatable whether T.A.R.R. interviews with elders even fit into any of Vansina's categories for oral traditions because (a) they are *interviews* rather than tales; and (b) they concern events which are much more recent than the sort of material he is dealing with. Therefore, many of Vansina's warnings may not even be applicable to our interviews.

these areas necessarily have to repeat what they have been told by their parents or grandparents, who were the actual eyewitnesses to treaty signings. In the case of the Treaty Eight elders, there are actually a few eyewitnesses still alive since this treaty was not signed until 1899. Altogether, about two hundred and fifty interviews, most of them in the native language, were conducted on various reserves and settlements throughout the province. A few interviews were also carried out in Saskatchewan, since the Treaty Six area extends into that province, and the actual sites of the treaty signing, Fort Pitt and Fort Carlton, lie within Saskatchewan rather than Alberta.

In many ways, the project was almost too large to handle in terms of being able to "cover everything." Because of financial and personnel limitations, some shortcuts had to be taken. These involved concentrating on the two main language groups in Alberta, Cree and Blackfoot, sticking more or less to the recognized "authorities" on the treaties in terms of who to interview, and emphasizing certain geographical areas because of greater population concentration or abundance of informants. Thus, T.A.R.R.'s approach in collecting interviews on the treaties has been geared towards flexibility and the ability to get to the sources of information on short notice.

As the interviewing project progressed, refinements in our methods became necessary. For example, at the outset, various respected elders interviewed other elders. The results were intriguing, though not particularly informative to the non-Indians because of the presence of so many shared, implicit assumptions and ideas about the treaties. The use of younger interviewers helped somewhat as they tried more to pin down the meaning of statements.

Another problem was that each treaty area seemed to have its own version of the negotiations. Thus, the same questionnaire could not be used everywhere, and each treaty area came to need its own. This division between treaty areas led to speculation that we were seeing differences based on culture, that is, a Cree version in the Treaty Six and Treaty Eight areas versus a Blackfoot version in the Treaty Seven area. Yet there were differences between Treaty Six and Treaty Eight interviews. Thus, the variations seem to reflect differences in the treaty negotiations themselves.

We also had to investigate whether we were obtaining fairly standardized accounts of the treaty within any one treaty area because all the interviews were being conducted in the same language. Would Chipewyans or Stoneys have a different view of the treaties? There was not time to pursue these questions in depth, nor to cover all the language groups in Alberta. However, we were able to carry out a few interviews in Chipewyan for the Treaty Eight area, while in the Treaty Seven area, we conducted a few interviews on the Sarcee reserve, and were able to read translations of interviews done in Stoney by the Stoney Cultural Education Program at Morley.

Analysis of these additional interviews did not reveal any major differences in interpretations from the other interviews within a treaty area. Such uniformities probably reflect real differences between treaty areas concerning the subjects emphasized in the treaty negotiations.

CONTENT OF THE INTERVIEWS

All of the interviews within a treaty area were examined for references to certain subjects related to the treaty which are of concern to Indian people. These subjects include land; hunting, fishing, and trapping; economic development; education and medicare; mineral and other resource rights. Although responses to interviewers' questions could be fairly varied within a treaty area, some general patterns did emerge.

Treaty Six

Treaty Six elders tended to agree that the treaty was an agreement to let white people use the land for farming, and in some cases to let them use timber for building houses and grow grass to feed animals. The treaty commissioners asked only for the use of the depth of soil needed for agriculture; so this is really all the Indians gave up in the treaty. The wild animals and fish were neither asked for, nor given up, as they are the Indians' livelihood. The treaty, then, can be said to concern peoples' livelihoods.

In return for allowing white people use of the land, Indians were promised help in learning new ways of living. Most frequently mentioned promises include agricultural implements and animals, as well as expert personnel to teach agriculture and be useful to the Indians without taking control away from them. This was to be done on reserves, places set aside for the Indians' own use where they would be safe from interference and encroachment. Free education and medicare were to be provided to the Indians, and most say this was to be done on the reserves. What education and medicare were to consist of is not clearly spelled out, though some imply that education should give the skills necessary to cope with white society.

Finally, where mineral and other resource rights are discussed, there is general agreement that Indian people have kept these, since they were never asked for and thus were never surrendered.

Treaty Seven

Treaty Seven interviews are very different. Not one elder mentions that the treaty had anything to do with giving up land or sharing it with white people. Rather, Treaty Seven is an agreement that was made to establish peace, to stop the Indians from killing each other, and to put an end to the disruptions caused by liquor. Indians were told that they would be able to hunt anywhere and were instructed not to interfere with each other. Land was only discussed in terms of each tribe being able to choose its own reserves. The Indians, however, felt fenced in when they actually settled on reserves and saw how much smaller the reserves were than what they had thought of as their own land.

In return for their promise to keep the peace, the Indians were promised they would be taken care of by the Queen. Rations would be provided and their needs would be met. Some Indians mention agricultural implements and animals, but there is no clear expression of the idea that these were to provide a new way of life for the Indian. Education as a promise is not dealt with to the extent it is in the Treaty Six interviews. It is not clear what is meant by the term, though some interviews imply that education should help Indians speak English. More is said about medicare in terms of a hospital or doctor to be provided free to the Indians, but many elders feel the treaty payment was reduced from twelve to five dollars to pay for education and medical services.

There is less discussion of mineral or other resource rights than in the Treaty Six interviews. Some mention that mineral resources were never discussed at the treaty negotiations, although there is agreement that Indians *should* receive more benefit from mineral wealth, since it comes from land they had occupied. There is also a fair amount of discussion on traditional uses of minerals, wood, and plants.

Treaty Eight

Treaty Eight elders gave the most varied responses as to what the treaty was about. This is not surprising since negotiations were carried out in many different places because people in this area tended to live in smaller groups that were more isolated from each other. Generally, the interviews are more similar to those from the Treaty Six area than to those from the Treaty Seven area.

It is agreed that the treaty involved surrendering land, though a few people express this as an agreement to share land or surrender the surface only. Land is the only thing that was given up, however. The main discussion of the treaty by most elders concerns hunting, fishing, and trapping and how rights to pursue their traditional livelihood were not given up and were even strongly guaranteed in the treaty to last forever. Giving up the land would not interfere with the Indian's pursuit of his livelihood, and the Indians only signed the treaty on this condition.

In return for surrendering land, Indians were to receive "help" in the form of reserves (places where they would not be bothered and could earn their livelihood) and assistance in farming, if they chose to do this (implements, seed, animals). There is a great deal of resentment over the fact that those who chose to farm did not receive the aid necessary to be successful and were never allowed to control their own affairs. Indians were also to receive education (knowledge of the white man's way of living) and medicare (termed "doctors, medicine, hospitals, medical aid") for free, as well as care of their old people.

Mineral and other resource rights are mentioned as things that the government never bought from the Indians, nor was agreement made on them. However, any consequences in terms of ownership of such resources are not clear in the interviews.

Common themes in the interviews from all three treaty areas centre around two main ideas: (1) the treaty was about relationships between peoples, whether this is phrased as the relationship between the government, or Queen, and the Indians, or Indian-white relations, or even, as in Treaty Seven interviews, between different Indian tribes; (2) the treaty was to provide Indian people with opportunities for a new way of life. This idea is most heavily emphasized in the Treaty Six area.

The actual interviews included in this book will clarify some of these points.

SAMPLE INTERVIEWS

The basis for choosing the nine representative interviews included in this book varies a bit in each treaty area. At first an attempt was made to choose interviews from as wide a geographical base as possible in case there were important local variations in stories about the treaties. This was not always feasible because of variations in the quality of the interviews; so we had to compromise somewhat and simply choose the best ones. These tended to be the most comprehensive or the best conducted in terms of interviewing techniques. Even though this method of choosing interviews did not really take geographical differences into account, we still seem to have included the major variations, which appear to have some regional basis.

The three interviews from the Treaty Six area, for example, only cover two regions. John Buffalo and Lazarus Roan are both from the Hobbema area south of Edmonton, while Fred Horse is from Frog Lake, located in the easternmost portion of Treaty Six within Alberta.

The Hobbema interviews express the more general view that the treaty was made to enable the whites to use the surface of the land for farming and that in return the Indians would be taken care of. The Frog Lake interview is a bit more specific in describing the treaty negotiations. For example, it is stressed that the treaty negotiator only asked for three things from the Indians: the surface of the land, grass for feeding animals, and timber for building shelter. Other facets of the negotiations mentioned exclusively in the eastern interviews are that the Indians were promised the protection of the North West Mounted Police; in some of the interviews from Cold Lake, it was mentioned that Sweet-Grass had sold the land prior to the treaty signing.

The Treaty Seven interviews include two from the Peigans (Annie Buffalo and John Yellowhorn) and one from the Bloods (Camoose Bottle).

Again, these particular interviews were not necessarily chosen on the basis of fair tribal or geographical representation, but rather as being the most comprehensive example of the two major themes appearing in the Treaty Seven interviews. All the interviews make clear that the Indians did not feel the treaty had anything to do with land, or surrender of land, except in being able to choose their own land for reserves. Also, most of the interviews express the idea that under the treaty the Indians would be taken care of, or as John Yellowhorn puts it, that ''the Queen has made the Indian people her children.'' The Blood interviews place more stress on the idea that the treaty was made to establish peace, both among Indian groups and between Indians and whites, perhaps reflecting the participation of many Bloods in American treaties. There is also much more emphasis placed on description of the negotiations themselves in the Blood interviews in terms of citing sequences of events and actual dialogue.

The interview with John Yellowhorn is unusual in that it contains stories of events not found in the other interviews, such as a meeting between Bull Head and Colonel McLeod and prophecies by an ''east Blackfoot'' about a new way of life. It has been included so as to preserve these stories.

The Treaty Eight interviews are again only from two areas, the Sucker Creek Reserve on Lesser Slave Lake (Jean Marie Mustus and William Okeymaw) and Fort Chipewyan (Felix Gibot). However, both these locations were actual sites of treaty signings and were considered to be important by the commissioners, particularly as Sucker Creek (or Grouard) saw the first signing of Treaty Eight and Fort Chipewyan supported a relatively large population of the Treaty Eight area. It is not surprising that more comprehensive accounts of the treaty would survive in these localities.

William Okeymaw gives the best of the actual eyewitness accounts of Treaty Eight, and he recalls the long discussions the Indians had prior to signing the treaty because of their worry that their way of life would change thereafter. Jean Marie Mustus, whose grandfather was one of the chiefs who signed the treaty, also relates how difficult his grandfather's decision was. The fear the Indians felt that their hunting, fishing, and trapping would be restricted if the treaty were signed is a constant theme in most Treaty Eight interviews and shows up again in the interview from Fort Chipewyan. In fact, many interviews make the point that without reassurance by the commissioners on this matter, the treaty would not have been signed at all.

The question of whether the treaty concerned surrender of land is unfortunately not as clearly answered in these three Treaty Eight interviews as in many others. William Okeymaw, like the Treaty Six elders, feels that the Indians surrendered only the surface of the land, while Jean Marie Mustus states that his grandfather ''sold the land.'' Felix Gibot, an eyewitness to the treaty, is not certain that the government bought the land, but feels the commissioners thought they were doing so. In any case, it is clear that Treaty

Eight elders feel the treaty did concern land, whether they were being asked to sell it or share it.

Another prevalent idea in interviews from Fort Chipewyan is that the treaty commissioners had heard that the Indians were starving, and that part of the reason for the treaty was to prevent this from happening again. Felix Gibot goes on to stress that the treaty negotiators themselves discussed the necessity of more friendliness and helpfulness between Indians and whites in the future.

In addition, two other statements are included; they were made by Peter O'Chiese and Pat Weaselhead at the Elders' Think Tank, in Hinton, Alberta. These statements add significantly to an Indian understanding of the treaties. Pat Weaselhead is a Blood elder, and Peter O'Chiese is an Indian elder whose forefathers never signed Treaty Six.

Obviously, the understanding of the treaties by Indian people is often radically different from that of the government or of the white people in general. The point to be made here is that no one interpretation need be accepted as reflecting what really happened. It is enough to understand that the treaties have meant very different things to different groups of people, and that subsequent actions of these people have reflected their particular understanding.

TECHNICAL ASPECTS OF DOING NATIVE INTERVIEWS *(Richard L. Lightning)*

Several interviews done in the native languages, namely Cree and Blackfoot, have been included. It seems appropriate, therefore, that the reader become acquainted with the basic difficulties the interviewer encounters in preparing, completing, and translating these unusual interviews—unusual in terms of the very different languages involved, and the age, culture, and integrity of the people interviewed. This article is based on information gained through my own experiences, and it would be unfair to conclude that all native interviewers are faced with the same problems.

It has been stressed by professional people that time should be taken in approaching the interviewee. However practical this may be in urban areas, when flying in and out of isolated communities, every minute must be put to good use. Often there is only limited time, and this becomes a major factor. Hence, it is important to bear in mind what approach or technique the interviewer must apply to each situation. It is not a simple matter of locating the interviewee, introducing yourself, and saying "let us get on with the interview." If possible, a visit prior to the interview should be arranged— this is essential, if time permits. It allows one to outline the purpose, intent, and possible results of the interview. Thus, the elder becomes acquainted with what is to take place, and is able to feel relatively relaxed. That this, in return, will provoke thought and usually co-operation is evident and overwhelming. Often during this initial visit, the elders will commence conversation with a great depth of historical background which inevitably follows the pattern of general story telling. Although authentic information will be requested of them, they have to be reminded that the interviewer is to return at a later date for a more detailed discussion. Again it should be stressed that the approach is of great significance when initial contact is being made with the elders.

When doing interviews, it is difficult to utilize the standard procedure used when doing interviews in English. The difficulty one is faced with becomes apparent when attempting to formulate a questionnaire. There is such a vast difference in grammatical structure between Cree and English that a prepared questionnaire often becomes useful only in obtaining personal vital statistics. Native elders are not accustomed to being bombarded with questions, and questions that follow a pattern are often disrupted by unavoidable answers covering the same topic. Many towns and historical sites are known to Indians by native names, and if the interviewer does not fully understand the name, it breaks the train of thought of the interviewee when asked to repeat and explain what he has said. Therefore, it is of the utmost importance to maintain a chronological and coherent interview as much as possible. In some interviews, it is noted that only one or two questions are put forth, and the responses are very lengthy. It is at this point that the questionnaire breaks down.

Problems also arise because many of the elders are unfamiliar with tape recorders and are greatly intrigued by them. Then familiarization with the equipment becomes a necessity. A playback of the interview is also greatly appreciated.

Mostly, it is the man who relates the interview, but the elder's wife plays a major role in remembering dates if the elder has a momentary lapse of memory. Ages and dates often are given within a month or two and will require clarification. Names, too, are forgotten, but recalled vividly when mentioned in Cree.

A final part of the interview is the gift. It is a known Indian custom to exchange gifts while visiting other Indians or friends, so often tobacco or cigarettes have been given to elders, not as a form of payment, but as a gift. They appreciate the exchanges of information and social visit.

Translation is another obstacle, as the transcribing must be accomplished with one listening in Cree and writing in English. This may appear a minor detail; however, to translate Cree literally would be totally unreasonable, as many of the Cree words and expressions are reversed in English sentence structure. There must be some form of word juggling for the interview to be comprehensible to the reader.

Another aspect of the Cree language is that there are two distinct dialects spoken in central and northern parts of the province. The basic conversational grammar is parallel; however, some words are totally unknown to one group or the other depending on where the person is from.

Very often key words from the Cree language related to historical events are misconstrued, and one must be careful how the interpretation is made. As in any other language, some Cree-speaking Natives are well versed and possess a high-calibre vocabulary which is seldom used in daily conversation. What the non-native reader cannot visualize are the expressions and hand gestures which tell a story of their own. The tone of voice also carries emphasis, not of bitterness, but of the sincerity with which the elders relate stories of past events. In doing native interviews, the dialogue on the part of the interviewee often becomes repetitious. This indicates the emphasis which the elders place on the topic being discussed.

It has been our policy to return a copy of the interview to the elder who will check for errors and proper translation.

In conclusion, I might add that the details and obstacles that have to be overcome are minimal, and it gives one a tremendous feeling when the elder shakes your hand and says, ''come and visit again.'' They are more than pleased to be able to contribute in such a manner their time and vast source of information. From these interviews one gains a feeling of accomplishment that would not have been possible without the able assistance of an elder.

THE IMPORTANCE OF THE SACRED PIPE CEREMONY *(Gordon Lee)*

In our field research, we have found that much significance is attached to the pipe ceremony conducted prior to the meeting with the treaty commission. In fact, we have found that, according to Indian tradition, religious formalities are as important and as significant as the subject of the matter at hand, whatever that subject may be. It is an Indian custom to conduct those formalities before undertaking any matters of importance. The purpose of this tradition is that the Indians have utmost and absolute belief in the *sacredness of the pipe*. In the presence of the pipe, only *the truth* must be used and any commitment made in its presence must be kept. In that sense, then, the only means used by the Indians to finalize an agreement or to ensure a final commitment was by use of the pipe. The pipe, of course, being an absolutely vital element of the Indian's spiritual beliefs, has many other purposes.

We have concluded, after discussions with some elders, that the pipe ceremony conducted prior to the meetings at Fort Carlton and Fort Pitt was one that was held only in preparation for matters of extreme importance. The importance of the meeting is evident by the number of Indians in attendance at a time when the people should have been out hunting for their winter supply of food.

To the extent that we are able to explain it at this time, the purpose of the pipe ceremony was: (1) to conduct certain religious rites in respect of the Indian's concept of ''Mother Earth''; (2) to conduct their ceremonial rites of finalizing agreements and commitments, in accordance with Indian traditions.

Men such as Mistawasis, Star Blanket, and Sweet-Grass truly believed that the treaty promises could never be broken. Today, the Indian elders still cling to that same belief.

Interviews with Elders

Name: Peter O'Chiese
Date: 1 March 1976
Location: Hinton, Alberta (Elders' Think Tank)
Interviewer: None (statement)
Translator: Harold Cardinal

There was one thing that we were asked this morning. I will try to give an answer to the councillors even though I do not know if I will succeed. I am happy today listening to all of you talk on the treaties, on all of the things you have heard from the old people. It is true that there were different old people from generation to generation. The treaties that we talked about today, the discussions that we had today really come from things that we have heard. I am not a treaty Indian, my forefathers have never signed treaties. Until today, I have not taken the scrip or the treaty. Today we talked about the power that we were given for as long as the sun was there, for us to use our minds. You were asked today what were the treaties. You have talked about the aboriginal man, the first man. It is because of him that we have what there is today. There were, at that time, two aboriginal beings, and they were given separate things. Our man or our people were given one thing and that was to be kind and to have a gentle heart. We were given something that was straight so that our lives could be straight, and we were given something that was strong so that we could be strong. All of that taken together is life, and that which is talked about is passed on from generation to generation. So when the first man from our people was given kindness, he shared that kindness with the first man in the white race. He gave to him something he could piece together. It was our first man to whom was given the gun. When he was first given the gun by our Creator, it was in the form of a test. He realized when he saw the gun that there were some pieces missing before the gun would work. After identifying a missing piece, he saw another missing piece and asked that it be put there. He needed only one more piece before the gun would fire, and when that piece exploded, it was then that the gun worked and was fired. For the Indian people, that gun symbolizes the wealth that this country has to offer, and it was because our man shared this wealth that we see all of the things that operate in this country and that have to be operated by fire. That is why the white man arrived here and asked if he could live on our land and live off our land. That is what we are talking about now when we talk about the treaties. At that time, our people did not know what money was; it was not talked about. That is what you call treaty payments. What they talked about when the treaties were signed is life and how people continued to make life in this country. Our people have been using the gentle spirit and the kind heart that were given to the first man to deal with everybody else, and they still continue to use it.

At the time of the signing of the treaties, the Indian people did not know the white man's system, but they knew from the Indian side what they had to get in order to satisfy their people. So that gift or power that Indian people have was given through their first man. They have always had that, and they will always have it in the future. They did not mind that the deal would work as long as the sun shines or the river flows.

Sweet-grass and incense are symbols for our pipe and stem, for the gentleness that has to be for all of us who are Indian. The stem symbolizes for our people the straight road that we have to follow. When you see the pipe made out of stone, it symbolizes for our people the strength that we must have in order to keep our faith and our way of life. The fire that is there symbolizes a source of life, wildlife, or food. So all of you who are sitting around the table talked about it today. When the old men said, ''we do not give you our timber,'' what they meant was that they did not give their pipe stem. When they said, ''we do not give you our grass,'' they meant that they did not give their sweet-grass or incense. When our people said, ''we do not give you the rock of the mountains,'' they meant they did not give their pipe stem. They use the term rock out of which the pipe is made. When they said, ''we do not give you our animals,'' it was meant that they did not give their fire, the fire that is used in our ceremony. All these things we have, and from there we should be able to talk about the discovery of things the white man wrote about our treaties. He wrote his treaties from his understanding and we wrote ours from our understanding. When we go back to the point of the original men with the Indian and the white, they were made by the same creator; the creator who made both these people was kind. Because he was a creator and he was good, he dealt with both the original men with peace and fairness, so that neither of the original men would have anything to be unsatisfied about. If we continue our discussion from this point, I will be talking again. The other thing we should keep in mind is that since the creator dealt fairly with both the original men, and since he tried to make them both equally happy, we also have a responsibility today, whatever we come up with, to make sure that both sides are happy. I would be particularly pleased if the young people would fully understand what this all means, the way the first man was made. That is all for now.

TREATY SIX

Name: Lazarus Roan
Date: 30 March 1974
Location: Smallboy Camp
Interviewer: Louis Rain
Translators: Louis Rain and Richard Lightning

Rain: First I will ask you your name and your age.
Roan: I am now seventy years old plus two months.
Rain: Your name and your birthplace?
Roan: South of Pigeon Lake is where I was born.
Rain: Your name?
Roan: I am called Lazarus Roan.
Rain: I would like to ask you about Treaty Six and the time the people negotiated with the government people. Could you relate to me your knowledge? Perhaps through your relatives you may have heard stories of the signing of the treaties?
Roan: I have heard of all those things. My father was at the first signing of the treaties, and so were two of my uncles. My father's name was Chabachian (Shortback); Wapusaup (Rabbit Eye) was my uncle, and the other uncle, the oldest, was named Simacguness (Policeman). During the first treaty, Simacguness was made a councillor.

This is the story they always related to us, the manner by which the chief was dealt with. He would indicate with his hands approximately one foot in depth: ''That is the depth that is requested from you, that is what the deal is, nothing below the surface, that will always belong to you. Only land where agriculture can be viable; other areas where nothing can grow, that will always belong to you. You will always be the owner of that land.'' That is what they were promised. That is why they were agreeable to treaty because the promises were so good. The government official was always making references to a woman (Queen) who had sent them. The Indians sympathized with the woman, the Queen, through her representatives. That is why it was not difficult to give up the land. It was said that not one piece of timber, not one stone was given up to the government. The only thing which was included in the bargaining was those portions of land where something could be sown by the white man. ''The area where nothing will grow, that will always be yours.'' This is the promise which was made to them. ''And when the negotiation has been concluded, and settlers begin to homestead, it will only be their property that will be fenced off, that you will not be allowed to enter. Other areas which are not homesteaded and remain open will belong to you as long as the sun shines.'' These are the promises that were made to our forefathers and our fathers. It was most obliging and sounded wonderful when they first dealt with the white man. ''You will always be cared for, all the time, as long as the sun shines,'' they were promised.

A very old man stood up and said, *''Ahow Okeymow* (chief), I do not believe what you are saying. Does the Queen feel her breasts are big enough to care for us all? There are many of our people.'' The government officials thought the old man was insane and suggested that he be taken away from there. They said that the man was talking nonsense. The official replied to him immediately. ''Yes, she has a large breast, enough so there will never be a shortage.'' It would be interesting to know how the old man would have replied to the officials. It is said that the old man was discussing a very important issue.

The negotiators were insistent that it was only the surface of the land that they bought and nothing else. The word bought was not used, but, they said, ''that is all that is being asked of you. We are not buying anything from you, we are bargaining for it.'' That is what I know about our forefathers.

There was another old man who witnessed the first treaty signing. I do not know where it took place, but he followed the treaty negotiations closely and his stories were the same as the stories told by my uncles. He related the story very accurately. He was already about seven years old then.

The first time the treaty payment was made, each person received twelve dollars, and then the children, boys and girls, were loaned to others: ''We would change clothing and appearance before we would sit next to a woman. She then would have a family of about eight or ten children.'' He also stated that there was never a question of name nor age. The only question they asked the woman was ''Are these all your children?'' The woman would say yes and she would then receive her money. When the treaty payment was made for the second time, the Indians were told that seven dollars would be put in trust for them. It would accumulate, and in the future when the Indians were faced with hardships, the money would then be given back to them. There would be lots of it by then. This is what they were told; from that time, the Indians received five dollars in treaty payment. That is what four of the forefathers told the people.

It was 1919 when my father died. He was 67 years old. My mother died years ago—she was 104 years old. She, too, told everything of the treaties. ''I was old enough then to remember how the treaties were made,'' is what she said. This is the information requested here by my grandchild, but he came with short notice. If I had had time to think of all the stories told by our forefathers, I would have given more information at this time.

Ahow, ek seh (okay). I am thankful that he came with these questions. Not one animal was given to the white man, not one piece of timber was given to the white man, not even the grass. That was not discussed in the agreement. Not one stone was discussed in the negotiations. Our forefathers always maintained that this country was ours, including the mountains. They were positive that they never gave up the land and the mountains. There was no agreement made. This includes the animals.

Now my friends, those of you who hear me, the white man is making us suffer. When we were placed on earth, there was also plenty of food and resources for our livelihood. Animals were abundant in the mountains and also on the plains. They survived on their own with food and water. They were placed on earth by the Great Spirit, our Father. They were even placed underwater for our sustenance and our children's sustenance. The white man helped himself to all of these things; they were not given to him. The white man was also given some animals, but if he does not look after them, they will starve to death. If he does not provide shelter for them, they will freeze to death. If he does not give them water, they will die of thirst. Those are his animals (domestic animals), the animals they brought from abroad. But for the Indians, our animals will never starve to death, die of thirst, or freeze to death. That animal (wild game) is ours. The white man is making us suffer, because he has taken these animals away from us.

It was known that in the future there would be tax, but the Indians were informed that they would not pay one penny for tax. Now we are receiving five dollars per year, and even myself, I have figured out the amount I pay for tax far exceeds that five dollars I get back. This is all for now, I greet you all.

Photograph by Richard L. Lightning

Name: John Buffalo
Date: 18 April 1975
Location: Ermineskin Reserve
Interviewer: Richard Lightning
Translator: Richard Lightning

Lightning: First of all, I will ask you your age.
Buffalo: Coming seventy five.
Lightning: Where were you born?
Buffalo: Hobbema
Lightning: The information you are about to relate to me, did that come from the elders and ancestors?
Buffalo: Yes, I knew and saw many of the old people, including old women, who had received the first treaty. My grandmother and grandfather were there at the first treaty payment. When they received their third treaty payment, they were camped by a lake called *Nipee Ka Pitee Qak* (Rumbling Water)—it is located straight east of Stettler. My grandmother was present at the time they received their final payment there.

That is also the time the chiefs and the councillors were given their authority. That is when Bobtail became a chief and Ermineskin wanted to become a chief also, but he was told that he could not become a chief because they were related. However, he was told that he could become a councillor, so he did. This was told to me by my mother-in-law, Mrs. Smallboy. She is over one hundred years old and she is being cared for in Edmonton. I heard this old woman telling the story of the treaty; she was there. Bobtail, the first chief, was her grandfather. It was also during that time that they came here to Hobbema. That is what the old Mrs. Smallboy said. She said that the reserve here at Hobbema was one whole reserve at the time. Then Ermineskin decided to separate to form the Ermineskin Band. His older brother Bobtail gave him a portion of the reserve. Ermineskin was then the chief, and his councillors were Louis Bull, David Headman, Johnny Ermineskin, and another man. Finally, Louis Bull asked Ermineskin if he, too, could have his own reserve. Ermineskin did give him some reserve land and he was the chief of that reserve. So there was the Ermineskin Reserve and the Bull Reserve. They wanted to be on their own.

When all that had taken place, Bobtail took enfranchisement. He left the reserve for his people; that was the Montana Reserve. My mother-in-law said that Samson also asked for some reserve land from Bobtail; that was a long time ago. So old Chief Samson also received some reserve land and Montana became a small reserve as a result. The people who now live there originally came from the State of Montana. They were transported here by freight train; they were wandering around before they were gathered and shipped here. The freight train stopped at Ponoka, and the Indians were brought to the Montana Band. They stayed there for one winter, and in the summer, they started to wander away again. Their excuse was that they were going berry picking, but they left for good, and today they are the Crees of Rocky Boy, Montana—those people are from here. Some of the older people fled to Montana during the rebellion. So that is how they made their homes in Montana, according to my mother-in-law.

At the time of the first treaty, my grandfather, Buffalo Chief, was a councillor, along with old Saddleback and Louie Natchowaysis; their chief was Samson. I used to listen to my grandfather. He, too, was issued with a councillor's suit, as they were included with the treaty promises. They were told that, if the land was not suitable for anything, then that portion would not be taken, only the land where the settlers could make their living through agriculture. The commissioners were not to take the game animals, the timber, nor the big lakes—that was for the Indians' means of survival. Also anything underground would not be given up, only six inches, enough for the settlers to grow crops. "If anything is discovered below the surface of the land, half of its value will be towards your benefit," the commissioner said, "you will be so well off in the future that you will not have to work." None of that exists today. They are even pumping oil from our reserve right here, and I would say we only are getting about twenty-five cents for it. Over half of the money is taken by the white man. As far as the game animals are concerned, the Indians were given the right to kill them any time, any place, even in town, because they will not be wearing a government brand. They were told that they belonged to them. This also applied to the timber.

When the negotiations were complete, the papers were taken away by the commissioners. The mountains were not even mentioned, according to my grandfather, because they would not be useful. These were the terms of reference made by the commissioners at first: "Anything that cannot be used agriculturally will be yours." When they took the papers back to Ottawa, they made them so that the government could claim all of Canada. They did not ask permission here to do that; so now Canada as a whole is owned by the white man. That is not what the commissioners said. That is what I heard from the elders, but I myself think it was their own arrangement that the whole of Canada would belong to them, including the timber and everything else. You will see sawmills all over. They did not ask us for the timber; the commissioners did not negotiate for the timber. Now they put the timber through the mills, make lumber, and make money, but they never even give us a dime. "We are not taking your animals," but now they are selling hunting and fishing licences. They make money from these; that is not what they promised us; those are things they took right out of our hands. I guess the government makes a great deal of money. I would say we are not getting anything out of it as our elders were promised—where are those promises? "As long as the sun shines, as long as the river flows, you will not have liquor," the commissioner said. Today, even when the chiefs do not want liquor, it is still legalized. The commissioners decorated them as chiefs, but it looks as if they do not have any authority at all. They try to stop the liquor without success. I wonder if the people in Ottawa have overruled the Queen to be able to do that. That is what I think.

Lightning: What about education and medicine, how were they arranged?

Buffalo: We used to receive medicines from the Indian agency; the medicines were sent there and we would get them from there, but we did not use them. Some people said that the medicines were made by the white man and were sent to the reserves to be tested. That is what some people said. I myself used to go and pick up cough medicine. Finally, I used up many bottles, but it did not do me any good. The ones I bought in town would be more useful. There used to be all kinds of medicines at the Indian agency; today there is nothing.

When Ermineskin took up his own reserve, he met with the priest to inform him that he wanted a school within his reserve. He told the priest that he wanted a boarding school and the priest helped him. There was a boarding school here on the Ermineskin reserve. The government provided food, clothing, and accommodation for sleeping; that is how the children were being educated.

Today there is none of that. I do not know who is responsible for doing away with the boarding school. Now the children are sent outside the reserve. They have to take their lunch. In my way of thinking, that is not the arrangement that was made by Ermineskin. In the situation we are in today, everything is very difficult. It is very hard, because we do not own anything, not even the animals—if we hunt too much, we will be put in jail. I am talking about treaty Indians. That is not what the Queen's commissioner told us. And the buffalo, the commissioners did not even ask permission to take the buffalo. The only thing they said was that they would not take the buffalo. I do not know why that is.

Lightning: Were they promised implements and garden tools for agricultural purposes?

Buffalo: Yes, they were. Ploughs and oxen were given to them; it was a twelve-inch walking plough with a disc. For the garden, they were issued hoes and scythes. With the scythe, they put up hay to feed their cattle during the winter. Everybody was involved in making hay stacks, but during the winter only two men were selected to care for the cattle. The two men would receive rations every Saturday. I remember when I was young I rode a horse every Saturday to collect the rations for my grandparents. It helped supplement our food supply.

Lightning: When the Indians were negotiating, did they really understand what they were getting themselves into?

Buffalo: Maybe they did, but I do not know what kind of interpretation they were getting, because there was an interpreter; I think he was a Métis. After the commissioner spoke and spelled out his promises, one old man in the crowd stood up and denied all that was said. He said it could not be possible; the commissioner would not be able to comply with his promises. So that is exactly what happened, that is how I see it.

Lightning: Did the Indians request anything from the Queen on their behalf when they were negotiating?

Buffalo: You mean did the Indians ask for anything? That I do not know. It was only the commissioner who promised to the Indians. That is the reason the elders were not in favour of it, because it would not happen. The Indians were informed that they could take reserve land any place they chose, while it was still open and they had a right to it. "Take reserve land any place and as much as you want." It was at this time that the Indian elders had a disagreement. My grandfather, Buffalo Chief, was there and several others. My grandfather said, "I will start riding from here and go to Buffalo Lake, then I will go west for a long way, then I will ride north and circle Pigeon Lake on its west shore, and I will keep travelling until I feel that I have travelled enough. I will turn east. I will be riding far north of Peace Hill (Wetaskiwin), and I will approach Dried Meat Lake from the north." That is how much they were going to take for a reserve. But that is when the elders disagreed with one another. Some of them said that it was too much: "Where are we going to get all the people to put into that reserve?" Others said, "We can use it in the future, it will be for the benefit of the future." Yet others maintained that it was too much and that they would not have any use for it. Again it was stated that, in one hundred years from that time, future generations of children could make use of it. So it resulted in taking the reserves east of Pigeon Lake, south of Wetaskiwin, and this side of Ponoka, because the people who wanted a large reserve were overruled.

Lightning: During that period, did the priests influence the Indians for their good, or did they influence them in the wrong way?

Buffalo: They encouraged them in the wrong direction; what they did was harmful to us. They did not help us to any great extent. The elders had said, "White man will come ashore on this island (Canada); the ones with the

black robes will be in front; they were sent forth to try to extinguish us.''
Sure enough, the priests arrived. They were amongst the Indians teaching
them prayers and other things, and thus they managed to discourage the
people. That is how the elders told the story.

Lightning: How did the buffalo vanish from the prairie?

Buffalo: The elders said that the buffalo just left when the land was taken
over; that is when they moved towards the southwest. The Indians moved
camps as the buffalo migrated. They were in search of food. During the
night, they could hear them, but the following day they would move again
until night fell, never reaching the buffalo. Some old men said that the
buffalo entered the earth somewhere, but I do not know. It must be true, as
there are none left. Some of them were cut off from the herd, but they were
hunted by the white man for the hide. The meat was left behind. The few
remaining buffalo were then protected. Finally, they transferred them up
north.

Lightning: Did the Indians experience any hunger during those years
before the treaty?

Buffalo: Yes, they did. And also when the buffalo left, some died of
starvation. They survived by eating horse meat.

Lightning: Would they have been encouraged to sign the treaty because
they were faced with hunger and starvation?

Buffalo: No, they were not.

Lightning: What do you know of the Indian livelihood before the white
man arrived?

Buffalo: They were doing good for themselves. There was no work. This
land had herds of buffalo; they were all over the prairies. During the
mid-summer, the land looked as if there was a prairie fire with the amount of
dust made by the buffalo. The elders said that if a person were to put his ear to
the ground by a hole, he would hear the loud rumbling of the buffalo. That
was the Indians' source of food; the hides were tanned for clothing, blankets,
and shelter. During the winter, they used the buffalo jumps. One old man in a
few was given this power to be able to attract the buffalo towards the jumps.
They would eventually get them in the jump by riding circles around the
buffalo. Those Indians who lived prior to the white man's coming never
experienced any disease—headaches, toothaches, stomach-aches—no sickness at all. When a person reached old age, such as one hundred and over, he
would just die in his sleep. That is what was said by the elders.

Lightning: When the treaty was made, did the Indian know of money or
its value?

Buffalo: No, the majority of Indians did not know money. As an
example, our grandmother received payment for three sons, two daughters,
and herself at $25.00 per head. She had the money in her hand, but she just
gave it to another woman for payment on a horse she bought. They told this
story themselves; they did not know money—she paid $150.00 for her horse.

Photograph by Richard L. Lightning

Name: Fred Horse
Date: 14 March 1975
Location: Frog Lake, Alberta
Interviewer: Richard Lightning
Translator: Richard Lightning

Lightning: Can you give me your name, age, and place of birth?

Horse: I was born here at Frog Lake, and I passed my sixty-fourth year in January. I have been raised here on the Frog Lake Reserve.

Lightning: Where did you get your information? Who told you about these things?

Horse: All the old stories I know were told to me by my father; he told me many stories. He also said that in the future the stories would be needed, the people would use them. I do not not know how he knew, but today people approach me for this information. I am under age when you compare me with older men, but they did not listen to their parents. They, too, were probably told these different things, but for that reason, when someone approaches them for information, they are unable to provide it. For me, it was different; I listened to my father; that is why I know a few of the stories.

Lightning: The term ''treaty'' as used by the white man, is it used in its proper context? The Indian understands it as payment of money, is that proper? Or is it a misunderstanding?

Horse: Yes, today almost everything is lost as it was promised at the treaty; it sounded very good at the time. Is that what you wanted to ask me?

Lightning: Do the terms *tipahamatowin* and *asotamatowin* mean two different things?

Horse: Yes, they are two things. *Tipahamatowin* means once a year, to last forever. At the beginning, fifty dollars were promised to each person; after about six years, that was reduced. They thought of a way to make the Indians believe that the money was being put aside for them. Then they received fifteen dollars per person; only the chief continued to receive fifty dollars; but the rest of the people, including the children, only received fifteen dollars. Then after about six more years, they reduced the payment again; the chief now was paid twenty-five dollars and the adults and children each received five dollars. That still exists today. The people wondered what happened to the rest of the money. They were told the money was kept at the government. Many people questioned that and today it is still the same way.

Asotamatowin referred to the land. Of that, too, nothing is seen around here. Even at my age, I have not seen anything that has anything to do with *asotamatowin*. The commissioner who came with the promises made it sound so good. They even made their promises in God's name (Manitou). He cheated Manitou, the white man did, and all the people to whom he made the promise. The promises were great—"If I get this land, you will have some very good food on your table."

Today I see myself only eating bread, that is all, when I cannot get anything else to eat. That was his promise; he even used the sun, which is sacred, to indicate the terms of his promises. So that is why it is very difficult today to try to make a living. The white man today is rich. He took the minerals with which we could have made money; he took that away from us. If that had not happened, for example, you would be driving a very fancy car today. It was stated: "In the future, whatever the white man makes will also be yours." Where is it? There is nothing; we have nothing. But he has everything; everything he has is nice. I should not have to be here telling you of all this misfortune. Today every Indian should be very well off, on every reserve.

Lightning: When you mentioned, before, the payments being reduced, did anybody bother to find out where the money was going?

Horse: Long ago, they tried investigating it, but then it was difficult. It was not like today; it is much easier; the people can just go to Ottawa. It was not that way; the people could not do anything. They told the agent, but he did not do anything. Some of our councillors wrote letters, but there was never a reply. Maybe the letters were thrown in the garbage. My father also tried to find out about that many times, but he, too, never received a reply.

Lightning: When the white man first came and asked for land for agriculture, some Indians say he asked for this much (open hand with extended thumb), some say one foot. How was it known how much land they were asking for?

Horse: When they first came to deal with the Indians, they wanted to buy three things: grass, timber, and land, nothing else. The surface of the land was half a foot. "If there is anything underground in the future, it will not be ours," is what they were told, "that will all be yours." My father said the same thing. Today, nothing that is underground belongs to us; they have taken that away from us. That is the reason the people are unhappy today. People often say that, just half a foot of ground. That is how the commissioner indicated with his hand (open hand with extended thumb).

"Half a foot, nothing more." The trees were for h ⟨...⟩ ind his animals;
the grass was to be used for feeding his animals ⟨...⟩ e three things.
Everything else the Indian uses for a living on this e ⟨...⟩ on the ground,
in the bush, anything that flies or is underwater. ⟨...⟩ not buy these
things from the Indians.

Lightning: During the time the promises were ⟨...⟩ d the Indians
request anything from the commissioners?

Horse: No, they did not ask for anything, becaus⟨...⟩ ses that were
made were so good.

Lightning: Do the Cree people have a relationsh ⟨...⟩ earth? The
Blackfoot relate to it as "Mother Earth." Does that app ⟨...⟩ ee as well?

Horse: Yes, we refer to it as our mother. We were ⟨...⟩ this earth,
from the dirt; we were formed from some water and di ⟨...⟩ ou; that is
why we refer to it as our mother.

Lightning: When the treaty was made, did the Indi ⟨...⟩ f money?
When they were being paid, they borrowed children fr⟨...⟩ er. Why
were they making up large families?

Horse: They did not know of money. My grandfath⟨...⟩ the first
time they saw money was during treaty time. They really ⟨...⟩ ooks of
the money. During the payment, some men who were b ⟨...⟩ rrowed
some children. They had handfuls of money, but they did ⟨...⟩ out it.
The children were playing with it, and they were also tear ⟨...⟩ he did
not know about it.

Lightning: Today some Indians have been charge ⟨...⟩ nting
violations. What promises were made to them regarding hunt ⟨...⟩ ng?

Horse: As I said before, they only wanted three things⟨...⟩ the
Indian may use for a living is his; the white man has nothin ⟨...⟩ it.
There will be somebody who will look after that for the India ⟨...⟩ ite
man will not steal anything from the Indian." If anything wa ⟨...⟩ se
men were going to protect us; but they sure protect the white m ⟨...⟩ re
supposed to protect us; that is what my dad used to tell me. To ⟨...⟩ ce
do not protect us.

Lightning: What about education for the children and medicine? What
can you tell me about those things?

Horse: Yes, education was discussed. "There will be a school on your
reserve; your children will go there to be educated" until they reach a high
degree of education. But they are always going away from the reserve to
school; that is not what was said. The same about a hospital—"You will have
a hospital inside the reserve," but we do not have one on the reserve. "A
doctor will take good care of you there with proper food. You will not leave
until you are all better. You will not have to pay for any of it."

Lightning: When the treaty was made, was it just verbal or was anything
written on paper regarding promises?

Horse: No, they did not write anything. They came to inform the people. After they had made all the promises, they said that it would be written on hide, and that it would be kept at three different places. They were to use some type of ink that would never come off. The chief would keep one, one would be kept in Ottawa, and one would be kept by the Queen herself. That is what was said.

Lightning: How did the Indian make his living before the treaty was made?

Horse: Before the white man came, the Indian made a very good living. He was also very durable, like an animal. He was very strong because he only ate meat; he never boiled it; he cooked it on an open fire; that is why he never suffered from sickness. Even the children were not sick, and they wore very little clothing, even bare legs.

Lightning: How did the buffalo disappear?

Horse: The buffalo was given to the Indian by Manitou, for him to make a living. The buffalo was placed here on earth with the Indian. He was to use it for food, clothing, shelter, and blankets. When the white man arrived, the buffalo gradually disappeared. My father told us that the buffalo just vanished. Grandfather said they were taken away; they entered some opening in the ground. Some people went after them when they realized they were disappearing. It is said they found a place where they entered an opening in the ground. So they disappeared from then on.

Lightning: After the buffalo disappeared, did the Indian change his life-style in any way? How did he make his living?

Horse: During the time when the buffalo disappeared, the white man came, and he brought with him food and the way of life that he knew. That is when the Indian started to change his way of life.

Lightning: Before Treaty Six was signed, there were about four treaties signed in Eastern Canada. Did the Indians in this part of the country know anything of the treaties coming to them?

Horse: No, they were not aware of a treaty that was to be signed. It was only when it was here they they realized what was hapenning. It was not like today, with the reserves we have today. This happened much later. Take this river—that was a boundary. The reserves were not separated. Even the Province of Saskatchewan and towards the east was all Indian country. That was not the agreement to make separate reserves. Right there the promises were already broken.

Lightning: Did the elders or ancestors know of the treaties in the United States?

Horse: No, they did not know of them. They only knew of what was taking place with them.

Lightning: Did the Indians at the time want the treaty?

Horse: Well, it was brought to them and that is how they negotiated with the Queen's commissioners. That is how it was completed.

Lightning: How did the Indians feel when the reserves were being made separate?

Horse: When the Indians were placed on reserves separately, they took them right away. They were told that everything on the reserves would belong to them; nobody would bother them; that is why they took them immediately.

TREATY SEVEN

Name: Pat Weaselhead
Date: 5 March 1976
Location: Hinton, Alberta (Elders' Think Tank)
Interviewer: None (statement)
Translators: Mike Devine and Harry Shade

My friends, I will just tell you a few things. I am speaking as if I were my father. I have to use interpretation because my tongue is not very good. I have Mike [Devine] and Harry [Shade] to speak for me. In 1877, at the Blackfoot Crossing, the Blackfoot translation of David Laird was ''Tall White Man.'' My father was ten years old at the time. During negotiations between the Blackfoot tribe and Her Majesty's representative, David Laird, there were two interpreters, and there were four different languages that these people spoke—Blackfoot, English, Cree, and French. Nobody knows today what language they used during the negotiations. The first words that David Laird told us were, ''our great Queen Victoria is the person who speaks; I am not the one telling you what I am saying, it is the Queen who says it. The reason the Queen sent me, or the reason for the treaty, is so that we can all be related as brothers and sisters, as one family. Whenever you see another tribe camping in your territory, you are not to chase it out. Or if any other tribe has killed the buffalo in order to survive, you are not to take away whatever it has. Instead of fighting, you should live in harmony and peace with it and share with it. And you are not to go to other tribes and steal their horses. Someone has said that, whenever you see a tribe with a different language, you try to kill the other tribe and scalp the Indians. No, these are the things we want to put a stop to. This is why I made a trip to Blackfoot Crossing.''

Then David Laird told the members of our tribe that just as they had watched the redcoats protect them, so would the Great Mother, the Queen, hold them in the palm of her hand, and protect them, and look after them just like a child. In other words, ''the Great Mother will become your mother, since you are accepting the treaty. As long as these things are there,'' and he pointed to the sun and the river and the mountains, ''as long as these things are there, then these negotiations will last. In the future, when the sun sets forever, the rivers run dry, and the mountains disappear, then these treaty agreements will come to an end.''

I will tell about a little story from thousands of years before this treaty came up. During Moses's time, the people ran away from the country and their leaders were chasing after them to kill them off. Our Creator was the one who helped these people on to the safe side, and we Indians recognize the sun as our Great Spirit or our Guide. When Moses came into the mountains, he told his people, ''Stay here; I will climb up this mountain and I will be back.'' When he reached the top of the mountain, he did not see God, but he heard somebody talking and it was God who was talking. And that is when God presented the Ten Commandments. And God told Moses that the Ten Commandments were written on a piece of rock, and this rock was hard. Some things quoted from the Ten Commandments are: "Thou shall not kill," "Thou shall not steal," and "Thou shall not commit adultery." These Ten Commandments today are still in existence and will still be in existence for thousands and thousands of years. This is just about how it looks with our treaties. Why did David Laird take an affidavit before the sun and the rivers and the mountains? Nobody knows when the sun will stop shining, nobody knows when the rivers will run dry, and nobody knows when the mountains will disappear. That is why the people that were there to listen to David Laird all believed in him because they took the sun as their guide; and they believed him when he said that the treaty would last forever. And David Laird did not mention that there would be a time in the future when we would dismantle these promises that I have read to you. That will be all for now. Thank you.

Name: Camoose Bottle
Date: 24 October 1973
Location: Blood Reserve
Interviewers: Harry Shade and
　　　　　　　Mike Devine
Translators: Harry Shade and
　　　　　　　John Smith

Photograph by John W. Smith

Bottle: I am Camoose Bottle. I am a Blood Indian. I was born on the Blood Reserve. I am going to talk about what my elders told me, on how in the past drinking was bad. The people who brought the liquor were white men from the United States; they put up drinking places on the Blood Reserve to the east where the rivers meet; that is where the place to drink was. A missionary by the name of Good Heart came and made friends with an Indian by the name of Rainy Chief, and he went around with the Indian teaching him religion or the way of praying. They came to the drinking place. They saw an intoxicated woman being wrestled and taken away by white men, while her husband passed out in their house. I do not know how many children they had. All the people in the camp were drunk. This is some of the damage the first white men did to our people. The bringing of this liquor was very harmful to the Indian people. This missionary went down to the Queen and told her how badly the Indians were living and he asked how it could be stopped. The Queen said, ''I will send my men down and they will try to stop it,'' and that is the time when the police first came to Fort McLeod. These things are what my father told me. This is when the red coats first came to Fort McLeod to stop the drinking.

The next summer, Tall White Man came to Blackfoot Crossing. Chief Bad Head was not around here. He was travelling in the United States. Tall White Man asked the tribe:

''Where is your head chief?''

''He is not here, he is travelling in the United States.''

''How can he get here?''

''We will get word to him.''

"The reason we have come to see him is very important."

I do not know how fast they sent for the head chief. I think they sent the message by pony express, which went on horseback and took messages from place to place. The head chief received the message and started his journey back. I do not know where they found him in the United States. The head chief had just camped at the border when a messenger came and told him, "You are to camp here for awhile; the police are coming here to meet you." The police came to the border where he had camped, and he moved his camp across the border. In moving camp, he was given police protection to Blackfoot Crossing. He was taken to the meeting.

He was told by the police:

"Bad Head, you can have your say in what we are to discuss. We have been sent here by the Queen to put a stop to your way of life, you must quit your wars and put away your guns and your weapons. You will be brothers to all your enemies. This is the message we bring to you from the Queen. The Queen said you will be her children for the rest of your lives. The Queen promises that she will give you all the help you may require and will look after you and take care of you for as long as your people live."

"This is all very good, but I will wait for my friend, Crowfoot."

Chief Crowfoot had camped where the monument at Blackfoot Crossing is today. I have been to this monument. The messengers were sent to Crowfoot's camp to ask him to come to the meeting. I guess he went by the four requests—one usually waits until he is asked four times before he goes. After the fourth call for him, he was told:

"Your friend Bad Head is waiting for you."

"Yes, I am going now."

"He has not said anything yet. When you get there, he will talk."

A big crowd was waiting. He was led out from his camp. The meeting was across the river from where his camp was. The chief came out of his *tipi*, and the procession started to come down from his camp. The guns were fired as a salute. When he came to the river, the police again fired their guns. When he arrived near the crowd, the police band started to play. At the gathering, the chiefs had all been seated in the middle. Tall White Man came up to the chief, shook hands, and said to him:

"It is very important that you have come here. Your friend has not said anything yet. He is waiting for you to talk. This is the reason we have asked you to come here. Your people have suffered very much from drinking. For you to be free from the danger of enemies and for you to live in peace with everybody, you must put your guns away and any weapon you may have, to live in peace, in harmony with all people, Indian and white. There will be no more fighting."

"Yes, that is very good."

"You see the palm of my hand. That is where the Queen will hold you. You will be her children and she will take the best care of you. Whatever you ask for will be given to you."

"Yes, what you have told me is really good. Yes, you are right. My land and my people have been ruined. We have just about beaten ourselves in killings because of our drinking. It is good what you have told; I have nothing to say against it."

Tall White Man got up and shook hands again with Crowfoot. While shaking hands with Tall White Man, Crowfoot said:

"Let me ask you this, are you telling the truth? Say it again." And Tall White Man went over the promises of peace again.

"Yes, it is very good what you have said to me. Are you saying that what you have told me is all truth? You look at the sun, the rivers, the mountains, and you say this will be the law for as long as the sun is shining, the rivers flow, and the mountains are seen; that you will take care of the Indians."

"Yes, you are right. That is what it will be. Let us shake hands." He told the officials to write down all of these things. It was a big vow.

"You will have equal share and equal use of your land. You cannot stop each other. You can camp and you can hunt for food where you have always hunted. This is the way you are going to live."

"Yes, this is very good."

"Tomorrow you are going to be given things."

They started opening boxes. The people were given food and tobacco. The chiefs were given their decorations (medals). Each chief got up and spoke on how he would try to get the people to have peace.

At this time, Bad Head said to Red Crow, "I am old now. You are much younger; you will be a leader for the Indian people for a much longer time. I now give you my leadership. You will make a good leader for the future generations. You have good knowledge of our way of life." That was the time when Red Crow was given chieftainship.

The next day, they were given money; the minor chiefs were given it first. The rest of the people were given money under their respective chiefs. Twelve dollars were given to each person. When treaty money was first given out at Fort McLeod, the people were only given five dollars (three years after the signing of the treaty). They were given twelve dollars just for two years. The government, which made the treaty, took seven dollars back. The government said these seven dollars would be put in the bank for us. Ever since that time we have said, "Our money in the bank, our money in the bank." The government said that anything we needed would be bought from this money in the bank, and the people were told, "Remember, there will be ten cents added to each dollar every year for the money that is put in the bank for you." Today, how can I count my money? How could I understand about my money in the bank? I am seventy-one years old now. That is the way it was told to me. Up to today, seven dollars a year was put in the bank for me, and I have not seen or used that money. I have not benefitted at all from my money in the bank. This is the way I was told of the treaty. At the end of the meeting, Tall White Man said to Bad Head:

"Where would you want to be living with your people? Are you going to stay around this land of Blackfoot Crossing?"

"No, my place of living is to the south, the Belly Buttes. My parents and relatives were buried over there, and I do not want to live in any other place."

"Yes, I see. You, Crowfoot, are you staying here?"

"Yes, this is my land; I will stay on this land."

"You, Sitting on the Eagle Tail Feathers, where will you have your land?"

"My place of living is the Porcupine Hills. That is where I will go to live. I know how to make a living by hunting on that land."

I did not hear what the Sarcee and the others wanted. This is what I was told. I do not want to add anything that I did not hear. Our chief (Bad Head) chose to have this land between the two rivers, Kootenay (Waterton) and St. Mary's. "I will be living and have this land between these two rivers." Today, we are not using our land by Kootenay River, and we own all the timber land at the mountains between the two rivers. Tall White Man said:

"You own all this land as far east as the South Saskatchewan River, you own all of this area; you will have all of this area to carry on your trapping and hunting for all your Blackfoot-speaking people."

The land across the river is land that we are not using. That is what I know about the treaty.

Down in the bottom area between the two rivers (where the Mormons are and south of the police line), Indian people once lived in log cabins, but rain came and flooded it in 1902. People moved up from the flooded area to the dry land. The police also moved up. There was a storekeeper in the bottom by the name of George, and he also moved up. When the water went down and the land dried up, the Indians moved back to their homes in the bottom. The head of the police told the Indians to move to the south side of the river, to build their houses, and to live there, for if it flooded again, it would be worse. So the Indians moved up from this part of their land to the other side of the river. I saw one of those log houses still standing where the police were. That was all our land between the rivers, as well as on this side where we are now. Then came Chief Child. The Indians cut and put up hay for him all along on that Indian land between the two rivers. The Indians put up hay all summer for this man, right up to this side of Waterton. Chief Child leased all this land after he quit haying. He leased this land to the Mormons. The Indians never gave up this land of theirs, they just leased it for haying.

Chief Child had a house built of stones by Glenwood Bridge. He was a big cattle rancher. This is what I know about that land of ours this side of

Kootenay River. We lived on and used that land of ours. The Indians never made any settlement with the government for the white people to take it away from us. The proof that that land was really ours is that the Indians put up Sundances in four different places, so we had four Sundance monuments as our landmarks for that piece of land. If the police had not sent the Indians up from the flood, we would still be living on that land. On the south side, our land is marked by St. Mary's River. We owned the land right to the American border. We did not say two miles short of the border. Our land was right to the border. We owned the land right to the mountains. We Indians named a lot of the places we owned, like Crow's Nest. White people are using all these lands that were taken away from us—sawmills, farm lands, and other industries. Cardston, where the Mormons are now, was our land, too. Chief Red Crow just let the Mormons camp for one night. The Mormons fed the chief the leftovers of their meal, gave him tobacco, and told him to come back the next day to have some more leftovers. When the Mormons saw the chief was crazy, they gave him some liquor. When the chief got drunk, the Mormons asked to stay for the winter and gave him more grub. Red Crow said, "You can spend the winter here." The Mormons started to cut logs and build their houses to live in for the winter. The chief was given grub, liquor, and tobacco all through the winter. By then, all the women were going over to the Mormons for liquor. Today, the Mormons preach to the Indians against drinking. Liquor is the reason we have lost our land. Somehow the Mormons got the chief to sign papers leasing that land to them, but he did not know for how many years. We have heard that the Mormons wrote ninety-nine years. They all now have made their wealth from our lands. Today, we have nothing to show for that land. This is what I have been told by my elders. Red Crow alone made a deal with the Mormons, not the people. This is all I know about the treaty.

Name: Annie Buffalo
Date: 12 March 1975
Location: Peigan Reserve
Interviewers: John Smith and
             Tom Yellowhorn
Translator: John Smith

Photograph by John W. Smith

Smith: What is your name?

Buffalo: Mrs. Buffalo. My Blackfoot name is Sitting Up High.

Smith: How old are you?

Buffalo: I am past ninety now.

Smith: Tom will now ask you these questions I have.

Yellowhorn: Those people who have left you, your old people, your father and grandfathers, did their lives depend a lot on the buffalo?

Buffalo: The buffalo? My mother lived at the time of the buffalo, and they really depended on the buffalo for their livelihood—living, shelter, and everything else like that.

Yellowhorn: When did the buffalo disappear, before the signing of the treaty or after?

Buffalo: I did not know the buffalo, but I heard the stories from my elders. They said that the buffalo disappeared shortly after the signing of the treaty. It was sometime soon after the first payment.

Yellowhorn: Did the old people talk about how the buffalo disappeared, or why it disappeared?

Buffalo: The old people said that the white people took away all the buffalo. That was the reason there were no more buffalo around here. The white people just took away all the buffalo.

Yellowhorn: Did the disappearance of the buffalo change the Indian way of life?

Buffalo: When the buffalo disappeared, the white man gave us cattle to eat. They fed us cow meat instead of our eating buffalo.

Yellowhorn: Did the signing of the treaty change the way the people were living?

Buffalo: The old people told me that after the signing of the treaty the Indian people's way of living changed. They no longer lived the way of the buffalo. It really changed their customary way of life.

Yellowhorn: Did the people from here hear anything about the peace treaties being made across the border?

Buffalo: We heard that everything was stopped. There was no more fighting between our relatives across the border and all the other tribes of Indians. They were told, "Now you are going to end all the fighting amongst yourselves. You are all going to be friends." My mother was one of the last people to receive a medal from the officials. It was a medal with a stamp of shaking hands and a peace pipe. This meant that the Indians had agreed to stop fighting amongst themselves. There would be no more wars between the Indians.

Yellowhorn: What did the old people think of the signing of the treaty?

Buffalo: At first they thought it was really good. This was right at the signing of the treaty. They said that was the time when they gave us the five dollars; the rest of the money was supposed to be put away for our later use.

Yellowhorn: Did the Indian people think they were going to go on using the land, as they had always done, after the signing of the treaty?

Buffalo: After the signing of the treaty, the leaders of each group of Indians chose the area in which they were to live thereafter. Each tribe claimed a tract of land for their own use. But as time went on, these areas claimed by the different headmen were reduced by the white man's fences and surveyors. The Indians had felt that they could go on living the way they used to. It was not until they were put on reserves that they realized they could no longer live the way they used to. And each tribe lost a lot of land after they were put on reserves. It was Chief Sit Against the Eagle Tails who chose this area, the Old Man River, the Porcupine Hills. He thought this area was going to be the land where his people would live. He was the head chief of the Peigans at that time.

Yellowhorn: There are papers of signed treaties that have recently been uncovered by the government; they seem to be different. We are trying to understand these written treaties now to see if they were true. Were the promises made at the signing of the treaty kept?

Buffalo: At the time of the signing of the treaty, our chief, Sitting Against the Eagle Tail, was promised that his people would get five dollars, and that the rest of the money would be put away until needed. And rations were promised as long as the river flowed. They have broken their promises. It is no longer so. They are saying that the old legislation has been wiped out, that it no longer exists. New laws have changed these promises; so they are no longer in effect.

Yellowhorn: Did the Indian people think that anything above or below the ground was of any value?

Buffalo: The old people said the land held much of which use could be made, that is, Indian use, not white man use. The old Indian people also found wealth from the land under the ground, in the form of paint and medicine.

Yellowhorn: Did the old people make any request as to what they wanted that was not in the treaty?

Buffalo: The old people said there were a lot of promises, and these promises have never been kept, such as the money that was set aside for ammunition—today we still have not seen any of it.

Yellowhorn: How was the treaty signed?

Buffalo: Crowfoot was made to understand that the people who signed treaty were to get twelve dollars. At about the third payment, the Queen's men said, "we will give you five dollars from now on; the rest will be put away for you until you need it." They understood that they had some money coming to them. To this day, they have not received this money.

Yellowhorn: Before they came to sign treaty, did the white people have everything on paper as to how the Indians were to be governed from then on?"

Buffalo: The Indians were not familiar with writing. That was the white man's form. The white man had been writing for a long time before we knew how to write. I do not know whether or not everything was written down before the signing of the treaty.

Yellowhorn: Was there anything that the Indian people said they gave up at the signing of the treaty?

Buffalo: No, they did not know that they gave up anything.

Yellowhorn: Was there anything they asked for that was not written in the treaty?

Buffalo: Yes, the people at the time of the signing of the treaty did ask for a lot of things. But I do not know whether or not it was written down.

Yellowhorn: What did you hear about the fur trade from the elders?

Buffalo: All the furs were tanned by the women and then taken to Hudson's Bay Company in Edmonton. They were traded for food and cloth to make clothing. There was no money given for them.

Yellowhorn: What did you hear from the old people about the whiskey runners?

Buffalo: They used their furs to buy whiskey.

Yellowhorn: When was the smallpox epidemic?

Buffalo: I do not know. But across the river, east from Fort McLeod, sometimes some of the *tipis* were empty, no one was living in them. Sometimes all the people from one *tipi* were wiped out by smallpox. They were struck really badly.

Yellowhorn: Was that before the signing of the treaty?

Buffalo: No, it was after the signing of treaty that the smallpox epidemic struck the people.

Yellowhorn: Do you know what it was all about when Sitting Bull was fighting with the white men in the United States?

Buffalo: I do not know. I have never heard what started the trouble.

Yellowhorn: Why did the Indian people refer to the land as their mother?

Buffalo: When we pray, we say ''help us our Earth, our Mother.'' It is part of the religion. This is where our life comes from, because we walk on this land. Whenever we pray for our relatives, whenever we want to wish them well, we tell them to walk happily on this earth as long as they live. I do not know who first called the earth our Mother. We always pray to our Mother the earth that we may ever live well, and ever travel in safety, and always be happy. Everything that the Indians thought was holy came from the earth—all their needs, such as tobacco and berries. It was often referred to as the earthly spirit, because whenever they offered anything in sacrifice, it always went back into the earth.

Yellowhorn: At the signing of the treaty, did they know anything about buying or selling land?

Buffalo: No, they did not know.

Name: John Yellowhorn
(hereditary chief)
Date: 10 March 1975
Location: Peigan Reserve
Interviewers: John Smith and
Tom Yellowhorn
Translator: John Smith

Photograph by John W. Smith

J. Yellowhorn: I am going to talk about the stories that have been told to me by my elders, those people who were there, who were living at the time, who knew about the signing of the treaty. These are the people to whom I have listened. There must have been at least four stories which Small Water Child told me. And an old lady, she must have been *gee-pip-os-stoi*, told me about four stories that were identical to the ones told to me by Small Water Child.

There were these people who just appeared at *Aganasko* and asked Bull Head questions. Bull Head was from here; he was a Peigan, a North Peigan. Here they were shown *Stabiska*. Bull Head liked camping along the Old Man River west of the mountains, north of High Prairie, and east of Cypress Hills, and that is the area he claimed as his. That was his land. And here on Bull Head's land, the North West Mounted Police walked. And there was Bear Child—he was their guide. They came upon Bull Head's camp. It was up north, near where the two rivers meet. There were not many *tipis*. When they approached this encampment, they asked where Bull Head's *tipi* was. The party was introduced. Bull Head was told:

"Here are the police, the Queen sent these police. The chief of the police was sent here to meet you."

"All right, allow him to enter."

It is an Indian custom to invite a stranger into your home. The Queen's man went in, sat down, and explained his reason for wanting to see Bull Head.

"The Queen has sent me here to make treaty with you. She has sent me here to keep peace amongst your people."

They made friends with one another, and this is when Bull Head gave McLeod his name. Colonel McLeod told him that he would give him a uniform the same as he was wearing.

"No, you will not give me this clothing. The trail you took to come here, you must follow the same trail back. You will not sign treaty with me."

"It will be winter soon, the place we came from is far away. May we camp where these two rivers meet? In the springtime, we will return to where we came from."

That place was across the river from where Fort McLeod is now. Bull Head gave him permission to camp there. And here they put buildings, because this is where they were going to spend their winter. Bull Head remained where he was camped. He must have been sick right after this meeting, because he died soon after. Summer passed, and there was no attempt made by the police to move their encampment. Here they remained.

They went to these tea parties that the Indians were having. There were Indian camps nearby where McLeod was camped, and it was there that they were holding these tea parties. Colonel McLeod and his men greatly enjoyed these tea parties. They came in 1875, and in 1877 the treaty was signed. There was no mention during these years that there was going to be treaty (1875-1877). All of a sudden, it was being said that there would be a treaty to be signed at Blackfoot Crossing. Red Crow and Sitting Against the Eagle Tails broke up camp and moved there. The Sarcee chief moved there. To this day, I do not know who their chief was. On one side, Crowfoot camped. On the other side, they [the Queen's representatives] were camped; they were camped for quite some time. Crowfoot was elected by the Indian people to represent them because he was a very intelligent man. For days the Queen's men were sent across the river to negotiate with Crowfoot. Crowfoot told his people: "I will hold off as long as I can, so that we may get as much for our people as we can." Finally, he signed.

The Queen's representative must have been an East Blackfoot who came to ask Crowfoot again. He turned his horse in the direction the sun goes, because the Indians were always following the sun. This East Blackfoot turned his horse around to the Indian people, and he went to all the different people and talked to them. This is when he talked to my grandfather and my father's mother. And this is what they heard him say: "All of you people, you have all given up. The reason I have not given up is that in the future our way of living is going to change. We will no longer live our nomadic way. Away in the future, there will be no more hunting or living from the earth." My grandparents said he was a very intelligent man because he knew what was going to happen in the future. There were three other people I spoke to who said the same thing about this East Blackfoot who knew how we would be living in the future.

They went ahead and met for the signing. And this same East Blackfoot who spoke of the future said: "My people, I will show off to you." He put on war paint, and he went and shook hands with Colonel McLeod. Colonel McLeod pulled his hand back quickly. His hand was burned on this East Blackfoot's hand. After this, they had the final signing of the treaty. There were no chairs and no tables. Crowfoot and Colonel McLeod stood together. There was no writing at the signing of the treaty. The writing about the treaty is all recent. I feel like taking a piece of paper and making my own writing now, to say what actually took place at the signing of the treaty. That is one reason I do not look at these books written about the treaty, because they are all recent and do not say what actually happened. What was discussed at the treaty and the promises that were made by the Queen's men at the treaty, that is what I believe in, that is what I go by. They were promised that each individual would get twelve dollars every year and rations. The Queen has made the Indian people her children. I do not fully understand what it means when the Queen makes us her children. I have been asking around, and to this day I still do not know. If I take someone as my child, and I already have lots of children, should my own children get better treatment than the one I have adopted? No. The Queen's man said: "The Queen will look after you from now on. The red coats will look after you, they will clean up the whiskey traders. They will protect you from the wrongs these whiskey traders are committing against your people."

They were promised all sorts of things to make a new life, such as cattle, medicine, education—"Your children will have an education." At that time, the Indian people did not understand all these things, but this is what they heard from the interpreter; this is what my grandmother heard the interpreter saying. Each person was paid twelve dollars. It did not matter what age they were. What does a one or two year old child do with money like that? There were priests, white men from the south, east, and north, and Indian chiefs at the signing of the treaty. And no one explained to the Indian what this paper money was for. They were told it was for trading, but they did not know its value. When they went to buy, even only a package of matches, they just gave all of it. They did not know how to count it, what it was worth.

T. Yellowhorn: What stories have you heard from the old people about why the buffalo disappeared? When did the buffalo disappear, before or after the signing of the treaty? Did the disappearance of the buffalo change the Indians' way of life? How were the Indians able to survive after the disappearance of the buffalo? Did the signing of the treaty change the way the Indians lived? How did the reserves change the Indians' way of life?

J. Yellowhorn: They say that the white people killed off all the buffalo. The Hudson's Bay Company was buying all the hides; the white people and half-breeds were killing all the buffalo, just to sell the hides to the Hudson's Bay Company. The Indians never killed more buffalo than they needed. The Indian would kill a buffalo and use just about everything on the buffalo. They would take the hide; some of the hides were used for their own needs, some were used for trade. That was the time when they were taught how to buy.

They would go to buy guns. There were guns with long barrels, and they used to pile their hides up until they were the same height as the gun. I feel that the northern people were cheated more, because the hides that they used for trading were very expensive hides, animals like mink, marten, and silver fox. This is one of the reasons I say that the Hudson's Bay Company really got rich off the Indian people. When the buffalo disappeared, they substituted cattle—the Indian people said these cattle were very soft, they were not strong. The buffalo was a strong animal which gave us strong bodies and made us very smart. These cattle are crazy; they just stare at us. We Indian people do not get strong bodies from them.

After the signing of the treaty, the Indian way of life was greatly changed. We no longer live the Indian way of life. The way they were showing us to live after the signing of the treaty was really different; and we still do not know the white man's way of living. There was a fellow by the name of Sepomaksika who talked about the treaty. He spoke of how the Indian way of life was going to change, how our way of gathering food and our way of getting medicine were going to change. They were told not to do this anymore by the police and the government people. These people told them it was the devil's medicine they were using, not to use it anymore. But the medicine in the old days was good Indian medicine. It was strong medicine, and it never poisoned anybody. It made the Indians strong.

For the amount of land the Indians used to have, the white people sure gave them very little land in return. The reason the white people settled so close to the reserve was to keep a close watch on the Indian people, so that anyone carrying on the Indian way of life, such as sun dancing, could be stopped. They kept the Indians from doing what they were used to doing and this really changed their way of living. There is no way we will get our way of living back. There was nothing an Indian person could do without the Indian agent looking over, watching what he was doing. They kept hearing from the agent, "The government says you cannot do this, and the government says you cannot do that."

On education, the individual was taken away from his reserve just to take away anything that was left of his Indian ways. He was not taught; he did not learn the white man's way of life either. He did not know either way of living; he was really lost. The people who went to school were not allowed to come home during the holidays. They were not allowed to go out of the boarding school; so they did not know how Indians were living. The treaty really changed the Indians' way of living. Most of the promises that were made at the treaty were never kept. The only two promises they kept were with regard to medicine and education. We have had education for a long time. It has only been the recently educated Indians who really have learned the white way of living. We were given self-government at a time when we did not know what it really meant. The young people were told to take over the government of the reserve and the older people were no longer consulted.

That was another mistake that the Indian people made. The Indians were divided into their respective bands, and each band had a chief and its own area. These were the areas they asked for at the signing of the treaty. The white man's way of living and the Indians' way of living are very far apart.

Smith: Who was the interpreter at the signing of the treaty?

J. Yellowhorn: James Bird was the interpreter at the signing of Treaty Seven. Bear Child (Jerry Potts) was not the interpreter. James Bird was an employee of the North West Mounted Police. I do not know whether or not he spoke good Blackfoot. I have heard a lot of half-breeds speak, but I have never known one to speak good Blackfoot.

T. Yellowhorn: Did the Indian people hear about the treaties that were being signed in the United States, and if they did, what did they hear of them? Who wanted to make treaty, was it the Indians or the white people? If it was the Indians, why did they want treaty? If it was the white people, why did they want treaty? Why did the Indians think the government wanted to make treaty?

J. Yellowhorn: It was the government that asked the Indians to make treaty. The Indians were told by government officials and priests before the treaty was signed that they were going to have a much better life if they made treaty. The treaty was good at least for the first three years. Education was especially good. The education received in the United States was very good. Everyone was given a chance to get an education. The promises made about rations in the treaties in the United States are still being kept. They are still getting rations. They were given horses and cattle. Now you should see the amount of cattle they have. During that treaty, there were even some Peigan and Blood people who were given rations, cattle, and horses.

They had not even signed treaty here when they heard that they were already fighting down east over who owned this land. The people from the United States and the people from Canada were arguing over who owned this land. The Indian people did not know there was going to be a border put on their land. That is why a lot of people have relatives down in the United States, because they were divided by this line. The Blackfoot from Canada hold ownership for the United States, because that was part of their territory. The people in the United States had very good education from the beginning. But the people from Canada only started to get education yesterday. The promises made to the Indians in the United States by the government were all kept. It was good for the Indian people there. These things I have been talking about make me begin to think of how hard it was for the people in the past.

TREATY EIGHT

Name: Jean-Marie Mustus
Date: 26 March 1975
Location: Joussard, Alberta
Interviewer: Richard Lightning
Translator: Richard Lightning

Photograph by Richard L. Lightning

Lightning: Can you give me your name, your age?
Mustus: I am known as Jean-Marie Mustus.
Lightning: What is your present age?
Mustus: I am seventy-eight years old.
Lightning: Where were you born?
Mustus: I was born here at Sucker Creek.
Lightning: Did you always make your home within this area?
Mustus: Yes, I have always lived here at Sucker Creek. There is also another reserve, Driftpile, where I spent some time. My children attended school here (Joussard); so I am back again. At times, I go back to the reserve, but I never receive any assistance from there; so I am back here again.
Lightning: Are you a treaty Indian?
Mustus: Yes, I receive treaty money.
Lightning: You are also related to this man Mustus. He was the one who signed the treaty and also he was chief when the treaty was made.
Mustus: Yes, he was my grandfather. He was the one who sold the land here at first. He sold it on this side of Grouard.
Lightning: Do you know of any story related to that sale of land?
Mustus: He used to tell me stories about it. He said it was very difficult during those years—the only foresight he had was to the end of his extended arm. He also said that he did not read, and there was no one to give him advice as to what he should do.

"It was difficult for me to communicate. I always had to have an interpreter; that is the only way I could do it. As the promises were made, there were many I overlooked and did not accept. I was very cautious as I began to understand what he was talking about. It was only after I was certain of what he was promising me and of what he was planning to do that I shook hands with him. What he said was written on a piece of hide, and he made reference to the sun and the water. That is when I shook his hand. They tried to make changes, but I would not let them.''

But since my grandfather died, changes have been taking place regarding the land. They received many things; they received hay meadows for raising cattle and also food. They got hay mowers and everything else. When the Indians became familiar with agriculture, they were given plows to grow better crops. But they did not do the work.

Lightning: Was he alone when he negotiated with the commissioners?

Mustus: There were two of them, he and his younger brother. His name was Kinosayoo. The Métis had a spokesman as well. He went with Kinosayoo while they were having discussions about what terms they would agree upon. There was also a priest. His name was Father Lacombe. He discussed everything with the people. I have not seen him. He was before my time. He used to live around here. In the town of St. Albert, there is a house there with different things in it; he made that house.

Lightning: What was the name of the Métis fellow whom you mentioned earlier?

Mustus: His name was Ferguson.

Lightning: Was he the interpreter?

Mustus: He was the spokesman for the Métis people. He spoke on their behalf as to how they would go about taking scrip. He told them what to do, as he also spoke Cree. My grandfather was related to him also. When the time came for the Métis to receive the papers (scrip), everybody in a family received them, including the children and grandparents. My grandfather figured that the Métis did not receive treaty money, which is why they were allotted colonies.

Lightning: Was it Ferguson who helped the Métis regarding land?

Mustus: Yes, but it was understood that they were not giving up their way of life. They lived in the same manner as the Indians. They took scrip, but they would continue to live with and as the Indians. After the scrip, they were the same as the treaty Indians, because they hunted as well as the Indians; they hunted wherever they wished. They shot ducks and other animals. I guess they paid two dollars for a licence.

Today it is easier for the young people to get land; there are two colonies around here and there are two others up north; there is another one at Peace River.

The treaty Indians were given reserves and surveying was carried out. This particular reserve of Sucker Creek contains a lot of water. Sucker Creek has a total of 55,000 acres, and Driftpile contains 65,000 acres. The reserves are adjacent to the lake and the water takes a large portion of the reserve. The reserve was 25 miles in length when it was given and each band chose to have

12 miles apiece. The Driftpile reserve is quite large, and so is Sucker Creek, but they have a lot of water. A large part of the 55,000 acres is not good for cultivation; so they will not have any use for it.

Lightning: When the treaty was first discussed with the Indians, did they understand what they were agreeing to? Did they understand property?

Mustus: Gradually, they began to understand—that is what my grandfather said. When the white man arrived in the area, he, too, was travelling on foot. He made friends with the Indian; he cut hay for his animals on Indian reserves. It is from that time that the Indian taught himself different things. This is a long time ago that I am talking about. The white man also faced hardships in those years when the treaty was first signed. At times he had to butcher cattle for food, although everything was low priced. The farming was really in bad shape. If the grain was of poor quality, he received ten cents a bushel. If a bag of potatoes was good, you would pay fifty cents per bag. Finally it went up to one dollar.

Lightning: Do you know how much land was given up or sold to the white man?

Mustus: The amount of land they gave up was written down on paper. I am wondering whether it was one foot underground or more. It was written down, but I do not know where the paper could be found.

Lightning: And you do not know how much was to be used?

Mustus: No, I do not know, but whatever they selected for themselves they kept; the rest was taken. I do not recall my grandfather telling me about the depth underground.

Lightning: Did he ever tell you anything about underground minerals or oil?

Mustus: Yes, these things were mentioned, as was the timber within the reserve; the Indians had a right to anything underground.

Lightning: Was that the agreement they made?

Mustus: Yes, it was the agreement.

Lightning: Do you recall or know anything about the Indian way of life before the treaty period?

Mustus: The main source of livelihood was from the bush or from the lakes. When the Indians were in the bush, they made *tipi* shelters of wood. They hunted and in the fall prepared food for winter. There was no other place to go, there was a Hudson's Bay Company store here, but the supplies were limited. The Indians used to kill moose for the Hudson's Bay Company storekeeper, and he would look after the crippled or sick Indians. He also cared for the young people who were not able to help themselves; he gave them rations. He did help them a great deal. That is how the Indians lived. The did not have horses, but they used dogs. After that time, people came back to this area. In the spring they took their furs to Edmonton. Later on, according to my grandfather, they travelled in a two wheel cart. They travelled as far as Washington via the Saskatchewan river. They would return with supplies on the boat; these supplies were to provide for many people. That is how the people of long ago made their living.

Lightning: Did the Indians ever experience hunger?

Mustus: Many times they were in desperate need. They had no other place to go, and there was only the one store in Edmonton. I saw it myself in 1912. The train was already in service. There were only three or four stores; today there must be many more.

Lightning: Were there any buffalo around here during that period?

Mustus: My grandfather told me that there were buffalo around here. We heard stories of buffalo around Grouard and also in the High Prairie area. They were plentiful in these areas. But it was not too long before most of them were killed off. They also were at East Prairie. Buffalo bones and skulls were found around here; the Indians would place them between the spruce trees; I saw them myself; They are bleached almost white by now. Someone must have killed the buffalo or they may have died of starvation. This area where the buffalo roamed was all prairie. About fifteen years ago, you would travel with a wagon through that area. Today you would not do that. There are trees and shrubs all over the place; there are cutlines—that is where the exploration crews come in handy.

Lightning: Did the Indian people want to give up their land?

Mustus: They were asked about it. The treaty took place at Hobbema, I think, with old man Ermineskin signing. After they made treaty, they then came here and asked if they could make treaty with the people. It was a long time before the people agreed. They did not come here and make the treaty right away; it took a few days. Finally they signed. There were reserves all over the place after that.

Lightning: Before your grandfather signed the treaty, had he ever heard of Indians making treaty elsewhere?

Mustus: He could have, because there were treaties made already, like the one I mentioned earlier that took place at Hobbema. Then there was no treaty until they arrived here and began the discussions and meetings. They were all together, including the half-breeds. Father Lacombe was also present and spoke a lot to the Indian people on how to live. My grandfather said that he took Father Lacombe's advice because he had travelled with him many times. His advice was to take the treaty because it would help him and the young generations in the future. "If you do not accept treaty, it will not be long until you will not be able to make a living. If you choose a reserve, you will have a better chance of living longer." So my grandfather took land right up to Grouard for a reserve. They fished in the lake and killed ducks, and no one bothered them. But after my grandfather died, other chiefs lost these things that were promised at the signing of the treaty. That agreement must still be kept in Ottawa today.

Lightning: Did the Indians receive fish nets?

Mustus: Yes, they used to get fish nets; as I said before, they did get much assistance. They were issued with food, nets, black powder, and ammunition. They then received rifle shells. They used to get plenty of supplies.

Lightning: Do they still get these supplies today?

Mustus: They get some at times; but I do not.

Lightning: How come you do not make your home on the reserve?

Mustus: There is no place there for me to live. The far end is not good. They cannot grow anything there. I could only live along the highway because I cannot work at farming, I am too old.

Lightning: Have the Indians around here lost any of their trap lines?

Mustus: I do not know. Some of them have given them up. As for myself, I pay ten dollars for my own permit, but it does not tell me to what I am restricted when trapping. I told the warden that I should be informed of what I could trap because I would not be able to sell the furs; but he told me that it was my trap line and that I could kill whatever I wanted.

Lightning: Did you hear of what was promised in education and medical care for the Indians?

Mustus: We do not pay for medicines in the hospital. My grandfather told me that hospitalization was not to be paid by Indians, nor were taxes, including land taxes. The children still do not pay for education and hospitalization. The only thing we pay in taxes is on food, but the Indians should not mind that because the women receive a family allowance and the old people receive a pension.

Lightning: In your own mind, did your grandfather do the right thing when he gave up the land?

Mustus: I do not know, but I think he did the right thing. He was not really restricted to anything. He was promised that he could use a hay meadow fifteen miles from Sucker Creek. He was given that agreement on paper. I do not know how he lost it. He also could go to East Prairie to put up hay. It was all prairie at that time, but of course today it is different. He was treated fairly in everything. He could kill anything, hunt ducks, and fish. He was not restricted.

Lightning: But was this not the way of life before?

Mustus: Yes, that is how they lived, and the Métis also. But now they are separated—the Indian on one side and the Métis on the other. There were some white people there also, and some of them married Indian women. The women did not lose their rights, but those people are all dead now. The husband was allowed to put his crop within the reserve, and he could also put up hay on the reserve. But today this is not allowed.

Lightning: When were the changes made?

Mustus: I do not know, but that was my grandfather's idea. He even allowed the white man to bring two bottles of booze so the people could have a social drink. He allowed that much.

Lightning: During the time of the treaty, did the Indians realize the value of money, and did they know what it was?

Mustus: No, my grandfather said they did not know of money, they did not know of coins. There used to be paper money, but the five cent piece was made of silver. All that I have told you happened long ago. The Hudson's Bay Company helped the poor with meat. If the people had not received assistance, they would have had no place to go; they would have starved to death.

Name: William Okeymaw
Date: 27 March 1975
Location: Sucker Creek Reserve
Interviewer: Richard Lightning
Translator: Richard Lightning

Photograph by Richard L. Lightning

Lightning: Can you give me your name, age, and place of birth?

Okeymaw: According to my mother, my birthday was two days ago (March 25). I think I am now eighty-seven years old. There are signs that I am definitely getting older, and that I will not be good for anything. We used to live close to Sucker Creek, towards Joussard. I think I was born around there, because I can recall my childhood days there until just prior to treaty, when we moved to this area. The knowledge I have about the treaty is what I am about to relate to you.

I was about twelve years old. We travelled by foot and by boat. We crossed the river here in a boat, then we walked the rest of the way. When we arrived, the commissioners were already prepared. Alongside them were about twenty-two North West Mounted Police. I was frightened because I was only a child. I even held my dad's hand I was so scared. A long memory is one thing I have. I can recall many things of long ago. I can recall a huge tent at the time with many people all around it. They were from different places far and near, but they had travelled for that special day, the treaty. They discussed it for three days to find out how it would work best, how the Indian would make his living when he accepted treaty. There were many things promised that we did not see; we saw only a few, such as the rations, and very little of those. The promises made to us are missing. In my situation and at my age, I am becoming concerned. A person who has a family and growing children should be able to get an extension to the reserve. This applies to the whole band, in case they become farmers, raise livestock, or undertake any other way of living or occupation. They should be able to show something by which they make their living. I am not talking about the way of life nowadays. We are overcrowded on the reserves, and we are being crowded by white people who are very close to the reserves. It would be very nice if something could be done about it. It appears that in the past the Indians were looked after. It was stated that the Indian agent would look after the people if they became destitute. I am not saying we are in that state at the present time, but something should be worked out because our reserve has potential for making money. The Indian people are not looked after well enough, not as compared to the Métis people. The Métis receive a good share of assistance when they are old; not so for the treaty Indians; in fact they get less. With a family, the little assistance the Indian receives is not enough, especially now with everything getting so expensive.

I do not know why they forgot the promises that they made to us. They have forgotten about them in Ottawa. We wonder about these things. The government people were very persuasive, and the promises sounded so realistic. That is the reason our chief signed the treaty and accepted a reserve. I was there listening at the time. If the Indian had anything of value on the reserve, it was his; the commissioners only requested six inches of the surface of the ground. All the treaty Indians in the northern and eastern part of Canada should be entitled to resources discovered underground; that should still be in effect. Even today the people expect these things because they are not being properly looked after. The timber was not sold, yet I see twenty trucks a day hauling logs from many different places. During the time of the negotiations, nothing was asked about timber; so why is it they are taking the timber? It would have been better for the Indians to make use of it.

The Indian people still have other promises coming to them. The government still owes them a lot and they should get more help. We cannot say how long this earth will last. The commissioner said: "This will be in effect as long as the sun shines and the rivers flow." He used these two oaths in sincerity. Today the river still flows, and when we get up each morning, we see the sun. I heard of many things that time that the people could depend upon in the future to make a living. The white man was receiving assistance. He could settle any place; he would get help from the government. Whose money is it they are using? Maybe it belongs to the Indians. The Indian who made his own living prior to giving up his land should also get some type of help. He is entitled to it more than anybody else. The chief would not have consented to the treaty if he had known his people were being tricked. The Indian people were not like that. They would not have said something and not done it. They did not lie to one another or cheat. I have not seen any of that, and I am an old man. Many times I have seen people who lost something, and whoever found it would hang it up. The Indians thought a great deal of one another, and they always shook hands.

Today they greet one another like the white man, and very little of the native language is spoken. I do not speak English, and my grandchildren confuse me with English. This makes me feel badly. It was better the way it was long ago when we cared more for each other. Even the commissioner shook hands with the people as they entered his tent. It would have been nice if he had accepted the Indian people like that all the time. There is still a great deal missing, and today we are experiencing difficulty. We will never stop thinking of our land because it had so much to offer. Today the white man takes the most out of our land to make his living. Why is it that we have to pay for trap lines? Indians have to pay to build a cabin on their line. Also, it was not mentioned that we had to pay for a licence to fish for a living in order to feed our children. We were not desperate. There was plenty of food around. I was hunting ducks long ago; I came upon an old man who had his *tipi* close to the lake; he just sat in the doorway of his *tipi* pulling in the fish. I am just relating how plentiful the food supply was long ago. There were also all kinds of game animals, but now there is an overpopulation of white man. It was not difficult to hunt big game and feed my children many years ago.

Today the game is scarce, and animals are shot from the roadside when they come out. Even the white men are doing that—they are the people who will kill off the big game. If the people who make the laws do not make changes, we will be in worse condition than we are now. It will be especially bad for the older people. Long ago a person of my age could make his living with two traps, but now the animals are becoming very scarce. If somehow this could be stopped, it would be much better. Today the young people get all the trap lines and there are none left for us older people. It has been about twenty years since I had a trap line, and I can say I am one of the people who has spent much time making a living in the bush; today this is not so.

Lightning: Did the Indian people want a treaty when it was first introduced to them?

Okeymaw: The commissioners were very persistent. They worked on the Indians for three days. They were talked into taking the treaty by the promises that they would not pay for anything and that they would travel any place free of charge "as long as the sun shines." We still often fall into traps, and we were promised that we would not have to fear anything. If many of these false statements had been revealed to the Indians, chances are that they would not have signed the treaty.

Lightning: Did they know what they were doing when negotiating with the commissioners?

Okeymaw: That is one thing I do not know. It appeared that Albert Tate, a Métis, was fluent in English. He was an interpreter at the treaty. He also spoke fluent Cree.

Lightning: Was he from around here?

Okeymaw: He was here for a long time; I think he grew up somewhere in the St. Albert area, but he was with us for a long time, and he stayed for awhile after the treaty, until his father died.

Lightning: Did the missionaries in any way help the Indians, or did they influence them in the wrong way?

Okeymaw: My way of thinking is that perhaps the missionaries were detrimental to the Indians. One priest thought he was the leader, placing himself in front of anybody else. I forget his name, but he still stands in St. Albert in the form of a cement block. I think his name is Lacombe; he was the one who was pushing the Indians: "Take the treaty, take the treaty." But now it is obvious why he was really encouraging the Indians: there was only one church at the time at Grouard. There would also be a school; so what he had in mind was to try to make the Indians accept the money. That is the reason for his encouragement. The people often said that he was doing us wrong.

There was a minister across the lake from here at Buffalo Bay—his name was Holmes—but he did not say very much. He tried to keep in touch with the Indians; he did not keep them away. His intention was to teach some of the treaty Indians; he taught some Métis children, and they were taught well. He even gave clothes to the Indians. I myself never did hear the priest ask any Indian to come into his house or offer him tea, but the minister did. They were responsible for messing up everything, and I have heard older people say the same thing. We felt he was a father to us, but on the other hand that was not so. Maybe if we had worked together, I would not be talking the way I am today. Maybe what I am saying sounds derogatory, but that is not my intention.

Lightning: In 1942 many treaty Indians were removed from the treaty Indian register. Do you have any knowledge of what happened there?

Okeymaw: I can only comment on one case, that of one of my mother's relatives. The husband of this family was working, hauling supplies from Athabasca. While he was away, it came time for the people who took scrip to leave the reserve, and the wife was approached. When that happened, the man still held his treaty rights. His two sons had to be taken off treaty. One was raised here. He was treaty once. His name is Henry Prince. He lives in the north. He is now getting old and he regretted losing his treaty rights. His older brother, Richard Prince, also lost his treaty status. As I was a councillor, I spoke up; I questioned why they could not be put back on treaty, because the mother was placed on treaty again. There is another man, Robert Walker, and several others. We never found out why this happened.

Lightning: Who was the man removing names from the treaty list?

Okeymaw: I do not remember his name, but Richard Prince would know. He would remember, and he also speaks good English.

Lightning: Do you recall any of the agents' names?

Okeymaw: There was one agent here for a long time. His name was Laird. He married a woman from here. Two of his children are still alive. The next one was Leroux, a Frenchman. The other one was M.F. Lapp, but he went to Edmonton.

Lightning: Did they get along well with the Indians?

Okeymaw: The first one, Mr. Laird, was very friendly and got along well with the Indians. He took into consideration what the Indian requested, but during that time everything was different, such as trapping, which was restricted. The Frenchman was very strict; he was the agent at Driftpile. The other one was fairly docile.

Lightning: Were there any buffalo around here long ago?

Okeymaw: Yes, there were many. That is why they called that place Buffalo Bay. I will tell you a story now about what happened. There were two people who left the Alexander Reserve or someplace close by the reserve. They made a boat from trees at St. Albert and made their way north and finally came upon the Lesser Slave River. They came ashore at the place that is now Grouard. They heard a rumbling noise, and upon investigation, they discovered a large herd of buffalo over the hill—we often find bones and skulls. On their way back, they stopped at an island on Slave Lake and found some people there. These people did not have any rifles; so they had no trouble capturing them. That is where Slave Lake got its name. Some of these people were killed there and the rest of them fled north to Great Slave Lake. I forget all their names, but one was Sewapegaham.

Lightning: How did the buffalo disappear?

Okeymaw: I think they left here and went up north to Fort Chipewyan and other areas.

Lightning: When the signing of the treaty took place, did the Indian know of money? Had he used it before?

Okeymaw: No, they were not familiar with it. I once travelled north with my father and my uncle Mustus, who was the headman, and we came across a road-building gang. This was before the treaty. They were white men. That is when I saw them trading. They gave us some money and told us we could trade it at the store. There was another case where a white man wanted a pair of moccasins; the old lady was not convinced that she was paid. She said, "What am I going to do with this piece of paper. I want to get paid." So from these experiences, I would say that they did not know money. Even during the treaty, the Indians were asking what it was they were receiving. It was Albert Tate, the Métis, who knew money. Albert Tate knew money because he had worked in the store. From that time on, the Indians became familiar with money.

Lightning: How did the Hudson's Bay Company people get along with the Indians?

Okeymaw: They must have gotten along well together because the Hudson's Bay Company manager did not hesitate when he sold a rifle to an Indian. The Indian stacked pelts from the floor until they measured up to the tip of the rifle barrel. That was his payment. You could say that the Indian was cheated because the pelts were valuable. If they were not, he would not have taken them.

Name: Felix Gibot
Date: 5 February 1974
Location: Fort Chipewyan
Interviewer: Richard Lightning
Translator: Richard Lightning

Lightning: What is your name?
Gibot: My name is Felix Gibot.
Lightning: How old are you?
Gibot: Nearly eighty years old.
Lightning: Are you a band member of some reserve? Are you a treaty Indian?
Gibot: I am a treaty Indian.
Lightning: Do you make your home here at Fort Chipewyan?
Gibot: I was raised at Moose Island; that is where our land was. My grandfather lived there until he was very old. My father lived there until he, too, was very old; My dad told us to bury him there when he died; so that is where he is buried.
Lightning: You say you had land there? Was that land given to you as a reserve then?
Gibot: That is where the Wood Buffalo officials allotted land to us when they first made a park out of our land. There were twenty of us when that land was first allotted to us. Our home still stands there. My older brother is there, and also some other people are still there.
Lightning: Do the people still live there?
Gibot: At the present time, my son traps there; when the men trap, they camp over there. We are being looked after here.
Lightning: Nobody stays out there permanently?
Gibot: During the summer, we stay out there. We never leave it because that is our land.
Lightning: Do you remember the size of your land?
Gibot: It was twenty-five miles in one direction and fourteen miles along the river.
Lightning: Do you recall anyone being a chief there?
Gibot: The fellow who was the owner was my younger brother, Alex Gibot. He is dead now. When he died, we were called by the park officials to find out who would be headman of that reserve. Ben Houle, who lives here, is the present headman of our reserve. Ever since that land was allotted to us, it has not had a bad name or reputation. It is probably the only one, even today, that has not got a bad name.
Lightning: Could you tell me what you remember of the time of the treaty?
Gibot: I will tell you the story from the time of the treaty until today. I did not hear it and I did not read it; I saw it take place myself. What I am

saying is the truth. During a time when we were in the bush, word got around that we were all invited. We were not aware what it was for. Everybody arrived here at Fort Chipewyan. Everybody arrived here for a meeting and to listen to the commissioner. "I was sent here by the government to read this document to you. Stories have reached the government that Indians have been dying of starvation in the bush. The government would like to take control of the Indian people and care for them. The government does not want to see you living in poverty in the bush. This is the reason I am here."

It was then that a man who was in charge of trappers was made chief. He, too, had something to say to the commissioner. He told the commissioner that he was getting on in age, and according to what the commissioner had said, he would become the chief.

"I am greatly impressed by what you have just told us, that the government is to care for us. It will be like a log that has started from the middle of the lake. With a breeze behind it, the log will eventually make its way to the shore. This is how I can foresee the laws of the white man in the future. I will not see them myself, but the people who will be alive in the future will see this taking place."

"Yes," said the commissioner, whose name was Carr.

Pierre Mercredi was the interpreter at the time, and also a priest was there. His picture is still here today. It was those two people who were the interpreters. The Indians were told that they would receive everything all the time, in perpetuity, as long as the river flowed and the sun shone. "You will never be mistreated and these provisions will never be taken away." There is one more thing that the commissioner told the Indians.

"When you are in the bush, if you see a white man who needs help, take him and bring him to some settlement. You will not get paid for it. On the other hand, if a white man finds an Indian in trouble, he, too, should help him. You will have to get along as one. You should not make enemies amongst Indians and white men. This goes for the Cree, white men, and Chipewyan. You should not hate each other, but be willing to help one another."

"I am really impressed with what you are telling me, but even in twenty years time, everything will be different."

The commissioner said that this was not so because it was the Queen's word that he was conveying. "It is this document that says it. She will be caring for you. You will no longer live in poverty. There is no reason you should not like it."

"I am really impressed with what you are saying, and would be very happy if this were to actually happen. But I will not see that day."

The following day, there was another meeting. The same promises were reiterated.

"You have worked on me for two days, and now on the third day, I will talk to you. What you are saying is that the promises are being made in good faith. My people will now be cared for by the government; but I will tell you one thing. I do not want my people to be sent away from our land; I want them to stay here at Fort Chipewyan. It is large enough that there is room for everybody.''

"This land now belongs to you; you can keep it. No land will be restricted for you. You can make your living the way it suits you best.''

"Yes.''

That is when they put the coat on the Indian, and he was officially made chief. He indicated that since he was now chief, he did not want the commissioners to say no to anything he requested. "When you make promises to me and I say yes, I have given you my word to last forever. If I agree to anything, that is my final word and I expect the same from you. I want the promise you have made fulfilled.''

"On this trip, I am representing the government. As long as the sun shines and the river flows, your requests for anything will never be turned down.''

"I will not see any of this, but my people will see it if they are alive. There will be constant changes taking place in the future. As these children grow up, they will see the changes. Myself, I will not live very long, because I am an old man. I do not want any of you here to forget these promises that have been made.''

He also told the commissioner that they would get along with the white man as long as they lived, and that he hoped the white man would do the same: "I will think of him as my younger brother when I see him.''

He said the same thing to his people: "If you see a white man in need, help him. If you are kind to him, he, too, will be kind to you. He will not force you into anything if you have respect for him. It will not be like being forced into the water.''

Today as I am growing old, I see the people being cared for: houses are built for them, food is given to them, wood is given to them. This is what the commissioner must have been referring to when he was talking. This is the way I am beginning to see it today.

Yes, white trappers were all over the place, and we were on very friendly terms with them. I went trapping with them many times. They enjoyed having me along. I would guide them and show them how to trap. They were very thankful for that as they took their pelts home. This is my story. While we made our home in Wood Buffalo Park, I never heard any gossip from the Métis people or the white man, not once. I, myself, as an individual old man, do not want to be on bad terms with the white man. What I am saying now was not written on paper. I saw it myself and heard people tell of it at the beginning as it was promised to us. I am telling it now exactly as the promises were made.

Lightning: What was the man's name who was made chief?

Gibot: Justin Martin was his name. That was the very first chief.

Lightning: At present you are living here, yet you were allotted land at the other place. How did the people get to this place?

Gibot: That came about on account of the school. We were never here; we were always in the bush making a living. There was never anybody here in this part of the country. The children used to attend the mission. They would be left there as boarders. Then the school was built, and after that all of the people stayed here. They left their homes in the bush where they had previously made their living. They now make their homes within reach of the school. That is also the reason we are here. But at least we still have our house on our land. It is very good land, and also good for farming; we do not want to leave it. There is no reason why one would not like it; there are no rocks on it. The land was meant for farming and we planted potatoes; it yielded good crops. But when the school was started here, we also made our homes here. We go to stay there during the summer. My brother goes there with his family, and I also go there. They still trap on that land.

Lightning: Does that land still belong to your family?

Gibot: Yes, it is still ours. There were many of us, but now many of the people are dead, especially the older people. There are only two of us left, my older brother and myself.

Lightning: Were the Crees always living close to the Chipewyan people? How did they originally get together?

Gibot: The Chipewyan people had land here originally; they had land here even before I was born. The Crees were always on friendly terms with the Chipewyan. All the elders are now dead. When we were youngsters and growing up, we were always friends with the Chipewyan, and we are still friends today.

Lightning: When were the treaties brought to their attention?

Gibot: The promises made to them were identical to ours regarding the land.

Lightning: The commisoner dealt with the Chipewyan at the same time?

Gibot: Yes, when the treaty was signed, there were Chipewyans already living here, but the Cree were dealt with first. We were the first to receive the money; we were paid fifteen dollars; they received the same amount. The following day, they officially appointed a Chipewyan chief. His name was Alexander Laviolette; he was the first chief for the Chipewyan band. They were promised exactly the same as we were. Nothing was different.

Lightning: Were there many people during the signing of the treaty?

Gibot: Yes, there were many people during that time, and many Métis people were there as observers when the treaties were made.

Lightning: Did the interpreter speak Cree and English fluently?

Gibot: Yes, he could understand the Cree language clearly. He was a Métis. His name was Pierre Mercredi. There was a priest, too. His picture is still here. The priest who is here now would know his name.

Lightning: Was there any mention of water, as it is plentiful around here? Did you find out if you could fish in the lakes?

Gibot: The commissioner said, "The Indian, Métis, and Chipewyan can fish in this lake as long as they are alive, and they will make a living out of it." That was a sincere promise.

Lightning: Do you recall any time when the people were not allowed to fish or were discouraged from fishing?

Gibot: Later on a licence was required, and even today one must have a licence to fish. Today, they do not allow fishing nearby; they have to go far out on the lake. If someone is fishing around here without a licence, the fish warden will confiscate the net.

Lightning: You claim that the land you mentioned before was yours. It was allotted to you. When the commissioner came here to make treaty, were his intentions to sign treaty on a friendly basis or was it to acquire the land?

Gibot: That is something that always puzzles me when I think of it. It appears as though he wanted to claim the land, to own the land for the government. That is why they took that action. This is what I think, anyway. How do you people think about this?

Lightning: Some of our elders seem to have doubts about what took place.

Gibot: At times, the Indian people get angry about that. The white man never bought the land. If he had bought it, there would have been large sums of money involved in order for him to claim the land. That is what some of the Indian people say, and as a result, they become angry.

Lightning: Did the Indians of long ago ever imagine or think that anything valuable would be found underground?

Gibot: You mean the elders of long ago? No, they never mentioned anything about *money* [gold or minerals] to be found underground or even petroleum to be found below the surface. I never heard my grandfather, although he was intelligent, mention anything. Even after my grandfather died, I never heard anything mentioned.

Lightning: They never told stories of the commissioner discussing these things?

Gibot: No, the commissioner never mentioned them. The only thing he mentioned was how the people would be cared for by the government as promised in the treaty. That is all that was mentioned.

Lightning: Were your father and grandfather here when the commissioner first arrived?

Gibot: When the commissioner first arrived, many were alive then.

Lightning: You remember it also?

Gibot: Yes, it is just like today as I am talking here. I never forgot any of the promises that were made to the chief.

Lightning: The Indians in Treaty Six are basically living in farming areas, and when they signed treaty, they were promised implements, so that they could make a living in farming.

Gibot: It was the same here. Yes, it was the same here. My father and uncle received implements. My uncle was Thomas Gibot. My dad was Albert Gibot. They were using farming implements from the government. That is the reason they were in agriculture. But it was the school that made it difficult. All the treaty Indians who stayed in the bush worked in agriculture, and they were proficient at it. When they started to move here, they lost it all. Today some of them do not even have a dog or a trap. There are many here and it is only the school that keeps them here.

Chapter Six

The Saulteaux and the Numbered Treaties: An Aboriginal Rights Position?

by
J.E. Foster

The concept of aboriginal rights has attracted the attention of Indians and non-Indians alike in the Canadian West. For its proponents, the concept substantiates claims of injustice made by Indians against the federal government and the white community. Further, should the dominant community and the government accept the validity of the concept, the way would be clear to end existing injustices, and to renew or to create the basis for a vital and just relationship between the Indian and white communities. Unfortunately for the supporters of aboriginal rights, the concept has as many opponents as proponents. For many Western Canadians, the apparent self-serving nature of the concept in the hands of Indian leaders renders it suspect. For others, there is a negative, emotional response to what appears to be the ''brown aristocrat'' who in Euro-Canadian eyes stands to receive much, but give little, should the concept be accepted.[1] In legal circles, where a significant element of the serious discussion has centred, aboriginal rights as ''personal and usufructory rights'' to the land appear valid.[2] Yet these same rights as ''vested rights'' may better serve the interests of Indians and non-Indians alike, as vested rights do not suffer to the same extent the taint of the ''aristocrat,'' and at the same time, perhaps reflect more clearly the Canadian historical experience.[3]

Fundamental to any discussion on aboriginal rights would appear to be the assumption of aboriginal sovereignty and ownership of land. Such an

---

[1] Douglas Fisher, ''Let's Re-assess Native Programs,'' *Edmonton Journal*, 4 December 1974; see also reply by George Manuel, ''Special Rights for Indians?—Yes,'' *Edmonton Journal*, 6 January 1975; and Douglas Fisher, ''Is the Patience of Job Enough?'' *Edmonton Journal*, 9 May 1975.

[2] Peter A. Cumming and Heil H. MicKenberg, eds., *Native Rights in Canada* (Toronto: General Publishing Co., 1972), p. 53.

[3] L.C. Green, ''Aboriginal Rights or Vested Rights?'' *Chitty's Law Journal* 22 (1975).

assumption would appear to underlie the closing speech of Mawedopenais, a Saulteau chief at Treaty Three:

> Now you see me stand before you all: what has been done here today has been done openly before the Great Spirit and before the nation, and I hope I may never hear anyone say that this treaty has been done secretly: and now in closing this council, I take off my glove, and in giving you my hand I deliver over my birthright and lands: and in taking your hand I hold fast all the promises you have made, and I hope they will last as long as the sun rises and the water flows, as you have said.[4]

Assuming that the recorded translation of Mawedopenais's words is reasonably accurate (a most presumptuous assumption indeed), there would appear to be little doubt that in delivering over "my birthright and lands," Mawedopenais was surrendering sovereignty and ownership of land. The evidence will not sustain an attempt to explain this surrender in terms of Mawedopenais as an ignorant Indian leader duped by the cunning and duplicity of land hungry whites.[5] In the documents, Mawedopenais is obviously the equal of any Euro-Canadian negotiator. What, then, is the meaning of his statement?

Terms and phrases, such as "sovereignty" and "ownership of land," unnerve the historian examining Indian participation in the numbered treaties signed during the 1870s. Such expressions, derived from the European tradition, may well explain events from the perspective of that tradition; but do they reflect an Indian conceptualization of what was taking place? At first glance, such might appear to be the case. Again the words of Mawedopenais seem to lend substance to an aboriginal rights view:

> All this is our property where you have come . . . . This is what we think, that the Great Spirit has planted us on this ground where we are, as you were where you came from. We think where we are is our property.[6]

Yet such remarks must be balanced against other evidence purporting to convey an Indian concept of community or national ownership of land. It is significant that there is amazing consistency between different eras and cultural areas.[7] Perhaps the best explanation of an Indian view of sovereignty and land ownership is contained in E.T. Denig's "Indian Tribes of the Upper Missouri":

> None of these . . . tribes claim a special right to any circumscribed or limited territory. There [sic] arguments are these . . . . All the . . . territory in the West

[4] Alexander Morris, *The Treaties of Canada with the Indians of Manitoba and the North-West Territories* (1880; reprint ed., Toronto: Coles Publishing Co., 1971), p. 75.

[5] Ibid., pp. 59-75.

[6] Ibid., p. 59.

[7] Cf. Jonathan Carver, *Travels Through the Interior Parts of North America in the Years 1766, 1767, and 1768* (London, 1781), p. 171, as quoted in Abraham Rotstein, "Trade and Politics: An Institutional Approach," *Western Canadian Journal of Anthropology* 3, no. 1 (1972): 3.

(known to them) and now occupied by all the Indians was created by Wakonda [Assiniboine Creator] for their sole use and habitation . . . . Now each nation finds themselves in possession of a portion of these lands, necessary for their preservation. They are therefore determined to keep them from aggression by every means in their power. Should the game fail, they have a right to hunt it in any of their enemies' country, in which they are able to protect themselves . . . . It is not land or territory they seek in this but the means of subsistence, which every Indian deems himself entitled to even should he be compelled to destroy his enemies or risk his own life to obtain it.[8]

In the Indian view suggested by Denig, the question of sovereignty and ownership of land is neither aboriginal nor is it a right. A Euro-Canadian who did not share a Woodrow Wilsonian view of nations and nation-states would have little difficulty accepting the pragmatic views of ''national'' interest conveyed in Denig's account.[9] Yet the question remains; at the signing of the numbered treaties during the 1870s, how did the participating Indians see their interests?

A perusal of pertinent sources describing the discussions that preceded the signing of the treaties suggests that two related, but separate, goals and their accompanying strategies influenced Indian leaders. Both goals envisaged a ''better'' future for Indian people in a world in which the white man was an increasingly significant factor. One goal emphasized the physical and cultural survival of the Indian people; the other goal emphasized improved material well-being. One strategy underlined the need for an alliance with the whites; the other strategy suggested the hard bargaining of horse traders in the market-place. At Treaties Six and Seven in particular, and to a lesser extent at Treaty Four, the strategy of Indian leaders aimed at creating an alliance with the government, a ''we'' relationship if you will, in which the government as ''brother'' or ''father'' would lend maximum assistance to facilitate the physical and cultural survival of the Indian people. Again and again the words of Indian leaders emphasized this goal. At Fort Pitt, to the evident satisfaction of the assembled Indians, Sweet-Grass addressed Lt. Gov. Alexander Morris:

> I give you my hand. If spared, I shall commence at once to clear a small piece of land myself, and others of my kinsmen will do the same. We will commence hand in hand to protect the buffalo . . . . Use your utmost to help me and help my children, so that they may prosper.[10]

In this same vein, Big Bear's ''rope to be about my neck'' speech reflected the goal that emphasized the preservation of Indian ways.[11] Again at Treaty

---

[8] E.T. Denig, ''Indian Tribes of the Upper Missouri,'' *46th Annual Report of the Bureau of American Ethnology, 1928-29* (Washington, D.C.: 1929), pp. 476-78.

[9] Green, ''Aboriginal Rights or Vested Rights?'' p. 1.

[10] Morris, *Treaties*, p. 236.

[11] Ibid., p. 240.

Seven, Crowfoot's "feathers of the bird" speech fit within the same context.[12] Notwithstanding the demands of Button Chief, the head chiefs Red Crow and Old Sun adopted a position virtually identical to that of Crowfoot.[13] Old Sun chose his words with care: "During the past Crowfoot has been called by us our Great Father. The Great Mother's Chief (Commissioner Laird) will now be our Great Father."[14] At the Treaty Four discussions, where the numerically superior Fort Qu'Appelle Saulteaux tried to coerce the Cree and possibly the Fort Ellice Saulteaux to their view,[15] the Cree chief Loud Voice emphasized the necessity of a co-operative relationship with the whites in the difficult days ahead. When Morris noted that the Queen "out of her generous heart and liberal hand . . . wants to do something for you, so that . . . you may be able to do something for yourselves,"[16] Loud Voice remonstrated with all of the assembled Indians: "I wonder very much at your conduct. You understand what is said and you understand what is right and good. You ought to listen to that and answer it, everyone of you."[17] But Loud Voice would be upstaged by the proponent of a different goal with a different strategy.[18] For the Gambler, a headman of the Fort Qu'Appelle Saulteaux, the treaty was not simply a question of Indian survival, but survival in the best possible material circumstances.

In the discussions at Treaties Six and Seven, and to a much lesser extent at Treaty Four, Indian leaders clearly pursued the goal of ensuring the physical and cultural survival of their people. To achieve this end, they sought an alliance, a "we" relationship, with the government. The frequent use of such terms as "father," "mother," and "brother" was not an inconsequential by-product of effusive Indian oratory.[19] Spokesmen carefully chose words which to their minds clearly and succinctly defined the nature of the relationship between Indians and the government. Subjects of immediate material benefit were of importance, as evidenced in the words of such spokesmen as Poundmaker and Starblanket.[20] But at no time were ambitious younger leaders, such as Joseph Thoma at Treaty Six and Button Chief at Treaty Seven, permitted to jeopardize discussions with material demands to which government representatives reacted negatively.[21] Yet at Treaties One through Four, views similar to those of Joseph Thoma and Button Chief

---

[12] Ibid., p. 272.
[13] Ibid., p. 273.
[14] Ibid.
[15] Ibid., p. 81.
[16] Ibid., p. 92.
[17] Ibid.
[18] Ibid., pp. 97-114.
[19] Ibid., pp. 171, 190-91, 266, 273.
[20] Ibid., p. 219.
[21] Ibid., pp. 220, 270.

predominated. The goal and strategy that these words sustained dominated treaty discussions at which Saulteaux bands were either the only or the majority of Indians present.

Immediate as well as long-term material benefits were the cardinal goals of Saulteaux leaders participating in treaty discussions in the early 1870s. From the beginning, the Indian commissioners seemed to experience difficulties in communicating the limits of what they could offer. At the Treaty One discussions, Lt. Gov. A.G. Archibald noted:

> They [the Indians] have been led to suppose that large tracts of ground were to be set aside for them as hunting grounds, including timber lands, of which they might sell the wood as if they were proprietors of the soil. [22]

The Saulteau goal and the strategy accompanying it were apparent at Treaty Three in the words and actions of the Fort Francis chief, Mawedopenais:

> We ask fifteen dollars for all that you see, and for the children that are to be born in future. This year only we ask for fifteen dollars; years after ten dollars; our chiefs fifty dollars per year for every year, and other demands of large amounts in writing, say $125,000 yearly. [23]

After Lieutenant Governor Morris declined such a request, Mawedopenais explained: "Our hands are poor but our heads are rich, and it is riches that we ask so that we may be able to support our families as long as the sun rises and the water runs." [24] Mawedopenais further emphasized that his demands were not excessive in view of what the Indians were offering. *"The sound of the rustling of gold is under my feet where I stand*; we have a rich country . . . ." [25] For Mawedopenais and most other Saulteaux, successful fur trappers and traders for generations, the circumstances of the treaty negotiations were a market-place in which bargaining skills determined material rewards. It is significant that Mawedopenais felt it necessary to explain or to justify his actions to the Indian commissioners. It is further significant that he offered explanations that would be comprehensible to the assembled whites. One such argument was the assumption that the Saulteaux owned the land. "It is the Great Spirit who gave us this; where we stand upon is the Indians' property, and belongs to them." [26] Coupled with this argument was another derived from previous experience: "The white man has robbed us of our riches, and we don't wish to give them up again without getting something in their place." [27] Similar explanations were offered by Saulteaux spokesmen at other treaty signings. At Treaty Four where The Gambler reflected a goal and

---

[22] Ibid., p. 33.
[23] Ibid., p. 60.
[24] Ibid., p. 61.
[25] Ibid., p. 62.
[26] Ibid.
[27] Ibid.

a strategy essentially identical to that of Mawedopenais, the same arguments of explanation were effectively presented in the guise of a discussion concerning the Hudson's Bay Company's past, present, and future relationships with the Indians.[28] On all occasions, it is readily apparent that Mawedopenais, The Gambler, and other Saulteaux spokesmen were particularly shrewd, intelligent, and competent negotiators, utilizing a strategy that they believed to be highly effective in discussions with whites.

In the discussions preceding the signings of the numbered treaties in the 1870s, it is the apparent "tribal" difference in goals and their accompanying strategies that attracts the attention of historians. It would seem obvious that there is no discernible difference in the negotiating abilities of Sweet-Grass and Crowfoot on the one hand, and Mawedopenais and The Gambler on the other. Their different performances stem from their different goals and strategies. If such be the case, then the historical question becomes what circumstances past and present account for the different goals and strategies? Are the records of the treaty discussions evidence of differences between Woods and Plains people? Does the explanation lie in a particular feature of their past experience? As the actions of the Saulteaux discussants seem to reflect an aboriginal rights view, the answer to this historical question has relevance today.

The immediate circumstances of the Indians with reference to the resource base of their lands and their particular adaptation to it is a significant factor in explaining the differences in question. From the evidence, it would appear that the Saulteaux did not see the impending crisis in food resources that to the Plains Cree and Blackfoot lay immediately ahead. The explanation for this Saulteaux view lies in the historical fact that they had adapted differently to the lands that they had inherited from the westward-moving Assiniboine and Cree.[29] Living in the forests and parkland in widely dispersed bands, apparently almost incessantly in motion in exploiting local resources, the Saulteaux saw no significant changes in the 1870s affecting their adaptation to the environment.[30] On the contrary, the Plains people saw the buffalo disappearing. As the western Plains tribes centred on the Cypress Hills in search of dwindling supplies of game, increased warfare and a smallpox epidemic rendered life more chaotic.[31] To the north and east, the Saulteaux did not face such circumstances. Quick action by the Hudson's Bay Company had stopped the smallpox epidemic of 1870 before it could decimate their ranks.[32] But for the leaders of the bands of the Blackfoot

---

[28] Ibid., pp. 81-82.

[29] Arthur J. Ray, *Indians in the Fur Trade: Their Role as Trappers, Hunters and Middlemen in the Lands Southwest of Hudson's Bay, 1660-1860* (Toronto: University of Toronto Press, 1974), pp. 101-3.

[30] Ibid. In comparison with Treaties Six and Seven, the question of the decline of game resources was nowhere as evident in the earlier numbered treaties.

[31] Ray, *Indians in Fur Trade*, pp. 191-92.

[32] Ibid.

Confederacy and the Plains Cree, no such respite occurred. Dwindling game resources, increasing warfare, and spreading disease heralded a crisis in which physical survival itself was in question. To bargain for a greater or lesser number of material goods not directly related to the question of survival would have been the height of political irresponsibility. What was needed was an ally to assist them through the crisis, not dollar bills. For the Saulteaux, who faced no impending crisis, political reality dictated hard bargaining for maximum material advantages.

Two incidents, one at Treaty Three and the other at Treaty Six, lend substance to the suggestion that Indian views of their own relative well-being influenced treaty discussions. At Treaty Three when an impasse developed between the Saulteaux and the Indian commissioners that threatened to terminate discussions, the Lac Seul chief broke ranks to adopt a position similar to that of the Indian leaders at Treaties Six and Seven.[33] Morris explained the split in Saulteaux ranks as follows:

> The Rainy River Indians were careless about the treaty, because they could get plenty of money for cutting wood for the boats, but the northern and eastern bands were anxious for one.[34]

It would appear that those bands whose material circumstances seemed relatively secure could adopt a ''hard line'' to the point of risking a rupture in relations. More distant bands, however, fearing for their future welfare or envious of the good fortune befalling their kindred living closer to the whites, were not willing to risk such a conclusion. For them the strategy of the alliance suggested itself. In this instance, it is significant that the words of the Lac Seul chief averted a breakdown in discussions. The Indians withdrew to establish a more moderate position to which the Indian commissioners could respond.[35]

At Treaty Six, we find a similar incident in the intervention of Joseph Thoma. On this occasion, however, the strategies were reversed. Thoma appeared to reject the alliance strategy of the Indian leaders at Fort Pitt. Thoma emphasized a dollars and cents approach, ending his speech with a cryptic statement: ''I have told the value I put on my land.''[36] Although Red Pheasant of the Battle River Cree rejected Thoma's approach,[37] his words take on added interest when compared with certain oral traditions among the Cree of the Treaty Six area in eastern Alberta. In one tradition, a Bush Cree named Sasakawapisk, Chipmunk or Striped Gopher, intervenes in Treaty Six to tell Lieutenant Governor Morris: ''You will never pay the price of our

---

[33] Morris, *Treaties*, p. 63.
[34] Ibid., p. 65.
[35] Ibid., p. 66.
[36] Ibid., p. 220.
[37] Ibid., p. 221.

land.''[38] In the tradition, the Plains Cree oppose him and prevent him from continuing his particular line of discussion. Perhaps Sasakawapisk is the Joseph Thoma of other accounts. But of greater importance is the fact that a Bush Indian could adopt a hard bargaining position, while the Plains people were fearful that such a tack might alienate the whites and end the opportunity of establishing an alliance.

Another factor which cannot be ignored in examining the circumstances surrounding the signing of the treaties is the particular interests of Indian spokesmen. Evidence on this subject is scarce. Nevertheless, some tantalizing morsels emerge with reference to The Gambler at Treaty Four. The evidence is by no means conclusive, but it does serve to demonstrate that the particular personal interests of individual Indian spokesmen may have played a prominent role in determining a particular strategy and goal. It suggests that the Fort Qu'Appelle Saulteaux, of whom The Gambler was a leading spokesman, used the threat of coercion to have the Cree and Fort Ellice Saulteaux follow their lead in manipulating discussion with the Indian commissioners.[39] Exploiting the desire of the government representatives to begin talking treaty, The Gambler and his associates successfully insisted that the status of the Hudson's Bay Company be discussed first. At issue, from the Saulteau view, was access to the £300,000 paid to the Company for its interest in Rupert's Land. Failing in this quest, The Gambler and his associates emphasized the action of the Company in surveying a reserve about their post without consultation or compensation involving the neighbouring bands.[40] Finally, it was The Gambler who requested that the Company be restricted to conducting business within its posts rather than travelling *en dérouine*,[41] Morris replied to the effect that the Company had neither more nor less rights than other traders in conducting its business.[42] What had been The Gambler's interest in such a request?

A seemingly unrelated incident involved The Gambler challenging Morris for his hesitation in shaking hands with a half-breed. Morris apparently satisfied The Gambler when he in effect declared that half-breeds living as, and with, Indians and accepted by them would be treated as Indians for treaty purposes.[43] Who was the particular half-breed who initiated the question? Unfortunately, he remains unidentified.

Such incidents involving The Gambler take on added interest when his brother, the noted Saulteau free trader Kissoway, is introduced into the

---

[38] T.A.R.R. Interview with Elders Program, interview with Simon Watchmaker, Kehewin Reserve, date not recorded.

[39] Morris, *Treaties*, pp. 81-82.

[40] Ibid., p. 82.

[41] Ibid., p. 111.

[42] Ibid., p. 112.

[43] Ibid., p. 99.

narrative.[44] Was the Gambler utilizing his position to protect a family interest? This same Kissoway played an important role a year later at Portage La Prairie in the difficult negotiations with Yellow Quill's band, involving additions to Treaties One and Two. Kissoway, a member of Yellow Quill's band, happened to be passing by during discussions; he stopped to render needed assistance in reaching an agreement.[45] A year later, in 1876, as the Indian commissioners were on their way to Fort Carlton to negotiate Treaty Six, who should give up to the lieutenant governor his place in the line-up for the ferry across the Saskatchewan but the ubiquitous Kissoway.[46] It must be noted that as a trader it would be most natural for Kissoway to be found among Indians discussing the terms of treaties. Successful discussions would be good for business. Another feature of Kissoway's activities must be noted as well. His actions suggest a classic illustration of the "moccasin telegraph." The Saulteaux and other Indians knew what had been discussed and decided at earlier treaty signings. Kissoway and others would carry the word. But did the moccasin telegraph go beyond merely providing information? Did it try to co-ordinate policy? It is known that Yellow Quill's band twice sent messengers with tobacco to Treaty Four to block negotiations.[47] How did this influence the leading Treaty Four spokesman, The Gambler, a leader whose brother Kissoway, a leading trader, was a member of Yellow Quill's band? The evidence available gives rise to far more questions than it answers. It does, however, demonstrate the possibility of a co-ordinated approach to treaty discussions among bands of different treaty regions. This co-ordination could have played a role in determining what the particular goal and strategy would be at each treaty signing.

It is obvious that the particular circumstances of individual bands in terms of how they saw themselves in relation to their resource base influenced the selection of goals and strategies at the treaty negotiations. Evidence would indicate that the particular interests of different Indian leaders played a role as well. Still, the major factor would be the previous experience of various bands in relationships with Europeans. As aspects of the Saulteau strategy with its emphasis on ownership seem to reflect an aboriginal rights position, their history becomes significant. How did a concept, essentially European in origin, become incorporated in the Saulteau tradition and not in the Plains tradition of the Cree or Blackfoot? The historical answer lies in the particular experiences of individual bands in the fur trade.

---

[44] Ibid., p. 141.
[45] Ibid., p. 142.
[46] Ibid., pp. 181, 187.
[47] Ibid., p. 141.

A rough typology of Indian experience in the westward moving fur trade would denote the following landmarks.[48] Initially, there would be contact with more eastern bands seeking an alliance. To cement the relationship, the eastern bands would offer European goods of significant economic value and accept in return pelts of apparently minor worth. Eventually, European traders would appear among particular Indian bands offering better goods at better prices than the previous Indian traders. In addition, the European traders held out special rewards to those leaders who contacted more distant bands and brought their furs to the trader. This was the golden age for most Indians. Undreamed of material benefits, coupled with immense social and political power and prestige, created a world of luxury virtually unfathomable, in their minds, a couple of generations earlier. But the golden age came to an end. The traders passed on westward to more distant bands. For most of the bands who had enjoyed the position of middlemen in the fur trade, the change necessitated adaptations that compared unfavourably with the golden age.

The downfall of Huronia ushered in the golden age of the middlemen in the fur trade for the Saulteaux. Their eastern kin, the Ottawa, succeeded the Huron as the middlemen in the St. Lawrence trading system. Through a network of alliances, the Ojibwa peoples took the chaos of change in stride. Nearly half a century later, the Cree experienced a similar occurrence when the Hudson's Bay Company established a post at York Factory. They, too, became middlemen, dominating the Saskatchewan, the arterial route of the Hudson's Bay Company trading system.[49] But with the role of middlemen in the fur trade came economic and political dependence.

With time, European goods ceased to be luxuries and became necessities.[50] Even alcohol and tobacco were incorporated into Indian ceremonial activities to become essential ingredients. But perhaps even more significant than European goods was the European alliance. As middlemen in the fur trade, particular Indian bands enjoyed the support of the power and prestige of the European trader in protecting their lands from would-be aggressors or in pushing their claims against enemies where the fortunes of war and the pursuit of furs led them.[51] Such dependence upon the European trader gave the trader much leverage over his middlemen partners. The Indian middlemen, in turn, as suppliers of pelts, possessed significant leverage in their relations with the trader.

---

[48] Such a typology emerges in Ray, *Indians in Fur Trade;* and in Harold Hickerson, *The Chippewa and Their Neighbours* (Toronto: Holt, Rinehart, 1970). The following narrative reflects the historical consensus emerging in recent publications.

[49] Ray, *Indians in Fur Trade*, chapter three.

[50] Ibid., pp. 85-87.

[51] Hickerson, *The Chippewa and their Neighbours*, chapter five.

The European trader was dependent upon the Indian not only for furs but for foodstuff and other goods, such as toboggans, snowshoes, and canoes. In addition, Indians often served as interpreters, guides and couriers.[52] While their numbers proved a liability to themselves in the sense that it was difficult to establish a consensus on a specific issue, these same large numbers demonstrated to the trader that his continuing presence among them was a function of their good will—effective political leverage indeed. Yet history is replete with examples of misplaced attempts to use various forms of leverage in a particular community's interests. In the fur trade, what prevented socio-political ''accidents''? What mechanism permitted the use of leverage by each party without inadvertently overstepping the limits of the relationship?

In essence, the regulating mechanism in relations between European traders and Indian middlemen was the political alliance cemented by mutual dependence. In effect, the alliance from an Indian view was the willingness of the Indian to treat the trader as ''we'' instead of ''they,'' on condition that the trader's behaviour reflect his acceptance of the ramifications of such a relationship. The elaborate fur trade ceremony of each of the two trading systems was simply a non-verbal statement of this political, social, and economic truth. Inherent in this relationship was the assumed equality of each community.[53] Indian middleman and European trader were equal partners in a politico-economic alliance that worked to both their advantages. The Saulteaux experienced this relationship in their golden age on the shores of Lake Superior; so, too, did the Cree and Assiniboine on the Saskatchewan a half-century later. But the equal partnership relationship that the Indian middleman enjoyed depended upon his position as middléman in the fur trade.

In the second and third decades of the eighteenth century, when Sieur de La Vérendrye crossed the height of land between Lake Superior and the Northwest proceeding westward to the lands of the Cree and Assiniboine, the role of the Saulteaux as middlemen was threatened. Yet La Vérendrye handled the situation admirably.[54] The lavish dispensing of presents ensured the stability of the alliance with the Saulteaux. In addition, his posts in the West served as sources of supply to Saulteaux bands moving into the vacated lands of the Cree and Assiniboine.[55] No doubt the political and economic leverage of the Saulteaux declined, but to all appearances the Franco-Saulteaux alliance remained an equal partnership. It was not until the defeat

---

[52] Glyndwr Williams, ed., *Andrew Graham's Observations on Hudson's Bay, 1767-91*, with an Introduction by Richard Glover (London: The Hudson's Bay Record Society, 1969), p. 192.

[53] Ibid.

[54] Arthur S. Morton, *A History of the Canadian West to 1870-71*, 2nd ed., ed. Lewis G. Thomas (Toronto: University of Toronto Press, 1973), p. 173.

[55] Ray, *Indians in Fur Trade*, pp. 101-3.

of New France and the replacement of the French in the St. Lawrence trading system with Anglo-Americans that the myth of equal partnership was shattered. The realization of this, provoked by inexperienced traders, bore fruit in the form of Pontiac's uprising.[56]

With the loss of control of the middleman position in the St. Lawrence fur trade system, the nature of the relationship between the Saulteaux and the trader changed. If anything, Saulteau dependence on European manufactured goods increased. The trader's leverage was increasing at the expense of the Saulteaux. No longer could an equal partnership be said to exist. It is at this time that the imagery of the family increased in importance in the ceremonial behaviour involving the trader and the Saulteaux. The trader became "father."[57] His rum became "milk."[58] The Saulteaux became his "children."[59] An impression arises from the literature suggesting that the strategy of many band leaders was to replace words of imagery with words of concrete fact. The trader hopefully would not only be an honourific father, but a father in fact. If not father, then some other relationship, such as brother-in-law or son-in-law, would do. Surprisingly, the traders reacted positively to this relationship, though their journals would be replete with negative comments noting the costs involved. Many traders, however, had strong ties to their Indian families.[60] In addition to their own cultural heritage, they would enjoy and appreciate their role as patriarchal head of an extended family.[61]

The trader's acceptance of this new, unequal relationship was crucial to providing the Saulteaux some leverage in their relationship with him. As father, he had to bear some responsibility for the band's survival. As children, the Saulteaux could make legitimate demands upon the time and purse of the trader. By the same token, a perceptive trader could recognize the significant influence he possessed over particular bands. Within the limits of the new relationship, he could make demands that at an earlier date would have proved unacceptable.[62] Did not the father determine where the bands would hunt?

By way of comparison, it is significant that the Cree of the Saskatchewan did not suffer the fate of the Saulteaux in the region between

---

[56] Alexander Henry, *Travels and Adventures in Canada and the Indian Territories Between the Years 1760 and 1776* (1809; reprint ed., Edmonton, Alta.: Hurtig Publishers, 1969), chapters three, four, five.

[57] Note the usage of this term in the treaty negotiations.

[58] Henry, *Travels and Adventures*, p. 242.

[59] This term occurs frequently throughout the fur trade literature.

[60] J.E. Foster, "The Country-born in the Red River Settlement" (Ph.D. diss., University of Alberta, 1972), p. 72.

[61] J.E. Foster, "The Indian Trader in the Hudson Bay Fur Trade Tradition" (Paper delivered at the Second Canadian Ethnological Society Annual Conference, Winnipeg, 1975), p. 7.

[62] After 1821 particularly, the Hudson's Bay Company would move bands into different areas as a means of conservation. The bands were given little say in such decisions.

Red River and Lake Superior. When the Cree lost their position as middlemen in the fur trade, they turned to the full exploitation of the buffalo in the parkland and on the Plains. Their dependence upon European goods and the European alliance, if anything, declined.[63] A period of significant readjustment occurred. But in essence, the golden age of the middleman in the fur trade carried over into the equestrian age of the Cree on the Plains. To the Plains Cree, the trader might be "brother," but he would not be "father."

The new relationship between the Saulteaux and the trader continues to evolve. To the Saulteaux, the direction of evolution decreased their power and influence. With the passage of time, younger, better-educated officers replaced the older traders. Reflecting the "modern" administrative practices arising out of the Industrial Revolution in Great Britain, they seemed to play down the familial context in which the Indians perceived their relationship. In addition, in pursuing their careers, they rarely remained in one place long enough for the familial imagery of the trading relationship to be connected to their individual persons. In Great Britain, their superiors looked askance at nepotistic practices surviving from earlier days in the fur trade.[64] From the viewpoint of the Saulteaux, these developments would eventually place them in a position little different from indentured servants or serfs. If the trader did not accept the familial context of the relationship, what little leverage the Saulteaux had possessed would be gone. To have any hope of improving their position, the Saulteaux had to find a concept that the trader would accept as operative in the relationship between the Saulteaux and himself. It did not matter whether the Saulteaux believed in the concept. It did matter that the trader accepted it and acted upon its premises. Such a concept began to emerge from the experience of the Métis, kindred of the Saulteaux, in the Red River Settlement during the closing decade of violence in the competition in the fur trade.

The years from 1810 to 1820 witnessed the intensification of a competitive struggle in the fur trade that traced its roots back more than a century. The economic advantages of the Hudson's Bay Company trading system had been matched by the entrepreneurial skills of the traders in the St. Lawrence trading system.[65] First the French and, after the fall of New France, the British, largely Highland Scots, successfully challenged the more cautious policies of their northern rival. The mixture of Highland Scot officers and French Canadian voyageurs that became the North West Company dominated the fur trade by the dawn of the nineteenth century. For the North West Company and the St. Lawrence trading system, victory

---

[63] Ray, *Indians in Fur Trade*, p. 168.

[64] Foster, "Indian Trader," pp. 10-11.

[65] Marjorie Campbell, *The North West Company* (1957; reprint ed., Toronto: Macmillan Co. of Canada, 1973), remains the standard work.

seemed assured. Yet a decade later, in 1810, new faces appeared on the Governing Committee of the Hudson's Bay Company to challenge such a verdict. Men such as Andrew Wedderburn (later Colvile) and John Halkett developed the "retrenchment policy" to defeat the North West Company.[66] The initial result was a decade of escalating violence which, in its final tally, would cost nearly half a hundred men their lives.[67]

An essential feature of the retrenchment policy was the plan of a young Scottish earl, Lord Selkirk, to establish a settlement at the confluence of the Red and Assiniboine Rivers, downtown Winnipeg today.[68] Selkirk's family and philanthropic interests envisaged new homes for displaced Highland Scot crofters on the edge of the Great Central Plain. His brothers-in-law, Wedderburn and Halkett, incorporated his ideas into their policy. The settlement would first serve as a haven for Scot crofters, retired officers, and servants with mixed-blood families from the Company's service. In time it would supply agricultural products and personnel to the fur trade.[69] Such was the plan for the Red River Settlement. Would the future bear it out?

The North West Company could not accept Selkirk's settlement in the Red River valley. Such a settlement would straddle the vital lifeline between the provisioning posts of the parklands and the fur trading posts of the Interior. In addition, the settlement was but a few short miles from the North West Company's main communication route across the continent.[70] To the North West Company, Selkirk's project was not philanthropy or *noblesse oblige*. It was a clever plan to threaten them at their most vulnerable spot. At all costs, the settlement had to be destroyed. For such a purpose, the North West Company turned to their most dependable ally, the Red River Métis.

Before examining the Métis interest in the Selkirk settlement, it is first necessary to determine who the Métis were in the Red River Valley in the second decade of the nineteenth century. Some scholars may suggest that the Métis as such did not exist at this time.[71] At best one may use the term proto-Métis. The virtue of such a position can be seen when the Métis are placed in the context of earlier Indian history in the region of the Upper Great Lakes. With the first appearance of the fur trade, a continuing series of Indian bands spun off from the forests and parklands of the northeast, journeying to

---

[66] E.E.Rich, *The History of Hudson's Bay Company, 1670-1870* (London: The Hudson's Bay Record Society, 1958-59), vol. 2, *1763-1870*, p. 291.

[67] The two incidents suffering the greatest loss of life were the Hudson Bay Company's Athabaska campaign in 1815-16 and the Battle of Seven Oaks, June 1816.

[68] A sympathetic and fair treatment of Selkirk can be found in Chester Martin, *Lord Selkirk's Work in Canada* (Oxford: Clarendon Press, 1916).

[69] A.S. Morton, "The Place of the Red River Settlement in the Plans of the Hudson's Bay Co., 1812-1825," *Annual Report of the Canadian Historical Association, 1929*, p. 106.

[70] E.E. Rich, *Hudson's Bay Company*, p. 316.

[71] It has been suggested that one cannot speak of the Métis previous to the arrival of the French-speaking, Roman Catholic missionaries in the region in 1818, and the first of the regularized buffalo hunts in 1820.

the Plains to adopt a way of life suitable to the Prairie environment. Beginning with the Cheyenne and followed by various bands of the Dakota peoples, the movement to the southwest onto the Plains continued. The general southwest movement of the Saulteaux or Chippewa people in the latter years of the eighteenth century was merely the most recent incident in this historical process. Pressures on the Saulteaux to move westward were intensified when a burgeoning population and diminishing resources, coupled with the loss of the middleman role in the fur trade, seemed to herald a crisis in survival. Warfare with the Santee and Yankton Dakota intensified. By 1800, however, the Saulteaux had passed beyond the forest through the parkland to the banks of the Red River below its confluence with the Pembina River. Here their westward move stopped. The equestrian bands of the Plains, armed with the Plains gun, would decimate the pedestrian Saulteaux armed with the Woods gun.[72] Such Saulteaux bands needed time and assistance in adapting to the new environment. They needed an ally; and what better ally than the one they, their fathers, and grandfathers had known previously, the fur trader?

The fur trader had preceded the Saulteaux into the lands drained by the Red and Assiniboine Rivers.[73] Their interest was not so much furs but provisions, pemmican, and dried meat to supply posts in the forests and the fur brigades on their annual dashes across a large part of the continent. Without the provisioning posts, the St. Lawrence trading system could not penetrate much beyond the Great Lakes. The principal difficulties in the provisioning trade lay in relations with the Plains tribes.[74] Virtually independent of the trader in terms of their need for European goods, the Plains tribes supplied provisions at their convenience and not that of the fur trade. As a result, in any given year should the Plains tribes decide not to come into trade, the fur trade's very existence was threatened. The circumstances of the Saulteaux who had reached the edge of the Prairie ensured greater regularity on their part. If they could acquire the means of hunting buffalo, they would be a most valuable ally to the trader.

The relationship that evolved between such Saulteaux bands and the trader recalled, to a degree, the time of equal partnership when the Saulteaux had controlled the middleman role in the fur trade. As in previous times, intermarriage between Saulteaux women and servants, largely French Canadian, cemented the relationship.[75] Upon retirement many of these

---

[72] Ray, *Indians in Fur Trade*, pp. 73-79.

[73] La Vérendrye encountered Cree and Assiniboine, not Saulteaux, in the region.

[74] The literature emphasizes that the most skilled officers were assigned to trade with the Plains tribes.

[75] See Elliott Coues, ed., *New Light on the Early History of the Greater Northwest* (Minneapolis: Henry & Thompson, 1965), vol. 1; numerous entries of Alexander Henry, *Travels and Adventures*, attest to this fact, including his own marriage.

servants remained in the country with their families.[76] On the demise of the XY Company in 1804, large numbers of servants were cast adrift in the region, adding to the numbers who were acquiring equestrian skills that would permit them to pursue the buffalo on the Plains. Such Saulteaux bands, as a result of their alliance with the fur trader as provisioners, were on the road of cultural change that would see them emerge as the Métis.

The initial reaction of the Métis to the appearance of the Selkirk settlers in 1812 appears to have been positive. There may have been some hesitancy towards greeting people who were "Anglais," the enemy in company affiliation, language, and religion.[77] But like the trader, the settlers needed the Métis to hunt for them; and they paid well for provisions.[78] Circumstances changed with the inappropriate actions of the settlement's governor, Miles Macdonell. His proclamations against hunting buffalo from horseback and exporting pemmican from the settlement threatened the way of life of the Métis. The settlers who had been welcomed as friends now appeared to be acting with seemingly little concern for the Métis. Many of the Métis turned to their old bourgeois in the North West Company for advice and explanation.[79]

A principal strategy of the Hudson's Bay Company in its conflict with the North West Company emphasized the validity of its charter, particularly "stressing its possession of the soil of Rupert's Land." From Selkirk's viewpoint, he inherited this same right when he acquired the region of Assiniboia from the Company. His strategy was "to prevent the North West Company from obtaining prescriptive rights through uninterrupted possession."[80] If the charter were valid, and legal opinion seemed to confirm it, the hands of the North West Company were tied. But the hands of the original inhabitants, the Indians and the Métis, were not tied. With little difficulty, the officers of the North West Company instilled in the minds of the Métis the view "that the land was theirs and that the English company was taking it away from them." In addition to agitating for a concept of aboriginal ownership of the soil, the North West Company assisted the Métis in organizing themselves to take purposeful action against the settlers. Accident and miscalculation culminated in the Battle of Seven Oaks, in which Selkirk's representative, Governor Semple, and twenty settlers died at the hands of the Métis under the leadership of Cuthbert Grant.[81] The intervention

---

[76] The "freeman" was encountered in the valleys of the Saskatchewan and Red Rivers from the 1780s onward.

[77] This aspect is not developed in the literature, remaining more a hint or suggestion.

[78] Alexander Ross, *The Red River Settlement* (Minneapolis: Ross & Haines, 1972), pp. 24-25.

[79] A.S. Morton, "The New Nation, The Métis," *Transactions of the Royal Society of Canada*, no. 3, pt. 2 (1939) p. 139.

[80] Ibid., p. 138.

[81] Ibid., p. 139.

of the Métis did not prevent the demise of the North West Company by the end of the decade; but it did initiate the use of the treaty in relations between whites and Indians in the region. In view of previous events, in 1817 Selkirk had the Saulteaux bands of the region surrender their interests and recognize his through a treaty.[82] This act in itself seemed to emphasize the validity of the position of the Métis and Indians that the North West Company had advanced.

For the Saulteaux bands in the region of the settlement who did not share the good fortune of their kindred, the Métis, the signing of the Selkirk Treaty must have been a significant event. At the time and in the years ahead, they could sense their lack of bargaining power with the Hudson's Bay Company.[83] For reasons cited earlier, they saw their position relative to others declining. But with the Selkirk Treaty a new possibility arose. The settlement seemed to accept responsibility for a debt to the original inhabitants. Customs, such as the appearance of the Indians at the doors of the settlers' houses on New Year's Day to receive, not to beg, food and drink, sustained the concept. In time, no doubt the Saulteaux came to honestly accept the validity of the first inhabitant or aboriginal argument. Such evidence would suggest that their additional enthusiasm was derived from the fact that since the whites acknowledged the idea it gave the Saulteaux additional leverage in relations with them. Initially the Saulteaux concept of aboriginal rights could well have been a political tactic. In time, like the Métis, they would come to accept it as an article of faith.

As the Métis were neighbours and often kinfolk of the Saulteaux, their subsequent experiences in the Red River Settlement were shared with the Saulteaux in such a manner that they can be considered a part of the Saulteaux experience as well.[84] The relationship between the Hudson's Bay Company and the settlement on one hand and the Métis on the other could be chaotic. In such circumstances, the Métis would fall back on a vague, ill-defined "original inhabitant" justification for their actions.[85] On all occasions, the Company sought to mollify the Métis with gifts, special favours, and a dialogue on specific issues. But at no time did the Company indicate acceptance of the aboriginal rights position. However, the Company's actions, in the eyes of the Métis, would appear to support such a position. What the Métis did not fully appreciate is that the Company gave way before Métis military power, not the sophistication of their argument.[86] During the

---

[82] Morris, *Treaties*, pp. 15 and 299.

[83] An excellent example is in the Treaty Three speech by the Lac Seul chief found in Morris, *Treaties*, p. 63.

[84] Evidence to date would indicate continuing intermarriage between the two groups. No doubt individuals passed with relative ease between the two communities.

[85] Several sources reflect this viewpoint. In addition to Morton, "The New Nation, The Métis," see Ross, *The Red River Settlement*, pp. 237-39.

[86] Ross, *The Red River Settlement*, pp. 166-68.

1840s when free traders amongst the Métis challenged the Company's monopoly, the aboriginal rights argument emerged with far greater clarity.[87] In defence, the Company publicly emphasized the position that it had always taken; the charter, not aboriginal rights, was the basis of legal and political right in Rupert's Land.[88] The battle was joined, climaxing in the trial of Guillaume Sayer in 1849 for illegally trading in furs.[89] The Company won the legal battle only to lose the political war. After the jury found Sayer guilty, the Company addressed the court, requesting that punishment not be implemented and that charges against three remaining Métis free traders be dropped. This "magnanimous" gesture[90] was misinterpreted to the armed mob of Métis outside the court house who discharged their guns in a *feu de joie* while shouting *le commerce est libre*. In their eyes their aboriginal rights concept had been accepted. There would be no reason for the Saulteaux, the neighbours and kinfolk of the Métis, not to share this view.

The 1850s reintroduced the importance of treaties to the Saulteaux in the region of the Red River Settlement. The Métis as well took a keen interest in developments as the influence of the American central government approached the forty-ninth parallel of latitude:

> Ever since the road to St. Peter's [Minnesota Territory] has been opened, it has been rung in their ears what large sums of money the Americans pay for Indian lands; and that half-breeds, being the offspring of Indians, come in for a good share of the loaves and fishes on all such occasions.[91]

For many of the Métis, the terms of the Pembina Treaty between the Saulteaux and the American government in September 1851 were a disappointment "after their long struggle to obtain a settlement, in the belief that they themselves would have been recognized by the American government as the rightful owners of the disputed lands of Pembina; on what grounds, however, we have always been at a loss to discover."[92] A provision in the treaty said that the half-breeds were entitled to what the Indians chose to give them.[93] As a result, a most interesting realignment in relations between the Saulteaux and Métis may well have occurred. The persistent remark of the Indian commissioners in the treaty discussions of the 1870s, to the effect that the half-breeds were most "helpful" in advising the Saulteaux, may have owed much to a particular provision in the Pembina Treaty.[94] The

---

[87] James Sinclair et al. to Gov. Alexander Christie, 29 August 1845, Red River Correspondence 1845-47, Provincial Archives of Manitoba, Winnipeg.

[88] Christie to Sinclair et al., 5 September 1845, ibid.

[89] The best account is given in Ross, *The Red River Settlement*, pp. 374-76.

[90] With an armed mob of 300 Métis outside, the Hudson's Bay Company could afford to be magnanimous.

[91] Ross, *The Red River Settlement*, p. 403.

[92] Ibid., p. 411.

[93] Ibid.

[94] See Morris, *Treaties*, pp. 51, 141, 187.

greater significance of the Pembina Treaty, however, was the manner in which treaties became a frequent topic of conversation in Red River.

The Selkirk Treaty of 1817 could not match the Pembina Treaty of 1851 in terms of the benefits it bestowed on the signatories.[95] Needless to say, ample reasons were advanced to question its validity. Alexander Ross explained:

> The Cree nation always claimed Red River as their lands; but Lord Selkirk, having found on the soil some Saulteaux as well as Crees, gave them an interest in the treaty, though, as they acknowledge to this day, they had no right to the lands, being originally foreigners. Errors of this kind cannot always be avoided, and the mistake having been made, the Saulteaux claim a sort of prescriptive right, rendered as valid, by mere lapse of time, as that of the Crees themselves. The latter, thus provoked, threaten to expel their rivals from Red River altogether, and the whites along with them, unless the names of the Saulteaux chiefs were expunged from the compact, and the annual payment be made to the Crees only.[96]

The threats of violence never matured to actuality; but they did have the desired effect in that no less a person than Alexander Ross recommended compliance.[97] This same Alexander Ross roundly criticized similar tactics on the part of the Métis.[98] Why would Ross not take similar umbrage with the Cree and later the Saulteaux? The simple explanation is that, from his viewpoint and quite likely the viewpoint of a number of other settlers, the Indians had a valid argument.

The Saulteaux entered the treaty negotiations of the 1870s with a half-century of experience with treaties. Their value was that they provided leverage in terms of interaction with the seemingly more powerful white community. As this community seemed to accord the claims of the original inhabitants, particularly the Indians, some validity, the Saulteaux enjoyed a degree of leverage unknown since their forefathers had a choice of traders during the the period of competition. Needless to say, the Saulteaux, as a result of their dependence upon European goods, expressed their new-found influence in terms of material benefits. The events of 1869-70 had virtually little influence upon their lives except to suggest that perhaps the Métis may have tried to subvert their interests.[99] The presence of the federal government in succeeding years merely provided an opportunity to apply a time-tested technique to improve the material well-being of the Saulteaux. All indicators suggested the traditional aboriginal rights approach of the Saulteaux would enjoy even more success in the future. Thus the goal and strategy of the

---

[95] Ross, *The Red River Settlement*, p. 411, contains excerpts of the Pembina Treaty.

[96] Ibid., p. 159.

[97] Ibid.

[98] Ibid., p. 167.

[99] Note particularly the pro-Canadian attitude of Henry Prince, chief of the Indian village at St. Peters.

Saulteaux at the discussions preceding the signing of the numbered treaties were derived from their previous experience.

There can be little doubt that the concept of aboriginal rights, in its narrow and particular sense, is European in origin. From what is known historically of Indian concepts in this area, aboriginal rights were simply the rights of any human collectivity to take all measures necessary to ensure physical and cultural survival in a particular environment. Yet it is equally apparent, when the behaviour of the Saulteaux at the treaties is examined, and when their history in the previous generations is viewed from a particular perspective, that the concept of aboriginal rights had become part of their technique for dealing with the larger dominant community. In this sense, aboriginal rights were as much a part of Saulteaux culture as any other aspect. The fact that the Plains Cree and the members of the Blackfoot Confederacy had not developed such a concept and technique is to be explained in terms of the absence of a significant degree of dependence on European goods and allies after they had lost their middleman role in the fur trade. Whereas the Saulteaux slipped into the familial alliance of increased dependence and decreasing leverage, the Cree had taken an opposite route. Thus it would be the Saulteaux, and not the Plains Cree, who would develop a concept of aboriginal rights by the time of the treaty signings in the 1870s. It is significant that in the discussions surrounding Treaties Six and Seven the language of the familial relationship emerged. The terms "father," "mother," and "brother" were evident. Perhaps the Cree and Blackfoot were facing a crisis familiar to the Saulteaux a century earlier. In such circumstances, an understanding of aboriginal rights as conceived by the Saulteaux could stand the Indian people of the Plains in good stead.

Chapter Seven

Indian-White Relations in the Prairie West during the Fur Trade Period — A Compact?

by
J.E. Foster

The concept of a "compact" between two or more communities is widely recognized in Canadian history. Its most cogent expression is found in the discussion surrounding the nature of Confederation. The concept of the compact has been used to understand the nature of the relationship between the federal and provincial governments and between the French and English communities in Canada.[1] In essence, we appear to have two interrelated compacts, one political and the other cultural. While at different periods and under varying circumstances one or the other of the compacts has tended to predominate, it is significant that both views have received recognition simultaneously. Speaking in the House of Commons, 20 March 1924, Arthur Meighen gave expression to this view:

> It could never be said that our constitutional position rests on a basis of contract merely as between the provinces and the whole Dominion . . . . it also rests on the foundation of a contract as between minorities and majorities, even not identical with provinces . . . .[2]

While historically such a view has tended to be used to articulate rights and responsibilities respecting relations between the French and English communities, one wonders whether in such a view there is not room for an Indian-white compact in Canadian history?

The compact concept receives wide, though not universal, acceptance because it performs two interrelated functions. First, it structures historical data in a meaningful manner. Put simplistically in its usual context, the

---

[1] The most recent, succinct discussion of the compact thesis is found in G.F.G. Stanley, "Act or Pact: Another Look at Confederation," *Report of the Canadian Historical Association* (1956).

[2] As quoted in G.F.G. Stanley, *A Short History of the Canadian Constitution* (Toronto: Ryerson Press, 1969), p. 81.

Canadian Compact is seen as the product of the learning experience of colonists and Canadians in the period between the Conquest and Confederation. The unfolding record of particular solutions to particular problems, engendered by changing circumstances and events, articulates specific understandings. At a particular time during the decades of the 1840s and 1850s, the specific understandings coalesce to create a general understanding in which each community recognizes the right of the other to pursue its ends, with the proviso that the ends and the manner in which they are realized are not antithetical to those of the other community.[3] Such a state of affairs implies continuing and frequent consultation between the two communities. Equally prominent in the general understanding is the view that in many areas of mutual concern the co-operation of both communities is required. It matters not that lawyers and political scientists cannot denote a document or documents constituting a clear and all-inclusive statement of the compact.[4] It existed in the words and thoughts of many Canadians. Needless to say, compact enthusiasts see the understanding continuing after Confederation, its pragmatic and dynamic nature permitting the redefinition or re-emphasis of specific understandings to meet the needs of succeeding generations.

For many Canadians, the second function of the compact arises out of its first function. The concept of a compact is not unique to Canadian experience, but the particular understandings of the Canadian Compact are unique to our experience. Many Canadians feel that this politico-cultural achievement is worthy of recognition and perhaps emulation by others. The survival of Confederation suggests its validity and utility today. The compact denotes reciprocal rights and responsibilities of each collectivity. While confrontation seems to be the order of the day in debate on specific issues with each party identifying its rights and ignoring its responsibilities, the existence of the compact usually elicits a recognition of the other's rights and thus an implied responsibility. Further, the criteria for a solution in the context of a compact are not administrative efficiency, the realization of a particular political philosophy, or the ''victory'' of one collectivity's interests over the interests of another. The criterion for a solution is a fair and equitable result embodying the interests of all parties to the compact.

Sufficient evidence has been amassed to demonstrate that the white community during the last century, principally through the actions of its government, has not recognized a compact in its relations with the various Indian peoples.[5] The reason may be quite simple: no compact existed. Yet

---

[3] Difficulty is encountered in locating a full and detailed articulation of the specific aspects of the compact. Nevertheless, its existence, implied or stated, is frequently found in numerous works examining Canadian problems. See Ramsay Cook, *The Maple Leaf Forever: Essays on Nationalism and Politics in Canada* (Toronto: Macmillan Co. of Canada, 1971).

[4] Readers will recognize my paraphrasing of Stanley, ''Act or Pact,'' p. 13.

[5] Examples are too numerous to list. One case study, however, is of particular note: A.D. Fisher, ed., ''Our Betrayed Wards,'' by R.N. Wilson, *Western Canadian Journal of Anthropology* 4, no. 1 (1974).

such a rejoinder ignores the very real dissatisfaction, perhaps even a sense of betrayal, expressed by many Indian people. No doubt much of their dissatisfaction and unrest can be explained in terms similar to situations experienced by other "third world" peoples.[6] But perhaps in the Canadian context there may be another facet to the so-called "Indian problem." While Indian dissatisfaction is often expressed in terms of specific issues, is there not an underlying thread of continuity? The Indian's litany of lament, revolving around such apparently disparate issues as hunting, trapping, and fishing rights, land claims, health services, control of education, and economic development has a common denominator. A sense of betrayal underlies the words of Indian spokesmen, be they relatively young, politicized leaders or elders on the reserves relating past experience to current circumstances. This sense of betrayal is in essence a historical interpretation. It suggests that at some point in the past an agreement, an understanding, a pact, a contract, call it what you will, existed between the Indian and white communities. With the passage of time, through acts of omission and commission, the white community has abrogated its responsibilities. It has failed "to keep the faith."

Another dimension through which Indians in the Prairie West express their dissatisfaction centres around their view of a special relationship with the monarch.[7] While not articulated with clarity to the white mind, the argument suggests an inviolable agreement between the Indians and the monarch. With the passage of time, officials of the monarch, not the monarch itself, have betrayed this understanding. Rather, the monarch is seen as a special protector against officialdom. Cynics may see this argument as clever manipulation of the sensibilities of some Euro-Canadians by Indian leaders. While this assessment cannot be totally discounted, it ignores the depth and breadth of the concept among the Indian people of western Canada. Dare we suggest the concept of a compact to explain this historical understanding? More important, will historical data support this understanding?

Time and space do not permit a thorough examination of this question on a national basis. In addition, detailed historical studies of specific issues and problems have not as yet been made. Sufficient materials exist, however, to provide some conclusions as to Indian-white relations in the area later known as the Northern Department of Rupert's Land (roughly the three Prairie provinces today) during the two centuries preceding Confederation in 1870. It is the contention of this paper that in the region under study, during the first century and a half of the fur trade, the essence of an understanding, a

---

[6] This emphasis is found in numerous works. Note particularly E. Palmer Patterson, *The Canadian Indian: A History Since 1500* (Don Mills, Ont.: Collier-Macmillan Canada, 1971).

[7] Outside formal addresses occasioned by a visit of the ruling monarch, I have not been able to find this view articulated in print. Yet conversations with Indians and with those who have worked with Indians attest to its existence and importance.

compact, emerged between Indian and white traders; that the compact was further clarified and delineated during the succeeding half-century when the Hudson's Bay Company enjoyed monopolistic control; and that the desire to continue significant aspects of this compactual relationship constituted an important part of the "mental set" with which the Indian leaders approached the treaty negotiations in the 1870s.

Before continuing the discussion, it is necessary to give some explanation as to the validity of the limits that delineate this study. "The Northern Department of Rupert's Land from 1670 to 1870" smacks of historical categorization from a paleface perspective. In the absence, however, of detailed tribal histories from an Indian perspective, such categories will have to suffice.[8] By the same token, with some flexibility, traditional categories may accommodate an Indian view. Obviously the different Indian bands would have a more limited territorial perspective than the Northern Department of Rupert's Land. The fur trade, however, which was a major influence in the lives of all Indian bands, including the Plains tribes, was structured and conducted on a "department-wide" basis.[9] Thus, while the Northern Department did not bear directly on the lives of Indian bands, the fur trade gave it an indirect relevance that cannot be ignored. Similarly, the dates that define the era of this study are equally defensible. 1670 marked the founding of the Hudson's Bay Company and the establishment of what would become the "Bay trading system." At the same time, the French and their allies were establishing themselves on the Upper Great Lakes.[10] From this base, the "St. Lawrence trading system" would penetrate westward. In a relatively few years, European goods, if not Europeans, were familiar to the Indian peoples of the West. Their impact economically, socially, and politically would be apparent to every Indian. For all practical purposes, the year 1820 marks the end of competition between the St. Lawrence system and the Bay system. While the Hudson's Bay Company was victorious, it incorporated many of the techniques and personnel of its vanquished rival. With monopolistic control, the Company took steps to stabilize its conduct of the trade and develop its long-range

---

[8] Recently, histories by Indians from an Indian perspective have begun to emerge. Note particularly R.M. Buck, ed., *Voices of the Plains Cree*, by Edgar Ahenakew (Toronto: McClelland and Stewart, 1973); and Chief Albert Edward Thompson, *Chief Peguis and His Descendants* (Winnipeg: Peguis Publishers, 1973).

[9] For a detailed history of the West to 1870, readers should consult Arthur S. Morton, *A History of the Canadian West to 1870-71*, 2nd ed., ed. Lewis G. Thomas (Toronto: University of Toronto Press, 1973). An excellent, detailed business history of the Hudson's Bay Company can be found in E.E. Rich, *The History of Hudson's Bay Company, 1670-1870*, 2 vols. (London: The Hudson's Bay Record Society, 1958-59). Both of the above works should explain historical data not fully elaborated upon in this paper. With reference to the Northern Department, see R.H. Fleming, ed., *Minutes of the Council, Northern Department of Rupert's Land, 1821-31*, with an Introduction by H.A. Innis (London: 1940).

[10] W.J. Eccles, *The Canadian Frontier, 1534-1760* (Toronto: Holt, Rinehart, 1969).

potential. The impact on the Indians was immediate.[11] The terminal date of the study, 1870, would have less relevance to the Indians outside the immediate environs of the Red River Settlement, although word of the disturbance carried into the Interior and had an impact. Possibly the greater significance of 1870 to the Indian was the fact that it marked the mid-point between the Company's decline and the signing of the treaties during the 1870s.[12] Thus it would appear at this time that both the area and the era under study are amenable to analysis from a Euro-Canadian and an Indian vista.

Fundamentally, the relationship between the Indian and the European trader was based upon the co-operative exploitation of the fur resources of the region.[13] From the beginning, each party specialized in what its heritage designated as the most appropriate tasks. The Indian harvested furs and provisions, prepared them for exchange, and transported them to a place where they could be exchanged for European goods. Europeans provided products adapted to Indian tastes and needs as well as auxiliary services required to ensure a successful hunt. To be successful, European traders had to recognize the Indian's view of the fur trade and act in an appropriate manner. It was the French on the St. Lawrence who first acquired this knowledge and later, through Pierre Radisson and Médard Chouart, Sieur des Groseillers, passed the essential knowledge to the English on Hudson Bay.[14]

Contrary to our dehumanized view of commerce as solely an economic exchange between buyer and seller, the Indian saw the commercial aspects of trade as inseparable from the more important political aspects of intergroup relations. To the Indian, trade was a mechansim for enhancing security.[15] It was the means by which alliances were established with other bands. From an Indian point of view, he was technically at war with all people with whom he did not have an alliance.[16] Political alliances were validated by the exchange of gifts and on occasion by the establishment of kin connections through

---

[11] One of the most immediate changes, though perhaps not the most important, was the drastic decline in the amount of liquor available in the Interior. Gov. George Simpson to Andrew Colvile, 20 May 1822, Selkirk Papers, Public Archives of Canada, Ottawa, vol. 24.

[12] I am marking the Company's decline as June 1863. See E.E. Rich, *Hudson's Bay Company*, 2: 816.

[13] The best account as to the economic structure of the fur trade remains Harold Adams Innis, *The Fur Trade in Canada: An Introduction to Canadian Economic History* (Toronto: University of Toronto Press, 1962); see also Arthur J. Ray, *Indians in the Fur Trade: Their Role as Trappers, Hunters and Middlemen in the Lands Southwest of Hudson's Bay, 1660-1860* (Toronto: University of Toronto Press, 1974).

[14] Rich, *Hudson's Bay Company*, 1: chapter 3; see also Sandra Nekich, "The Feast of the Dead: The Origin of Indian-White Trade Ceremonies in the West," *Western Canadian Journal of Anthropology* 4, no. 1 (1974).

[15] Abraham Rotstein, "Trade and Politics: An Institutional Approach," *Western Canadian Journal of Anthropology* 3, no. 1 (1972).

[16] George T. Hunt, *Wars of the Iroquois: A Study in Intertribal Trade Relations* (Madison, Wis.: University of Wisconsin Press, 1960), p. 20.

marriage and adoption.[17] The individual's participation in these exchanges constituted an expression of his agreement with the decision of the band and his personal commitment to the relationship. In Indian eyes, what was true for Indian participants was true for whites as well.

The exchange of gifts was crucial to the establishment or revalidation of any alliance. In 1684, a Huron had murdered a Frenchman. A Jesuit priest recorded the ceremony revalidating the alliance with the French:

> Our Christians [Hurons] had informed us of all their customs and exhorted us to observe them exactly, unless we would arouse prejudice. . . . The Captains divided the sticks among them, so that every nation should contribute toward the presents which we asked. For this purpose every one went to his own village. No individual was obliged to make this contribution, but they vie with one another, according as they are more or less rich, in sharing those public burdens, in order to show their devotion to the common weal. . . .
>
> The following morning, in the presence of a great multitude assembled from every direction, they made a sort of stage in a public square, where they suspended 50 gifts, which form the principal satisfaction. . . . In return we also made gifts to each of the eight nations, to bind up again and to confirm the old friendship; to exhort them to be always united and at peace, both among themselves and with the French, in order the better to resist their enemies; . . . to console them for the loss of some of theirs, killed by the enemies; and finally to assure them that . . . all the French would forever forget that murder, for which they had, according to their custom, made full satisfaction.[18]

Similar ceremonies fit other situations. The Huron Feast of the Dead, held every eight to twelve years, utilized gift giving as an essential part of the ceremony, cementing relations within the confederacy and with Algonkian-speaking allies to the north. In point of fact, it would appear that this ceremony became the basis of the fur trade ceremony which swept across the continent.[19]

In effect, Indian alliances for the major purpose of security required a ceremony in which gift giving played a crucial role. The ceremony was the vehicle through which participating bands recognized each other as classificatory "we" rather than "they." Cultural differences of course remained as, for example, between the Algonkian hunters and the Huron farmers. Yet for the purposes of intertribal relations, each would regard the other as "we." Similarly, for the fur trade to succeed, the Indian had to be able to regard the trader as "we." This in turn demanded appropriate

---

[17] The importance of these factors has not been emphasized in historical works dealing with the fur trade. Yet from the time of Champlain, both marriage and adoption have been important mechanisms for facilitating relations between Indian bands and between Indians and whites. See Alexander Ross, *Fur Hunters of the Far West*, ed. Kenneth A. Spaulding (Norman , Okla.: University of Oklahoma Press, 1956), p. 195, for a fur trader's views on the importance of an Indian wife.

[18] Reuben G. Thwaites, ed., *Jesuit Relations & Allied Documents: The Travels & Explorations of the Jesuit Missionaries in New France, 1610-1791*, 73 vols. in 36 (Lotowa, N.J.: Rocoman & Littlefield, 1959), 38: 273-78.

[19] Nekich, "Feast of the Dead": 15.

behaviour on the part of the trader. He had to demonstrate in his words and deeds that he accepted the responsibilities and obligations inherent in the alliance.

Particular circumstances played a significant role in determining the particular nature of the "we" relationship between various Indian bands and the traders.[20] At a vast distance from the traders were the hunting and trapping Indians who rarely, if ever, saw the European trader, although they were intimately familiar with his goods. Their indirect link with the trader was the "Upland" Indian, who functioned as the middleman in the fur trade. In relatively large expeditions, bands of Upland Indians made the annual journey to trade at the posts of Europeans. They returned to the Interior using their newly acquired European wares before trading them to the trapping Indians for their furs. A third category of Indians participated in the fur trade as well. Known as the "Homeguard" or "House" Indians, such bands supplied provisions in addition to furs. With time, other country produce, such as leather, snowshoes, and goose quills were traded at the fort. The Homeguard Indians supplied services in addition to country produce. As couriers, guides, and interpreters, they played an increasingly significant role in the overall conduct of the fur trade. Living in close proximity to the European traders, they would enjoy the most material benefits. Also they would harvest the bitter fruit of disease and alcoholism.

Those Indian bands who functioned as middlemen in the fur trade knew they were essential to its success. Even more important, they seemed to know that the trader saw them as the linchpin in the politico-economic alliance system that constituted the fur trade. As both parties to the system, the middlemen Indians and the European traders, were armed with this knowledge, the nature of the relationship evolving between them emphasized the treatment of each by the other as an equal. Neither party, in his own mind, saw himself as inferior to the other. This relationship in turn determined the nature of the demands that each party could make upon the other. Political skill in the fur trade, for both Indian and white, involved pressing demands in a manner that the other party could not deny while as the same time parrying, in an appropriate fashion, the demands of the other party. On all occasions, however, whether in pressing demands or parrying those of the other party, the strength and stability of the alliance had to be preserved, or better still, enhanced. A demand that placed a strain on the alliance was a political *faux pas* of the most serious consequences.

The "equality" emphasized in the relationship between the middleman Indian and the European trader and the nature of the demands that this relationship permitted were apparent in the ceremonial actions and the

---

[20] Ray, *Indians in Fur Trade*, chapters two and three, provides a detailed examination of the subject matter introduced in this paragraph.

conduct of the trade at York Factory near the mid-point of the eighteenth century. It is noteworthy how European practices and symbolic actions had been interwoven into the ceremony. It is further noteworthy that the European practices were modelled upon ceremony derived from relations between friendly nations in Europe. Chief Factor Andrew Graham began his description of the conduct of the fur trade with the arrival of the Upland Indians at the fort.

> Several fowling pieces are discharged from the canoes to salute the Fort, and the compliment is returned by a round of twelve pounders, less or more for each division, and the Great Flag flying from the Fort, as it continues to do every day they stay.
>
> The Governor being informed that Leaders are arrived, sends the Trader to introduce them singly, or two or three together with their lieutenants, which are usually eldest sons or highest relations. Chairs are placed in the room, and pipes with smoking materials produced on the table. The captains place themselves on each side the Governor, but not a word proceeds from either party, until everyone has recruited his spirits with a full pipe. The silence is then broken by degrees by the most venerable Indian, his head bowed down and eyes immovably fixed on the floor, or other object. He tells how many canoes he has brought, what kind of winter they have had, what natives he has seen, are coming, or stay behind, asks how the Englishmen do, and says he is glad to see them. After which the Governor bids him welcome, tells him he has good goods and plenty; and that he loves the Indians and will be kind to them. The pipe is by this time renewed and the conversation becomes free, easy and general.
>
> The guests being now equipped, a basket of bread and prunes is brought and set before the captain, who takes care to fill his pockets with them before it goes out to be shared amongst his followers; together with a two gallon runlet of brandy, tobacco and pipes. The Second had one gallon of brandy.
>
> Everything being prepared he is conducted to his tent with a procession. In the front are the spontoons and ensigns, next the drummer beating march, then several of the Factory servants bearing the bread, prunes, etc. Then comes the captain, walking quite erect and stately, smoking his pipe and conversing with the Governor and his officers; then follow the Second, and perhaps a friend or two who was permitted to come in with the Chief. The tent is all ready for their reception, and clean birch-rind or beaver coats are spread on the ground for the Chief to sit on; and before him are deposited the prunes, etc. The Chief then makes a speech to his followers, and then orders his lieutenant, or some respectable person, to distribute the presents, never performing this himself. I must take notice that the women and children are last served; the slaves get a little also. . . .
>
> The league of friendship must be renewed by smoking the calumet, and the guns, tobacco, and other goods are to be viewed, and the measures examined, before anything else is purchased. In order to do this, the captain collects the Puc'ca'tin'ash'a'win which is a collection of a skin or two from each man to form a present for the Governor. As the ceremony of smoking the calumet is necessary to establish a confidence, it is conducted with the greatest solemnity, and every person belonging to the gang is admitted on the occasion. The captain walks in with his calumet in his hand covered with a case, then comes the lieutenant and the wives of the captains with the present, and afterwards all the other men with the women and their little ones.
>
> The Governor is genteely dressed after the English fashion, and received them with cordiality and good humour. The captain covers the table with a new beaver coat, and on it lays the calumet or pipe; he will also sometimes present the Governor with a

clean beaver toggy or banian to keep him warm in the winter. The Puc'ca'tin'ash'a'win is also presented. Then the Governor sits down in an arm-chair, the captain and chief men on either hand on chairs; the others sit round on the floor; the women and children are placed behind; and a profound silence ensues. The calumet being lighted by the Governor, a servant holding the bowl and applying the fire, it is pointed towards the east, south, west and north parts of the hemisphere, also to the zenith, and nadir. Every man takes a certain number of whiffs as fixed by the owner of the pipe, and thus it passes round the circle. When out, it is delivered again to the Governor who repeats the manoeuvres as when he lighted it; at which all the men pronounce the monosyllable Ho! which is expressive of thanks. The women never touch the calumet, but smoke the common pipes as usual. A respectful silence again reigns for a few moments and then the captain makes his speech in a low voice at first, but rises as he proceeds, his hands are placed on his knees, and head hung down.

"You told me last year to bring many Indians, you see I have not lied, here are a great many young men come with me; use them kindly, use them kindly I say! We lived hard last winter and hungry, the powder being expended, the powder being expended I say. Tell your servants to fill the measure up to the brim; take pity on us, take pity on us I say. We paddle a long way to see you. We love the English, let us trade good black tobacco, moist and hard twisted, let us see it before opened; take pity on us, take pity on us I say. The guns are bad; let us trade light guns, small in the hand and well shaped with locks that will not freeze in the winter, and red gun-cases. Let the young men have more than measure; roll tobacco cheap; kettles thick, high for the shape and size, strong ears and the bale to lap upon the sides; give us good measure in cloth, let us see the old measure: do you mind me, the young men love you by coming to see you; take pity I say and give them good goods; they love to dress and be fine; do you understand me."

All the time he is speaking his eyes are fixed on the ground, and the hearers all silent except the Chief [Factor] who now and then pronounces Hawoko (i.e.) very well, or listen to what you say; and at the end of all speeches made either by the Factor or Indians the bearers pronounce Ho Ho Ho o o. The Factor in his turn tells them that the great man in England loves the Indians so well, that with great trouble and danger, sends the great ship yearly full of goods to supply their wants, and strongly talks to them not to be lazy but get furs in the winter, and all the young men to come down with their canoes full of beaver, etc., and not to bring moose skin pelts, and he tells the women to bring down the castoreum and he will trade it with them for beads, etc., and harangues upon the largeness of the measures, and the smallness of the Canadians, strongly advising them not to deal with them, etc. After the Governor has done speaking they begin to tell what hardships they undergo in coming down, from the long distance and want of food, etc. If they have lost any friend by war or otherwise they set up a howl and crying without shedding a tear, which often surprises the English that have not been used to them and their manners. Then the measures for powder, shot, cloth, and tobacco are produced and examined, and thus ends the ceremony . . . .

At the departure of a captain and his gang, the cannon from the Fort is fired and every kind of respect paid them that is in our power. What else has prevented rupture on either part these hundred years past? It certainly must be attributed to the justice, kindness and affability which has always been annually directed by the Company, and followed by their Factors.[21]

---

[21] Glyndwr Williams, ed., *Andrew Graham's Observations on Hudson's Bay 1767-91*, with an Introduction by Richard Glover (London: The Hudson's Bay Record Society, 1969), pp. 316-24.

At the time Graham recorded his description of the fur trade ceremony, the ceremony and the relationship between Indian and white that it entailed had existed for over a century. In parts of Canada, the essence of this relationship would survive for at least another one hundred and fifty years. This time span is of the utmost significance. Not only does it signify its success as a mechanism to facilitate Indian-white relations, it demonstrates the acceptance by Indian and white alike of a compactual relationship. Clashes, often violent, occurred; but they remained incidents.[22] The norm was the relationship spelled out in the fur trade ceremony, the classificatory "we" relationship. Between the middleman and the trader, the relationship tended to emphasize equal status and permitted each to make particular demands on the other.

In the dialogue recorded by Graham, it is significant that in comparison with the St. Lawrence trading system, economic factors rather than political factors were emphasized. This state of affairs was a function of both geographical circumstances and the Hudson's Bay Company's "coast-side factory" trading policy.[23] Yet the political relationship implied in the ceremony cannot be ignored. This political relationship continued to be important when the Company penetrated the Interior to meet the competition of traders from Montreal.

The conquest of New France had an impact upon Indian-white relations conducted through the St. Lawrence trading system. Whereas the French had placed heavy emphasis on the political relationship, the British tended to place more emphasis on commerce. In many instances, the French fur trade appeared more as a tool of, rather than a reason for, French imperial expansion in North America.[24] Nevertheless, the British government continued to recognize the importance of Indian alliances for over half a century after their initial mishandling of Indian relations as evidenced in Pontiac's uprising.[25] From the Indian viewpoint, the nature of the relationship appeared to remain the same. In 1811, Nathaniel Atcheson of the North West Company wrote:

> It is to be understood, though it may be difficult to convey the idea, that the relations of buyer and seller, of trader and consumer, hardly enter into the view of the Indian—of the Indian, at least, who lives remote from European settlements; . . . he hunts, and through friendship and in the spirit of generosity he brings his furs to the trader: the trader he regards as a representative of His Majesty, through whose friendship and goodwill manufactures are permitted to be brought, and to be

---

[22] The myth of non-violence in the West during the fur trade period belies the facts. Nevertheless, the "message" of the myth, violence as isolated incidents rather than the normal state of relations between Indian and white, is essentially valid.

[23] Rich, *Hudson's Bay Company*, 1: 436.

[24] Eccles, *Canadian Frontier*, p. 145.

[25] Hilda Neatby, *Quebec: The Revolutionary Age, 1760-91* (Toronto: McClelland and Stewart, 1966), p. 10.

presented to him in return. Here, therefore, are less of the cold relations of trade, than of the warm one of national and individual attachment . . .[26]

The penetration of the Interior by the Hudson's Bay Company and the North West Company altered many of the circumstances in which the fur trade was conducted. Among the changes were the disappearance of the trading bands and an increase in the numbers of bands who lived as Homeguard or House Indians.[27] These bands, in becoming increasingly dependent upon the traders, were fairly intimately associated with the trading post. Often, ties of kindship linked them to the personnel of the fort. In many ways, the commercial aspects of the trade were accentuated, with the trading post tending to become a general store and recreation center. But it is significant that on every visit a form of the trading ceremony, albeit much abbreviated, was observed. As one trader noted:

It is unnecessary telling always in the journal that every Indian who arrives, whether good, bad, or indifferent, gets a bit of tobacco and a dram; it suffices to tell, once, that it is the custom of the place, and anyone who reads of an Indian's arrival may suppose that this custom is followed . . .[28]

Would not this ''custom of the place'' sustain, in the mind of the Indian, the compact concept of the relationship?

From 1820 to 1870, the Hudson's Bay Company enjoyed a legal monopoly of the fur trade in what they designated as the Northern Department of Rupert's Land. In frontier areas where they faced competition from American-based traders, they met and successfully fought, except for the last two decades, all competitors. In these areas, it would appear that the historical relationship between Indian and white in the fur trade withered and died. To a significant degree the European market-place of buyer and seller became the normal state of affairs.[29] But this was not so in the Interior where the Company maintained its monopoly. There the Company and the Indian maintained and further articulated the traditional relationship.

The particular features of the fur trade relationship differed in various regions of the Northern Department. Among the Bush Indians, where their numbers and particular circumstances of dependence gave the Company a position of dominance, the relationship took a particular form. Among the Plains Indians, particularly the Plains Cree and the members of the Blackfoot Confederacy, where numbers and circumstances allowed the Indians to be virtually independent of the Company's influence, the relationship was

---

[26] Rotstein, ''Trade and Politics'': 13.

[27] Williams, *Observations on Hudson's Bay*, p. 192.

[28] L.F. Masson, *Bourgeois de la Compagnie du Nord Ouest: récits de voyages, lettres et rapports inédits relatif au Nord-ouest*, 2 vols. (Atlantic Highlands, N.J.: Humanities Press, 1960), 2: 381.

[29] Gov. George Simpson, British Parliamentary Select Committee on the Hudson's Bay Company, 2 March 1857.

expressed in a manner reminiscent of Graham's description of the conduct of the trade with the Upland Indians. Rev. Robert Rundle described such a ceremony at Rocky Mountain House in 1841:

> A large party of Blackfeet and Pegans arrived and their entrance into the Fort presented a very novel appearance. The first party that came were the Pegans. Before they started from their camp which was near the Fort they sang and then sedately marched in order to the Fort. The chief leading the van bringing with him a white horse, the head of which was stripped [sic] with red ochre, as a present to Mr. Harriott. On his approaching near the entrance Mr. H. went forward to meet him and when they met a salute was fired by the Chief's band behind him and the horse given in charge of one of the Company's servants. The party then marched on to the Fort and on the Chief arriving a salute was fired by men stationed there for that purpose.[30]

Henry Moberly described a similar occasion at the same post in the 1850s.[31] For the purposes of trade, the members of the Blackfoot Confederacy viewed and treated the personnel of the Company as classificatory "we."

With the Bush Indians, the particulars of the relationship were altered. The Company, with its control of European goods, was a major influence in the lives of small Indian bands, in the person of the trader. With this position of influence went some sense of responsibility. In part this sense of responsibility reflected social concerns expressed in Great Britain through the plethora of societies created to facilitate good works in Britain and in the Empire at large. Among these societies were several who looked to what they thought were the interests of various aboriginal peoples. This increased social consciousness had an impact on the directors of the Company and the officers whom they appointed.[32] This impact served to reinforce the traditional manner ("by fayre and gentle means") in which the Company believed it had treated the Indian.[33] This in turn served to reinforce not only the Company's view but the Indian's view of their relationship. It was in this period that some traditional practices were regularized and structured. An example in what might be termed the field of health and social welfare was given in the testimony of Dr. John Rae before the Parliamentary Select Committee on the Hudson's Bay Company, on 23 February 1857. One of the committee members began his interrogation of Rae as follows:

> 673. In a letter from Sir George Simpson, which is to be found in some papers laid before Parliament in 1842, he says: "Our different trading establishments are the resort or refuge of many of the natives who, from age, infirmity, or other causes, are unable to follow the chase; they have the benefit of the care and attention, free of

---

[30] H.A. Dempsey, "Western Plains Trade Ceremonies," *Western Canadian Journal of Anthropology 3*, no. 1 (1972): 30.

[31] Ibid.: 31.

[32] To varying degrees, the directors of the Hudson's Bay Company reflected this interest: see Rich, *Hudson's Bay Company*, 2: 345-46. For the criteria used in selecting officers, see Edward Ellice, M.P., British Parliamentary Select Committee on the Hudson's Bay Company, 23 June 1857.

[33] Rich, *Hudson's Bay Company*, 1: 145.

expense, of our medical men, of whom about 12 are usually employed in the service; every trading establishment being in fact an Indian hospital.'' How far does your experience as a medical man in the service of the Company bear that out?—Wherever we act as medical men our services are given gratuitously. We go to a distance if an Indian is at a distance, and have him taken to a fort, and he is fed and clothed there. And it is no uncommon thing to hear the old Indians, when unfit for hunting, say, ''We are unfit for work; we will go and reside at a fort.'' That is the ordinary feeling which prevailed in the country. Although there are no medical men up at the different posts (there may be the number Sir George has mentioned scattered over the country), yet medicines are sent up to all the posts in regular supplies . . .

676. Then, in short, you think that if a statement were made, that the Directors of the Hudson's Bay Company considered that it was their business to attend to the Company's own servants, but not to any other class of the population, it would be a false charge?—Perfectly erroneous; in fact the Indian is more readily attended to generally then the others.

677. And as a rule the medical men appointed by the Company would not consider it their sole duty to attend to the Company's servants?—Certainly not; they are there for the Indians as much as for the Company's people . . .

679. During that time what was the average number of the worn-out hunters who lived there upon your charity?—I cannot exactly tell that. The population of the place was, I think, about 180 altogether; few Indians came there; but there were generally two or three or four old families, or six sometimes, pensioners at the place. They called at the Fort; they were there regularly every week; they had their encampment at the place, and they went and hunted at intervals as they were able, and if they were not able to get food enough, they had it given to them . . .

683. Mr. Labouchere (Chairman of the Committee) wishes to know whether anything is done with respect to vaccination?—Yes; vaccine matter is sent to all the posts. I may mention a curious fact, which is, that in the year 1835 the small-pox was brought up by a steamboat from the States. A gentleman at the Saskatchewan vaccinated all the Cree Indians that came in; and there was scarcely a single case occurred among the tribe; we supposed it was because they had all been vaccinated; whereas deaths took place amongst the more distant tribes, near the Missouri. The small-pox was brought up by steam-boat up the Missouri, and was brought over to the Saskatchewan by a quantity of horse stealers, who heard that the disease was at the Missouri, and went to steal horses there. They found the Indians dying by hundreds; they took the disease with them, and most of them died upon the road.[34]

Gov. George Simpson, in his testimony, expanded upon this field in terms of Indian-white relations. As with Rae, Simpson's testimony applied largely to the Bush Indians.

1526. I will direct your attention to arms; in what way are they sold; are they sold by barter or for money?—They are sold by barter.

1527. For so many skins?—For so many skins.

1528. When you sell a gun to an Indian, do you ever take inferior skins for that gun?—We outfit the Indian.

1529. Cannot you answer me that question?—We do not sell a gun for skins; we give the gun to the Indian, as everything else, on credit and he pays for those supplies in the spring of the year.

---

[34] Rae, British Parliamentary Select Committee on the Hudson's Bay Company, 23 February 1857.

1530. Supposing a gun is sold to an Indian, would you take in payment an inferior kind of skins?—We take in payment whatever he can give us.

1531. If an Indian had nothing but musk rat skins, you would take those?—Yes.

1532. Do you mean to tell me that?—I mean to say that we would take from an Indian whatever he could give us. The Indian must have certain supplies.

1533. My question is a very plain one; would you take musk rat skins in payment for a gun from an Indian?—Certainly, we take whatever the Indian can give us.

1534. And you mean to state that to me, that guns are sold to Indians with the full understanding that they may pay you back in musk rat skins?—If an Indian has nothing but musk rat skins, we will take musk rat skins.

1535. Supposing that were to occur with an Indian once, would he be likely to get a second gun?—Yes, decidedly, if he required it.

1536. And you say that notwithstanding that, he (the Indian) is better off in the interior than he is on the frontier, because in the one case he gets spirituous liquors, and in the other case he does not?—And in other respects. The Indian in the interior depends upon us for all his supplies; whether he is able to pay for them or not, he gets them; he gets his blankets, he gets his gun, and he gets his ammunition. If from death in his family, or any other cause, he makes no hunt, it cannot be helped.[35]

In terms of the Indians in general and their political relationship with the Company, further testimony by Simpson strengthens the impression that has emerged previously:

1747. What privileges or rights do the native Indian possess strictly applicable to themselves?—They are perfectly at liberty to do what they please; we never restrain Indians.

1748. Is there any difference between their position and that of the half-breed?—None at all. They hunt and fish, and live as they please. They look to us for their supplies, and we study their comfort and convenience as much as possible; we assist each other.

1749. You exercise no authority whatever over the Indian tribes?—None at all.

1750. If any tribe were pleased now to live as the tribes did live before the country was opened up to Europeans; that is to say, not using any article of European manufacture or trade, it would be in their power to do so?—Perfectly so; we exercise no control over them.

1751. Do you mean that, possessing the right of soil over the whole of Rupert's Land, you do not consider that you possess any jurisdiction over the inhabitants of the soil?—No, I am not aware that we do. We exercise none, whatever right we possess under our charter.

1752. Then is it the case that you do not consider that the Indians are under your jurisdiction when any crimes are committed by the Indians upon the Whites?—They are under our jurisdiction when crimes are committed upon the Whites, but not when committed upon each other; we do not meddle with their wars.

1753. What law do you consider in force in the case of the Indians committing any crime upon the Whites; do you consider that the clause in your licence to trade, by which you are bound to transport criminals to Canada for trial, refers to the Indians, or solely to the Whites?—To the Whites, we conceive.

1754. Are the native Indians permitted to barter skins *inter se* from one tribe to another?—Yes.

---

[35] See footnote 29.

1755. There is no restriction at all in that respect?—None at all.[36]

The testimony of Rae and Simpson was obviously favourable to the Company's interests. Yet other witnesses, hostile to the Company, did not destroy their evidence. The particulars of the relationship between Indian and trader that Rae and Simpson articulated did in fact exist.

Beginning in the 1840s and gathering momentum as the years passed were developments that spelled an end to the relationship existing between Indian and trader. The appearance of the missionary heralded the beginning of the end. With his goal of evangelization and civilization, he tended to prove disruptive in terms of the traditional relationship between the Company and the Indian.[37] In later years, however, certain individual missionaries would prove to be able friends of specific bands during the difficult years of transition.[38] The free trader followed the missionary. Often of mixed blood and frequently related by blood and marriage to the bands with whom he traded, the free trader lacked the means, though he could well have had the inclination, to provide the auxiliary health and social services available at the Company's posts.[39] All too frequently his major stock in trade was alcohol. A change in the ownership of the Hudson's Bay Company in 1863 further compounded a deteriorating situation. The directors, who could trace back their connection with the fur trade for generations and who had some understanding of the traditional relationship with the Indian, were gone. In their place, perhaps well meaning, were men who looked at profits arising not from furs but from settlement. The actions of these men as they affected the West in the later part of the decade of the 1860s left some bitterness and a sense of betrayal in the minds of many Indians.[40] Into this disintegrating world two crises appeared to threaten the Indian; furs and game, the basis of physical survival, were disappearing; and the Canadians, a threat to cultural survival, were coming.

The subject of negotiations leading up to the signing of each of the treaties requires detailed studies. Nevertheless, sufficient materials exist to suggest an answer to our question as to whether the concept of a compact had meaning for at least some of the Indian leaders involved in the negotiations. An examination of the proceedings, as recorded in Alexander Morris' *The Treaties of Canada with the Indians*,[41] suggests two predominant views

---

[36] Ibid.

[37] While the missionary was disruptive, his actions often represented what he felt were the "Indian's interests" in relation with the Hudson's Bay Company.

[38] Note particularly Rev. George McDougall and Rev. John McDougall at Morley, and Rev. H.B. Steinhauer at Whitefish Lake and Saddle Lake.

[39] The role of the small free-trader has never been adequately examined in this period.

[40] The problems within the Hudson's Bay Company at this time are reflected in D.D. Tway, "The Wintering Partners and the Hudson's Bay Company, 1863 to 1871," *Canadian Historical Review* (1952); see also the words of The Gambler at Treaty Three in Morris, *Treaties*, pp. 101, 109.

[41] Alexander Morris, *The Treaties of Canada with the Indians of Manitoba and the North-West Territories* (1880; reprint ed., Toronto: Coles Publishing Co., 1971).

which have a bearing on the compact concept. The predominant attitude expressed by the Indians at Treaties Six and Seven centred upon physical and cultural survival. They could see that a crisis in game resources was imminent. To this end, they had decided that they would have to make significant changes; thus their requests for agricultural implements and, in the case of the bands of the Blackfoot Confederacy, cattle.[42] Among the Cree at Treaty Six, some concern was expressed that the assistance promised to the Indians was not adequate to make the transition. Poundmaker, in particular, possibly familiar with previous agricultural projects initiated by the missionaries, reiterated his concern in this area.[43] In exchange for having their demands in this area met, the Indians appear to have recognized the legitimacy of the government's right to make demands. Although they probably failed to comprehend fully the nature of the reserves and the white man's legal system, the right of the government to make such demands was recognized. Big Bear most forcefully expressed reservations in this area. In his famous speech in which he dreaded "the rope to be about my neck," it would appear that he was questioning the extent to which the Indian had to culturally adapt to ensure a viable agreement.[44] But at no time did Big Bear question the right of the government to make such a demand.

It is interesting to note the extent to which the Indians made reference to the previous relationship that they had enjoyed with white representatives of the Queen. At Blackfoot Crossing, the emphasis was on the North West Mounted Police.[45] At the Treaty Six signing, it was the Company by implication. In two speeches, Teeteequaysay provided evidence of the importance of the past relationship. His demand "to make some provision for the poor, unfortunate, blind and lame"[46] lent support to the testimony of Dr. John Rae and Gov. George Simpson given before the Parliamentary Committee of the Hudson's Bay Company in 1857. At a later point, Teeteequaysay again made reference to the past relationship: "When we look back to the past we do not see where the Cree nation has ever watered the ground with the whiteman's blood, he has always been our friend and we his; . . . "[47] In other words, we have treated the whites and they have treated us as "we" not "they."

The concept of a compact extending into the future is clearly evident not only in the ceremonial actions that accompanied the signing, but in the words of both whites and Indians. On numerous occasions both Alexander Morris

---

[42] Morris, *Treaties*, pp. 209-14, 268-72.

[43] Ibid., pp. 210-19.

[44] Ibid., p. 240.

[45] Ibid., p. 272.

[46] Ibid., p. 215.

[47] Ibid.

and David Laird emphasized the sanctity of the treaties.[48] Similarly the Indians expressed their appreciation of the treaties as an ongoing relationship. At Treaty Six, Mistawasis emphasized:

> What we speak of and do now will last as long as the sun shines and the river runs, we are looking forward to our children's children, for we are old and have but few days to live.[49]

Another chief, Wawekaninkahootamahote, expressed similar views, adding the ideas of ''sharing the land'' and respect for Indian ways:

> Pity the voice of the Indian, if you grant what we request the sound will echo through the land; open the way; I speak for the children that they may be glad; the land is wide, there is plenty of room . . . have compassion on the manner in which I was brought up; . . . [50]

No discussion of the treaties would be complete without reference to Indian views that suggested compensation and payment for the land and its resources. At Treaty Seven, there was the incident of Button Chief demanding compensation for the white's use of wood for fuel and lumber.[51] Button Chief's views appear to be consistent with what is known of the Indian's concept of land and resources.[52] The land and its resources were open to all who were viewed as ''we,'' but should one party use a resource to the detriment of the other's interests, there should be compensation. Laird's reply that the ''Indians ought to pay us, rather, for sending these traders in firewater away'' caused the assembled Indians to indulge ''in a general hearty laugh at this proposition.''[53] I would suggest that the ''hearty laugh'' recognized Laird's debating skills rather than the rejection of the concept on which Button Chief based his argument. This view found expression at each of the treaty signings. Among the Saulteaux this aspect of the negotiations took on a particular dimension. It is most evident at the negotiations for Treaties Four and Six, where the views of Saulteaux speakers differ rather sharply from those of their Cree allies.

The aboriginal rights aspects of the views of the Saulteaux were evident at treaty signings where they were present. At Treaty Six, Joseph Thoma later repudiated by Red Pheasant, used the phrase ''I have told the *value* I have put on my land.''[54] Nuswasoowatum, in arguing against the treaty, told Morris

---

[48] Ibid., pp. 208, 267.

[49] Ibid., p. 213.

[50] Ibid., p. 215.

[51] Ibid., p. 270.

[52] To date, the best explanation of an Indian concept of land and land ownership is found in E.T. Denig, ''Indian Tribes of the Upper Missouri,'' *46th Annual Report of the Bureau of American Ethnology, 1928-29* (Washington, D.C.: 1929), pp. 476-78. The view is remarkably similar to that expressed in the Valley of the St. Lawrence early in the seventeenth century.

[53] Morris, *Treaties*, p. 271.

[54] Ibid., p. 220.

that "through what you have done you have cheated my kinsmen."[55] At Treaty Four, The Gambler, in contrast to the Cree chief Loud Voice, expressed a strong sense of bitterness and betrayal towards the Hudson's Bay Company. The company's surveying of a reserve of land was criticized as "these Indians you see sitting around report that they only allowed the store to be put up."[56] Earlier, The Gambler expressed himself more forcefully: "The Company have stolen our land."[57] A colleague, Pisquia, pointing to a Company officer, stated: "You told me you had sold your land for so much money, £300,000. We want that money."[58] Yet at the same time the Plains Saulteaux also gave recognition to the traditional Indian view of the relationship with the Company. Later in the negotiations, The Gambler emphasized: "This Company man that we were speaking about, I do not hate him; as I loved him before I love him still, and I also want that the way he loved me at first he should love me the same; . . . "[59] After Morris' reply, The Gambler stated:

> I do not want to drive the Company anywhere . . . . Supposing you wanted to take them away, I would not let them go. I want them to remain here . . . we always exchange with them, and would die if they went away.[60]

At Treaty Six, Nuswasoowatum based his accusation of "cheating" in part on an argument voiced by Button Chief at Treaty Seven. The Indians had their ways; the whites had theirs. Both parties had shared in the past, but now the whites were encroaching.[61] Thus in all fairness, there must be adequate compensation. It is significant that, in the years subsequent to the signing of the treaties, the Saulteau view, a combination of the historical Indian understanding and the aboriginal rights idea from the Métis, seems to have received increased recognition among Indians. It would appear that the failure of the white community to observe the traditional relationship led the Indian to examine seriously the idea, European in origin, of aboriginal rights. The concept provided a vehicle for expressing a sense of betrayal and injustice, and at the same time, seemed to furnish white tools to be used in the Indian's interests.

The historical record of Indian-white relations in what was termed the Northern Department of Rupert's Land between the years 1670 and 1870 confirms the existence of a compact. The fur trade, the basis of the relationship between Indian and white, had its origins in Indian practices that

---

[55] Ibid., p. 224.
[56] Ibid., p. 108.
[57] Ibid., p. 101.
[58] Ibid., p. 106.
[59] Ibid., p. 110.
[60] Ibid., p. 111.
[61] Ibid., p. 223.

facilitated peaceful interaction between bands. The fundamental concept involved was the classificatory "we" rather than "they." Without this exercise in logic, the fur trade as history records it could not have been. European goods in themselves are not a sufficient basis on which to explain the historical record. The alliance, the classificatory "we" must be added to understand the full dimension of the fur trade. With the passing years, the train of events and changing circumstances altered particular aspects of the relationship. But in the Indian mind and, to a surprising degree, in the minds of white traders, the essence of the relationship, a compact, remained. Two peoples, culturally distinct, interacted upon a fair and equitable basis. Each party to the pact could make recognized demands upon the other. During the half century in which the Hudson's Bay Company enjoyed its monopoly in fact as well as in law, the compact basis of Indian-white relations continued to be recognized. The particular nature of the relationship differed with specific peoples. With the Plains tribes, notably the Plains Cree and the members of the Blackfoot Confederacy, the relationship was reminiscent of that between the company and the Upland Indians. On the other extreme, there was the relationship with the Bush Indians, where in fact the Company enjoyed a dominant position. Yet even in these circumstances, the form of the traditional relationship was recognized. At the same time, particular practices, such as those elaborated by Dr. John Rae in what might be termed the area of health and social welfare, further elaborated the nature of the compact. Provisions in the treaties for "medicine chests" and other services demonstrate this historical continuity.

It is not so much in the terms of the treaties but in the negotiations before the signing of the treaties that evidence of the compact concept emerges again. Granted, some question must arise as to how accurate our record of the negotiations is. Are the translations accurate? If they are accurate, how well do we comprehend Indian expressions suggesting a compact? Yet even with these reservations it becomes apparent, as the record of negotiations unfolds, that a compact interpretation encompassed the views of many of the Indian leaders. Many of the expressions of both Morris and Laird would reinforce such a view in the minds of the Indian participants. To the Indian leaders, words in council were as important, if not more so, than words on paper. Negotiating from a position of instability and potential chaos and crises, the Indian leaders sought to reaffirm the traditional basis of Indian-white relations—a compact. In this they believed they were successful. They believed the representatives of the white community saw it in a similar light.

One further point remains to be noted. If a compact did not exist in the minds of at least some of the Indian leaders, how then are we to explain their words and actions during negotiations? In the absence of a compact, the Indian becomes a simple, unsophisticated child of nature victimized, perhaps unintentionally, by the more knowledgeable white. If not racist, such a view suggests at least a cultural supremacy. The knowledge and skill of Indian leaders pass unrecognized and appear in the guise of child-like and largely meaningless rhetoric. To this view, Big Bear, after his remarks concerning "the rope to be about my neck," would have been satisfied with the offer of a firing squad. To anyone having an acquaintance with the history of Indian-white relations, such dated views are no longer acceptable. The historical data incorporating an Indian view become comprehensible only when they are conceived in the context of an Indian-white compact. This compact was "betrayed" in the years following the signing of the treaties.

List of Authors, Indian Elders, and Interviewers

Richard Price
— Research director, T.A.R.R., 1973-76
— Consultant, Indian Association of Alberta, 1977-78
— B. Comm., B.D., M.A. (Political Science)
— "Indian Land Claims in Alberta: Politics and Policy-Making (1968-77)" (M.A. dissertation, University of Alberta, 1977)

John Leonard Taylor
— Researcher, Canadian Indian Rights Commission
— "The Development of an Indian Policy for the Canadian North-West, 1869-79" (Ph.D. dissertation, Queen's University, 1976)

Richard Daniel
— Assistant director of Archival Research, T.A.R.R., 1975-77
— B.A., M.A. (Sociology)
— "Indian Rights and Hinterland Resources: The Case of Northern Alberta" (M.A. dissertation, University of Alberta, 1977)

John Foster
— Historical consultant, T.A.R.R., 1973-76
— Associate professor, History Department, University of Alberta
— Ph.D. (History)
— "The Country-Born in the Red River Settlement 1820-1850" (Ph.D. dissertation, University of Alberta, 1972)

Lynn Hickey
— Assistant to the director, T.A.R.R., 1975-77
— A.B., A.M. (Anthropology)
— "The Nunamiut Eskimos: An Ecological Perspective" (A.M. dissertation, Brown University, 1969)

Richard Lightning
— Assistant director, T.A.R.R., 1975-76
— Director, T.A.R.R., 1976-
— Interpreter

Gordon Lee
— Assistant director, T.A.R.R., 1973-75
— Chief, Ermineskin Reserve, 1976-

Indian elders

— Peter O'Chiese, Hinton
— Lazarus Roan, Smallboy Camp
— John Buffalo, Ermineskin Reserve
— Fred Horse, Frog Lake
— Pat Weaselhead, Blood Reserve
— Camoose Bottle, Blood Reserve
— Annie Buffalo, Peigan Reserve
— John Yellowhorn, Peigan Reserve
— Jean-Marie Mustus, Joussard
— William Okeymaw, Sucker Creek Reserve
— Felix Gibot, Fort Chipewyan

Interviewers

— Louis Rain, Cree, Louis Bull Reserve
— Richard Lightning, Cree, Ermineskin Reserve
— Harry Shade, Blackfoot, Blood Reserve
— Mike Devine, Blackfoot, Blood Reserve
— John Smith, Blackfoot, Peigan Reserve
— Tom Yellowhorn, Blackfoot, Peigan Reserve